INJUSTICE AT WORK

THE YALE CULTURAL SOCIOLOGY SERIES
Jeffrey C. Alexander and Ron Eyerman, Series Editors

INJUSTICE AT WORK

François Dubet

With the collaboration of Valérie Caillet, Régis Cortéséro, David Mélo, Françoise Rault

*Translated by
Eric Rosencrantz, Anita Conrade, and Mark McGovern*

Paradigm Publishers
Boulder • London

First published in French: *Injustices. L'expérience des inégalités au travail.* Paris: Editions du Seuil, 2006, 498 pp.

Published in the United States by Paradigm Publishers,
2845 Wilderness Place, Suite 200, Boulder, CO 80301 USA.

Paradigm Publishers is the trade name of Birkenkamp & Company, LLC,
Dean Birkenkamp, President and Publisher.

Library of Congress Cataloging-in-Publication Data

Dubet, François.
  Injustice at work / François Dubet ; in collaboration with Valérie Caillet ... [et al.].
    p. cm. — (The Yale cultural sociology series)
  Includes bibliographical references.
  ISBN 978-1-59451-687-0 (hardcover : alk. paper)
  ISBN 978-1-59451-688-7 (pbk. : alk. paper)
  1. Discrimination in employment—France. 2. Equality—France.
3. Social justice—France. I. Caillet, Valérie. II. Title.
  HD4903.5.F7D828 2009
  331.13'30944—dc22

                                                        2009007361

Printed and bound in the United States of America on acid-free paper that meets the standards of the American National Standard for Permanence of Paper for Printed Library Materials.

Designed and Typeset by Straight Creek Bookmakers.

13 12 11   1 2 3 4 5

Contents

Foreword

Injustice at Work is an essential contribution to the analysis of the interpretive frames through which individuals make sense of the realities that surround them. We are very fortunate that Paradigm Publishers has made this book available in English. Researchers and students of organizations, labor, culture, inequality, and social psychology (among other topics) have much to gain by reading this book.

Injustice at Work concerns the set of principles that structure the perception of injustice in the workplace. François Dubet and his collaborators/students identify three dominant and complementary principles concerning equality, merit, and autonomy (or dignity and recognition). They define the diverse manifestations and "lexicons" of these principles, illustrating them with individual and group interviews and with statistical evidence. Dubet et al. describe the tension and contradiction that are inherent in these principles. The result is an analysis that illuminates a new angle of a well-known reality, and in this way considerably enriches our understanding of the subject. Particularly persuasive is the analysis of the rejection of the relevance of the merit principle, which in other contexts, notably the American context, would be an uncontested principle of justice.

In its intention to reconstruct a series of critical postures taken by social actors in relation to situations in daily life, this book is theoretically influenced by Luc Boltanski and Laurent Thévenot's work on the principles of justification. But *Injustice at Work* is more directly and systematically empirical and less anchored in philosophical tradition. Additionally, just as it is the case for Boltanski and Thévenot, the argument developed by Dubet et al. does not have explanatory (or causal) aspirations. Rather, as Erving Goffman did, Dubet offers an analytic description that informs a new understanding of a well-known reality,

rendering it less nebulous and more linked to the functioning of fundamental social processes.

The authors' point of departure is that injustices do not exist as
such—rather, there exist social situations perceived as unjust, or "unjust
injustices," or "unjustifiable." We are more and more attached to the principle of equality, even though neoliberalism reinforces inequality, creating
evident tensions. We are also confronted by a multiplicity of inequalities
that are linked to our diverse identities and appearances. In this context,
we mobilize diverse and often incompatible principles of injustice. This
results from the normative activity that is the object of this book and that
also complements other recent works that deal with morality as it is lived
and constructed. I am thinking here of the works of Jeffrey Alexander,
Robert Wuthnow, Alan Wolfe, and Andrew Sayer (among others) in the
English-speaking world and of those from the *Groupe de Sociologie Politique et Morale* in France. It goes without saying that these contributions
form an essential complement to the works of Rawlsians and other moral
philosophers such as Michael Walzer and Robert Nozick. They also form
a complement to the classic approaches that deal with exploitation and
alienation as nurturing class consciousness and social mobilization; and
in this, they complement my own work as well as the work of others who
have revisited the subject of dignity in the workplace.[1]

The general impression we are left with after reading this book
is of the complexity and breadth of the French vocabulary associated
with the denunciation of injustice—a vocabulary that seems to include
numerous dimensions that are absent from its American counterpart, at
least so far as I perceive it through my own work. The complexity and
breadth give me hope for the French case, in as much as it is a source (or
"supply-side" symbol) for nurturing social forms of contestation such as
the *alter-mondialization* movement (or *alter-globalization* movement),
which remain weaker on this side of the Atlantic. It would be necessary
to link these national differences, if they exist, to different modes of gov-
ernmentality, which are more or less integrated or tight-knit. To consider
how the languages of fear and consumption complement that of injustice
and articulate themselves in the French and American contexts would
be a harmonious complement to the intellectual agenda suggested by
François Dubet's book. Thus, this book should be read by many American social scientists, not only for what it teaches us about French ways of
understanding injustice but also for what it teaches us about ourselves—
about the taken-for-granted limits of how Americans think about what's
fair and what's unfair.[2]

—Michèle Lamont, Robert I. Goldman Professor of
European Studies and Professor of Sociology and African and
African-American Studies, Harvard University

Notes

1. Lamont, M. 2002. *La dignité des travailleurs.* Paris: Presses de Science Po; Hodson, R. 2001. *Dignity at Work.* New York: Cambridge University Press.
2. I thank Eva Rosen for her assistance with the preparation of this foreword.

Acknowledgments

I wish to thank warmly all participants of the interviews on which this book is based. My gratitude also goes to the students and colleagues of the department of sociology of the Université Victor-Segalen in Bordeaux who participated in this work and to my colleagues at the Cadis in Paris for their encouragement prior to the writing of this book. Finally, my grateful thoughts go to Mireille Gaultier who administered this research and prepared the manuscript. The research was funded by the French ministry of family, health, and solidarities.

Introduction

"Real-Life" Injustices

INJUSTICE IS PRIMARY (Moore 1978). Though we may not all be capable of saying clearly what is just and what a just world should be, we all know what is unjust and why. Suffice it to ask, "Why do you think the situation or conduct you object to is unfair?" and everyone will be able to elaborate arguments based on principle and, in so doing, "play the philosopher." It is in this sense that criticism is a natural social activity (Walzer 1990). Injustice benefits from a sort of existential primacy over the justifications, arguments, and generalizations that evince the principles of justice grounding or underpinning the primary emotions (Boltanski/ Thévenot 1991). Everyone acts as a theoretician in this domain—not because we are capable of condemning injustice, but because our criticism will always involve or imply arguments based on principles that are perceived as being more or less universal, and therefore bound by the obligations of coherence and reciprocity. That is not fair because we're all equals, because I'm being exploited, because they're flouting the rules, because they're ignoring merit, because they're disrespecting me as a human being … and because what goes for me goes for everyone else, too.

To understand social injustice, it is not enough to describe and decry inequalities of the sort reported in surveys and statistics, for the only inequalities that count are those the subject finds unfair. An inequality we deem fair is hardly noticed since it seems self-evident and "natural." Measuring real inequalities is a Sisyphean task for empirical reasons—which ones do we pick?—and for moral reasons, as certain inequalities may be perceived as being perfectly fair. Hence, an analysis of social injustice presupposes that we put ourselves at the juncture between objective inequalities and the principles of justice according to which a given situation, act, or omission will be defined as unjust.

The connection between situations and judgments seems particularly strained and inscrutable nowadays. As regards "objective" social injustice, we are experiencing a trend reversal with the aggravation of certain inequalities, and the exclusion and weakening of a large part of the population, to which all the surveys show a heightened public sensitivity.[1] The swelling ranks of the poor, the long-term unemployed, and those without job security give one the sense that inequalities are becoming generalized. Not only is the unemployment rate close to 10 percent in France, but if we put the poverty line at 50 percent of median income, 7 percent of French households—i.e., 4.5 million people—are poor, and this figure doubles if we place the poverty line at 60 percent of median income (Observatoire national de la pauvreté 2003). Temporary employment has become widely established as more or less "normal" (INSEE 2005; Clair 2001). In addition to these few statistics, it is disappointing to note that the disparities in income are perpetuated, if not accentuated, when we take income from financial and real estate investments into account (Maurin 2004).

Geographic inequalities have increased as wealth and poverty become concentrated in certain municipalities and neighborhoods (Donzelot 2003), and the recent urban riots present an explosive image of these inequalities. Mass access to education, which was expected to reduce inequalities, seems to be incapable of doing so (Duru-Bellat 2002). Sociological surveys reveal new inequalities every day—and the perpetuation of past inequalities we thought were gone for good. The public feels the future will be worse than the present—and that the present is worse than the past. What is more, the plight of the homeless, the jobless no longer eligible for benefits, youths in urban slums, immigrants without papers or rights, and the working poor is sufficiently visible to rouse our ire and indignation, while certain top managers and celebrity stars appear to be reconstituting an aristocracy that is proof against the common human condition. Ultimately, our feeling of injustice may be a matter of course, for it seems patently obvious to many that we are living in an—increasingly—inegalitarian society.

But things are not that simple, for we are also probably becoming increasingly sensitive to inequalities and injustices. For example, although the situation of women has markedly improved over the past 50 years—what with access to higher education and employment, equal rights, and birth control—never before have the inequalities between the sexes been deplored as vehemently as they are today. Plenty of inequalities have diminished in France, such as the divide between the working population and the retired, for instance, and yet these inequalities seem more and more unbearable. Although most immigrants and their families are no longer confined to shantytowns and to working conditions more akin to slavery than paid employment, we balk at discrimination in the housing and job markets far more now than we used to.

Furthermore, the often asserted view of the ongoing degradation of the workers' plight is not entirely justified. In inflation-adjusted euros (reference year 2000), the statutory minimum monthly wage (SMIC) rose from €282 in 1960 to €350 in 1978 and €823 in 1999, so the *Trente Glorieuses,* as the French call the boom period from 1945 to 1973, can hardly be hailed as a golden age. As working hours have grown shorter since then, leisure time has increased—along with consumption and life expectancy. French society has continued to grow more affluent over the past 30 years, and even if some have enriched themselves more than others, the majority have benefited from economic growth, albeit meager, but growth nonetheless. Whatever we may think, things could be, and have been, worse.

And yet our society seems more and more unjust to us because we grow more and more attached to the principle of equality, though we are living in an economic and social world that is incessantly generating inequalities of all sorts. In fact, our representations fall somewhere between Marx and Tocqueville. The social structure, the division of labor, and the workings of the economy seem like machines designed to produce inequalities; and the mechanism is accelerating, driven by the globalization of trade and the opening up of national economies, hitherto hegemonic and relatively protected, now facing foreign competition. But the democratic revolution is still a powerful force, and we grow ever more zealously attached to our fundamental equality and averse to castes, privileges, and exclusionary trends that eject individuals from our circle of elementary equality. The clash between the two philosophies has become all the more violent now that the balanced system laboriously constructed by the welfare state appears to be in jeopardy, its safety nets fraying and the whole nation overwhelmed by the brutal changes in the global economy. This analysis, which is at the heart of most latter-day social criticism and condemnation of the damage caused by free-market policies, also shores up a critical stance that happens to be every bit as one-sided and conformist as the conformism it is combating.

For one cannot simply declare every form of inequality a priori unjust—period. Three facts belie such a facile reduction.

First, individuals and social movements are hardly egalitarian. As a matter of fact, they find many an inequality perfectly fair: It's fair to grant higher pay for seniority or academic credentials, it's fair to protect certain professions. Furthermore, social struggles are not necessarily any more about reducing inequalities than maintaining entrenched positions. Hence, the problem of justice is less about inequalities than about unjust inequalities, or, to put it more clearly, about just inequalities.

Second, the individual is not an indivisible monad. Each of us moves in several spheres, in several registers that are each subject to specific inequalities. We may or may not be equals in our respective capacities as workers, women, teenagers, college graduates, etc. And each of these registers places us on a different scale of inequality and of criteria of legitimacy. The inequalities are not only more and more potent, they are also multifarious. Take an impecunious student leading a free and active life, for instance: Is he getting a "rawer deal" than an ageing and overworked executive tormented by the fear of being sidelined or sacked (Dubet 2000)?

Third, every time we assess the fairness of a situation, we apply, more or less consciously, different principles of justice. The selfsame situation may appear grossly unfair through the lens of pure equality but perfectly fair through that of individual merit. Inequalities and injustices are not *facts,* they are the product of normative activities that give them meaning. This composite nature of inequalities that may seem now fair, now unfair, obliges us to consider them from the angle of the philosophy of justice and from the sociological angle.

What, then, are the component elements and general rules of a syntax that could form the basis—the vocabulary and grammar, as it were—of the normative activity of workers describing the inequalities and injustices they witness and/or suffer? Spanning the multitude of criticisms and denunciations is an overarching "theory" of just inequalities, for individuals clamor not so much for absolute justice as for a more pragmatic and complex conception of just inequalities.

So, despite the diversity of individual situations, career paths, ideologies, and resources, we advance the hypothesis that there exist some principles informing the experience of injustice in the workplace. Our intuitions, opinions, and moods are guided by stable principles that are usually shared by others. For an injustice to be recognized as such, one has to adopt the same criteria as those one wishes to convince of the injustice of one's lot (Nagel 1994).

In this regard there is neither a radical break nor a seamless continuity between commonplace and theoretical judgments, for social agents are neither weathervanes turned this way and that by the mercurial winds of public opinion, nor moral surveyors. Our feelings of justice generally rest upon stable principles that provide the reasons, if not the Reason, for our criticisms (Boudon 1996; 2004). The argumentation is of the essence here because the wrongs I have suffered are not wrongs unless others, putting themselves in my place, can be convinced of the reality thereof. I am not truly the victim of an injustice unless I can convince others of that injustice, which presupposes the existence of an "impartial spectator" who is capable, as Adam Smith put it, of detaching himself from his own interests, putting himself in another's place, and sharing his terms of reference. There is probably more regularity and stability in normative and symbolic systems than there is in all the accidents and arrangements of life in society. "The customs of a community, taken as a whole, always have a particular style and are reducible to systems. I am of the opinion that the number of such systems is not unlimited and that—in their games, dreams and wild imaginings—human societies, like individuals, never create absolutely, but merely choose certain combinations from an ideal repertoire that it should be possible to define" (Lévi-Strauss 1955, 205[2]).

The principles of justice do not loom above social experience like so many justices of the peace; rather, they engage the critical activity of individuals, their *normative activity.* The normative dimension of social experience may then be discussed in both senses of the word *normative* (Pharo 2004): that of a set of principles deemed legitimate—or "obligatory" in Durkheim's terms—and that of the practice of autonomous reflection and evaluation that gives our judgments the seal of their true morality. Each principle of justice is independent of the agent and precedes him, preexisting him, and "imposing itself" on him. But the polyarchy of these principles, associated with the diversity of social situations, leads individuals to develop their own moral activity within frameworks, rules, and combinations.

Criticism of working conditions and workplace relations comes all the more naturally because the set of social mechanisms and relations that crystallize at work is particularly conducive to manifestations of feelings of injustice. What is this archeology of work (Méda 1995), this sedimentation of strata of significations that solidify in the experience of work? Work is at once *status, exchange value,* and *creative activity,* and each of these "natures" refers to a principle of justice.

Equality

Work confers status, it assigns a position in the social order and thus integrates the worker. Of the people we surveyed, 21 percent see that as its essential value.[3] In democratic societies this integration will necessarily be gauged against the yardstick of an *equality* to which everyone is supposedly entitled. And yet, though even the most ordinary criticism of the workaday world will dwell on its inequalities, at work no one demands pure and radical equality. As Supiot remarks (1994, 119), "a contract of employment establishes a hierarchy among equals." Managers and manual laborers are not equals, and yet they are when, in certain circumstances, the latter decry the injustice of their lot in the name of equality. So what is the nature of equality in this case?

Because work assigns each individual to a place in the hierarchy, workers gauge their social equality there in terms of lifestyle, rights, political participation, and access to what are deemed elementary goods. They may denounce the state of exclusion and disdain in which they are kept as citizens or as human beings. For a long time, manual laborers were "camped outside the walls of the community"—and of the nation—for they were denied most democratic rights, and they fought first for their equality and their rights: The right of association, the right to vote, and the right to strike were conceived of as the preconditions for the workers' struggle itself. The affirmation and extension of social rights has been defined as the transformation of the "formal" equality promised by democratic revolutions into "real" equality. More diffusely and routinely, demands of this type are always involved in labor disputes, which consistently condemn excessive inequalities—those that threaten the fundamental equality of individuals, that is, when sexual or racial segregation, poverty, and unemployment exclude a segment of the population from what are deemed the fundamental equalities. This raises the issue of acceptable inequalities: minimum wage, welfare, and the desirable disparities between welfare benefits and earned income. Are these social rights a debt owed by the state or a form of state charity?[4] At any rate, work is expected to ensure the social integration of individuals and their fundamental equality in a democratic society.

The equality in question cannot be absolute. As Walzer points out (1997, 13), "Equality literally understood is an ideal ripe for betrayal." Or as Sen asserts (2000), the question of equality is always that of the "equality of something." Equality being relative, one family of criticism of unjust inequalities can be summed up in a very simple argument: A given inequality is unjust because it conflicts with my conception of a just hierarchical order. To wit, it's not fair to pay new recruits as much as "old hands" because long years of service in a given post entitle the latter to a just inequality. On the other hand, it's not fair to pay women less than men, for in principle we're all equals. In reality, these two seemingly conflicting arguments are of the same nature insofar as they both reflect an a priori conception of the inequalities that are deemed just in any given society. The "pure" equality we are attached to adapts perfectly to a hierarchical order we find legitimate.[5]

Thus, every social group—in brief, every society—proposes a hierarchical order of just inequalities, allotting to each what he is entitled to according to his position. Justice, then, consists in giving each his due according to his rank, age, sex, nationality, academic credentials, etc. At work as elsewhere, unjust inequalities break these hierarchical rules: It is wrong for the young not to show due deference to their elders, for skilled workers not to be better paid than the less skilled, for foreigners to be treated like nationals, and so forth. All these violations of the hierarchical order are in breach of the respect owed to individuals, more specifically of the respect owed to the positions individuals hold. To put it simply, what is just is what custom, as internalized by each of us, defines as just in terms of respect for positions, rights, and duties. The feeling of injustice does not arise because equality is not guaranteed, but because legitimate hierarchical inequalities have been breached.

Consequently, in democratic societies, equality does not do away with legitimate hierarchical orders. To follow Tocqueville in this, we may say that the democratic order affirming that all individuals are fundamentally equal is less the abolition of aristocratic hierarchies than the extension of the aristocratic model (d'Iribarne 1996). Basically, democratic equality would be but one hierarchical order among others, only it would be an order that flattens out the "natural" hierarchies to replace them with a paradoxical hierarchy in which all individuals are "naturally" equal though occupying unequal positions. Since fundamental equality is led to accommodate de facto inequalities, it must be transformed into a conception of what are considered just hierarchical inequalities. We might therefore conjecture that the experience of inequalities reflects, in part, our conceptions of legitimate hierarchies, even if this hierarchy enlarges the sphere of equality by defining the community of equals as the democratic space (Dumont 1985). And any infringement of this equality or these just inequalities, for the two often coincide, gives rise to a moral type of criticism since it is the basic cohesion of society that is at stake.

So it is that workers generally criticize inequalities when they are excessive; when they disturb the civil peace and the community, the *fraternité*; and above all as soon as they challenge the appropriateness of inequalities arising from the "normal" division of labor. We chiefly denounce inequalities that exclude people from the social community because they create too great a rift between the principle of equality and the conditions imposed on individuals, when, in Rawls or Dworkin's terms, "primary goods" are not guaranteed. Such is the case, for example, with gender- or race-based inequalities or unequal access to health care, which appear to be denials of fundamental equality. So, too, economic inequalities are considered shocking because they produce separate human categories: The mighty become gods of a sort, while the excluded become "subhumans."[6] What outrages us, far more than the inequalities themselves, are the vast chasms separating the richest and poorest, the countries of the North and South, the differences in status between the protected and the precarious.

Merit

In addition to being an assignment to a place in a hierarchical order, work is also an exchange between labor power, of whatever nature, and income. Hence the ongoing play of comparisons, of measures of contribution and retribution, resting on a conception of *merit,* which, in turn, is apt to produce what we deem just inequalities.

No agent is the simple product of his or her socialization. Each is *also* a strategist seeking to control his or her interests in a social situation defined in terms of competition and therefore of distributive justice, in terms of the commensurability of contributions and compensations (Deutsch 1985; Homans 1974). Here, the norm of just inequalities is that of merit and therefore that of the justice of the tests on which merit is based. Thus, it is a matter of combining fundamental equality with a merit-based inequality. In this case, the feeling of injustice does not derive from merit as such, since everyone seeks to gain recognition for his merit, but from the fact that the tests determining this merit— productivity, competitive examinations, promotion by selection, bonuses, etc.—are supposedly unjust or "rigged." The realm of work is probably particularly sensitive to this meritocratic aspect of inequalities, which, it should be underscored, often conflicts with hierarchical conceptions of status, as shown by the ordinary example of tensions between the qualifications acquired at school, well prior to entry into the working world, and the skills that come into play in the workplace, or between promotion by seniority and promotion by selection. It may also be posited that the intersecting frustrations that pit the public sector against the private sector, like those that pit the generations and groups who run a higher risk of unemployment against those at lower risk, ensue from this dialectic of equality and merit.

Merit is a norm of justice and not just a convention or a method of management because it is not contested as such by the agents. There is a simple enough reason for this: merit appears to provide the sole basis for the introduction of fair inequalities into a society that as a rule promotes the fundamental equality of individuals. Assuming that we are all equal, and that every society nevertheless ranks and classifies individuals, the only way for it to do so is by evaluating the talents, energy, and efforts of free and equal individuals. Without merit, we would have no means of situating individuals on a stratification scale and would have to fall back on birth or drawing lots. We regard examination and competition results, skills, energy, and the various talents as equivalents of merit, although on a fundamental level we often wonder if individuals are really responsible for the qualities that make them different from others. However, Article VI of the Declaration of the Rights of Man and of the Citizen considers merit to be a direct consequence of the equality of individuals,[7] whereas Rawls, despite his fundamental doubts about merit (Am I more responsible for my penchant for effort than for my physical handicaps?) cannot conceive of any other method for building fair inequalities into a world where equality and freedom are the primary principles of justice. The fact that merit is the only way to combine equality and freedom in a society in which the division of labor holds sway makes it a principle of justice that is as fundamental as equality.

The view that workers are free to sell their labor power, thereby cutting themselves loose from the bonds of personal dependence in feudal societies, should be taken seriously, despite the manifold doubts that have been expressed about the reality of this freedom. Not only did the classical political economy of the English Enlightenment (particularly Locke and Smith) define free contract employment as a substitute for social bonds between unequal agents, but it also thereby established a criterion and measure of the justice between individuals who are theoretically equal, because each possesses a property he may use freely: his labor power. Although the inequitable nature of these "contracts" has since been widely criticized, and although community ties and solidarity have since been set against this purely wage-based relationship, work was nonetheless promoted as a principle of justice, as a balanced exchange between "free and equal" employers and employees. This is, of course, a fiction, but this construct has hardly ever been questioned in terms of the principles of justice: to each according to his utility, equal pay for equal work, etc.

Considered a universal equivalent, work reconciles the two contradictory dimensions of democratic and capitalist societies, namely the fundamental and ontological equality of individuals who may use their labor power freely, and the inequality of their positions in the division of labor. Inequalities are deemed to be just when they result from unequal work, and when individuals have "decided" to work longer or shorter hours. Am I paid fairly or not enough for the work I sell to my employer? I am the victim of an injustice because I am not paid enough, because others are better paid for the same job, and that is all the more unfair because I am fundamentally equal to everyone else and my merit is the test of my equality and my freedom. The judgment here is based not on a hierarchical order, but on the arithmetical equity of an exchange (Kellerhals et al. 1988; 1997).

Just as equality is linked to a conception of social integration, merit is not justified by itself alone, but is supposed to produce collective efficiency in terms of both production and the "wealth of nations." The free competition of merit, talents, and interests is said to generate wealth and inequalities that are deemed good and fair, as in Mandeville's fable where the free play of selfishness yields a collective good. Meritocracy in education produces elites whose qualities are useful to everyone. Merit-based pay stimulates work, efficiency, and the production of wealth. In this sense, merit is undeniably linked to capitalist modernity, though it cannot be confined to it because in many cases the diverse spheres of merit are opposed to one another. For example, those credited with scholastic merit tend to disparage those whose merit lies in business, whereas the latter consider academic degrees a sort of unearned pension. University graduates may clash with self-made men, but both groups base their legitimacy on the same standard of justice. Specifically, they both believe inequalities are just if there is fair competition and equal opportunity, and they both affirm that the free expression of merit yields a collective good. Merit may, then, appear to be a moral good. On the one hand, it is a manifestation of human freedom and therefore of fundamental equality when we consider that equality is defined in terms of freedoms of action. On the other hand, merit is moral because it requires rational, controlled, ascetic, and essentially virtuous action; the *doux commerce* (or "gentle commerce") envisaged by Montesquieu was also associated with a project for universal peace (Hirschman 1980). This bourgeois utopia was echoed in an equally peace-loving socialist international, which believed that the society of workers would be wholly devoted to "the administration of things."

The principle of merit plays an important role in the critique, which is still quite current, of *exploitation* (Baudelot/Gollac 2003). In fairly "Marxist" terms, a sense of exploitation is engendered by a mechanism and a system of relations that enable agents from dominant groups to "selfishly" appropriate the utility of work and make it their own private property, and in so doing dispossess the exploited worker and the community of the wealth created by labor. One does not have to be a Marxist to appreciate the critical reasoning of poorly paid workers whose employers appear to be "excessively rich," or of those who feel the wealth produced is not being reinvested in collective utility when managers opt to reward stockholders instead of employees. In our day and age, still plagued by financial speculation and stock market bubbles, we have not forgotten that powerful sense of injustice, which is only the critical reversal of the connection between merit and utility. But this connection must be critiqued in the name of merit itself, of a true and justly rewarded merit.

Autonomy

Work is not only a vector of social integration and an exchange value, it is also an *ethic*. There is no need to rehearse the theories of Weber here except to recall that the work ethic extends well beyond the realm of Protestant values, for social thought in industrial society has also added an ethical and moral value to the objective exchange value of work. From Hegel to Marx, work has been considered the quintessential means to self-fulfillment and the supreme representation of human creativity in a secular society dominated by science and technology. This conviction is a veritable anthropological theory asserting that man achieves recognition and fulfillment in his works and, in consequence, through the bonds forged with others and with nature. It matters little whether this is a secularized doctrine of salvation or a bourgeois ideology, for this belief has been a central tenet of industrial society, initially imposed by management and later reappropriated by the workers' movement, which championed genuine, expressive, personal work as against mechanical, dehumanized, "abstract" work on the factory floor.[8]

It may be said that employees, as opposed to workers *stricto sensu*, are more directly involved in the struggle for equality and merit, and for fair wages. Yet feelings of injustice also arise from working conditions that are harmful to the health and dignity of the individual worker when she is treated merely as labor power and not as a human being. Autonomy becomes a central principle of justice here, the focus of criticism shifting from inequalities to the alienation of workers who have become the helpers of the machines. Latter-day changes in the workplace have not diminished the importance of this principle of justice in the struggle for better working conditions, as evinced in the widespread criticism of new management techniques, and related issues of pressure, stress, fatigue, and suffering in the workplace. These issues are increasingly coming to the fore, not only because working conditions have deteriorated as the balance of power shifts away from workers in unemployment-ridden economies, but also because the desire for autonomy and self-expression has, in all likelihood, lowered the threshold of tolerance for unsatisfactory working conditions.

The worker may no longer be the collective subject of history, but each of us judges the fairness of his or her work in terms of the freedom, autonomy, and self-fulfillment it affords. A full 41.5 percent of those questioned in our survey gave first priority to self-expression in their work. The historical quest to emancipate the workers has been transformed into a desire for individual autonomy and development, as unanimously confirmed by research in the field. Work puts to the test my creativity and my ability to feel myself the author of a work. When work ceased to be a curse—or a form of bondage, suffering, torture, or punishment—the worker became a subject. Of course, this conception immediately triggered a critique of actual working conditions, but such a critique cannot be undertaken without faith in the creative capacity of the subject at work.

Workers define as unjust situations and relations that deprive them of their creativity, uniqueness, and dignity, and therefore resent any obstacles to self-fulfillment in the workplace. In such cases, the norm of judgment is not a cultural principle similar to hierarchical equality, nor is it an understanding of equity based on "calculations" to establish merit; it is based on personal and strictly subjective experience in which the subject gauges the quality of his or her work against an aspiration for autonomy and personal development of which he or she is the only judge. Justice comes in the intrinsic rewards work offers in terms of professional interest, the quality of social relations, and the possibilities for personal development. At the other end of the spectrum, a sense of injustice results from situations and relations that give rise to what the sociology of work has long defined as a sense of subjective alienation: fatigue, "burnout," a lack of interest in the task, and feelings of contempt and powerlessness with regard to one's work (Seeman 1967).

Right action demonstrating "autonomy of will" can have no other source than the subject himself (Dworkin 1986; Kant 1984; Renaut 1989). From a sociological point of view, this logic clearly does not posit a non-social subject preexisting the action, but it does imply that the agents are motivated by a cultural model that values the realization of the subject. Whether or not this representation of the subject is really about exaggerated pride, it exists whenever individuals adopt this ideal of autonomy or, in more metaphysical terms, this ideal of freedom. Just as the gods exist because men believe in them, the principle of autonomy exists whenever workers prize what each perceives as his or her own authenticity, self-fulfillment, and power to be the master of his or her own life. This representation of justice, understood as the individual's capacity to build a life he or she finds desirable for him- or herself, is very close to what one sociological tradition called "accomplishment" and Amartya Sen termed "capability": "the realization of goals and values that a person has reason to pursue, whether or not they are connected with her own well-being[. . . .] Capability is, thus, a set of vectors of functionings, reflecting the person's freedom to lead one type of life or another" (Sen 2000, 46).

We may consider these remarks rather abstract, vague, and quite incompatible with sociological realism, which usually focuses on the rational utility or cultural determining of behavior. But there is a scale of job satisfaction that goes beyond financial inducement and a sense of social integration, a scale on which autonomy is the ordinary secularized heir to the Protestant vocation. So an independent logic of subjectivization has to be posited to explain the force and regularity of grievances expressed about suffering at work. Without this "negative theology" linking suffering to a standard of autonomy, these grievances would simply be impressions and not judgments on justice.

Principles, Values, or Ideologies?

What is the nature of the three principles discussed above? Are they opinions, ideologies, or a kind of intermediate fiction between social categories and philosophical concepts? The ambiguities are exacerbated by the fact that most of the theoretical edifices proposed by philosophies of justice are built on three major principles: equality, merit, and freedom, which we have chosen to call autonomy in order to stay closer to the categories broached by workers and to avoid becoming enmired in the metaphysics of freedom. Let's clarify this terminology.

Are these principles of justice cultural principles or codes, just like any other values? So-called communitarian thinkers claim that principles of justice are inscribed in specific cultures and societies. They hold that equality, freedom, and merit are not independent of the cultural contexts from which they emerge (Kelley/Evans 1993). To theoreticians of liberal equality whose sole focus is the question of justice, they point out that such a position is inadequate for characterizing a good society because equality and freedom alone cannot define the common good. Freedom— or, for our purposes, "autonomy"—cannot be based on "an unqualified concept of the self" since the cultural and social integration of the individual is essential for the development of an autonomous self, and even more vital for a self that is capable of conceiving of its autonomy. In short, for freedom to be more than an abstraction, we have to lead the type of life we want to lead (MacIntyre 1997). This objection is perfectly admissible, especially for a sociologist at times "annoyed" by the abstraction of many philosophical theories of justice. However, the fact that norms of justice are rooted in cultures does not negate their plurality, their level of generality, or their systematic but contradictory nature, unless we regard them simply as customs or mere attributes of groups and genders (Gilligan 1986). Ultimately, the contention that principles of justice are cultural attributes is not convincing because all agents move toward higher levels of generality in their argumentation, levels that are by nature decontextualized, and because the same principles obtain despite the diversity of situations, career paths, and identities. What varies is not the principles, but what agents make of them and how they apply them to specific social contexts.

Does the fact that principles of justice are invoked by unions and management alike imply that we should regard them as ideologies (Kruegel/Smith 1986)? Given that "our own interest is a marvelous instrument that we use for putting out our eyes" (Pascal 2000, §78), can we agree with Engels that justice is "the glorification of existing conditions"? We define ideologies here as systems of beliefs, values, and justifications whose object, more or less consciously and "cynically," is to justify the dominating social order by disguising it to those who are subjugated to it. Of course, our research, like most research in this field, shows that workers favor equality while managers favor merit, but the two groups are attached to both principles, which means they are not mere ideologies. There is, moreover, a significant argument against relegating the principles of justice to the ranks of ideological expedients: namely, their critical reversibility. Although there is little doubt that the principles of justice do legitimize an order and therefore a form of domination in the workplace—merit gives meaning to exploitation, autonomy appeals to the worker's commitment, equality defines what is intolerable and, by inference, a number of acceptable inequalities—each of these principles is reversible and can be used to oppose the order it is supposed to justify. We combat the inequalities we find unjust in the name of equality, we criticize contracts of employment and pay scales in the name of merit, and we object to the worker's alienation in the name of autonomy. In other words, the principles of justice are principles because agents can use them to construct two-sided ideologies to reflect their interests, even if their interests are conflicting.

Neither customs nor ideologies, the principles of justice can be defined as "necessary fictions," beliefs that are indispensable for the development of action, without which one could not act together with others. We must "believe" in merit, for example, if we wish to combine equality and autonomy. By the same token, we must believe in the equality "of something" if we wish to construct a relatively rational organization in which individuals are interchangeable. Finally, we have to believe in the creativity of individuals if we want workers to handle unforeseeable situations so that the organization can respond effectively to its environment. In other words, the principles of justice are "functional frameworks" that we do not have to "truly" believe in to construct stable relations and credible, shared orders of judgment. But we have to act "as though" we believed in them. In short, although the use made of principles is infinitely malleable, the fact remains that the principles of justice are principles and not mere beliefs derived from mores or ex post facto rationalizations.

The Polyarchy of Principles

There is no preeminent principle of justice because each of them operates in a specific dimension of social relations: From the point of view of equality, the *other* is a member of a community; from the point of view of merit, he or she is a competitor; from the point of view of autonomy, he or she is a *subject.* Contrary to analyses that assign a principle of justice to a sphere of activity—the family, politics, the economy, etc.—our hypothesis is that individuals apply all these principles to their experience of work. As they are attached to all of these principles, which are all interconnected, the agents develop an autonomous normative activity that leads them to combine them: Although we are all equal, we all have different levels of performance, and at the same time we are all unique individuals in a tightly woven web of social relations. It is in this sense that we can speak of a system or syntax of principles of justice, but it is a very unusual system, not only because the various principles are necessarily interlinked—i.e., merit implies equality and autonomy—but also because each of the principles contradicts, and calls for criticism of, the others.

Merit can be criticized from the standpoint of equality and autonomy, considerations of equality are naturally opposed to merit and autonomy, while autonomy cannot abide a purely merit-based system and dismisses the reign of equality as a form of egalitarianism. It is this dialectic that grounds the normative activity of agents.

These propositions lead us away from theoretical strategies that prioritize a single principle of justice. For Nozick (1988), the primacy of equality is simply a dimension of freedom because what makes us equals is the freedom at our disposal. And if we are equally free, any restriction of freedom undertaken in the name of equality is an ipso facto violation of the most fundamental equality, which is our equality of freedom: "that equal right that every man hath to his Natural Freedom without being subject to the will or authority of any other man" (Locke 1984, §54). But freedom also prevails over "needs," in any case over needs as defined by utilitarianism, because it is the indispensable condition for the formation of a subjective sense of action that enables us to value things, emotions, and experiences. Freedom is a property of the self, assuming that the individual chooses activities that he considers to be worthwhile experiences, and injustice is therefore anything that limits his choice.

For the purposes of sociology, however, Nozick's philosophical strategy of according priority to one principle of justice over the others is less convincing than strategies that attempt to construct a combinative system of more or less mutually antagonistic principles. Kymlicka (1999, 10) says a theory of justice would do well to incorporate bits and pieces of most existing theories. Again from a sociological point of view, it is hard to imagine social agents facing a variety of principles of justice and tracing the chain of those principles back to a single principle that subsumes all others. At one and the same time, workers want their equality guaranteed, their merit recognized, and their autonomy ensured. And it is because "they want everything" that their social experience becomes a dynamic normative force, for to want everything in this domain is "to want everything and its opposite."

The assumption of a plurality of principles is also a departure from the framework proposed by Walzer, though the latter is situated at the opposite end of the theoretical spectrum. Walzer's model of complex equality postulates that each sphere or major field of activity sets up a specific type of dynamic between equality, merit, and need—which may be associated with autonomy for our purposes. When a sphere of activity is dominated by a single principle of justice, what Walzer calls a problem of monopoly arises. For example, when the economic sphere is dominated by merit alone, it is very likely that equality and need will be neglected. However, though management will, admittedly, favor merit and efficiency, there is no evidence that workers do likewise, for they will "resist" the preeminence of merit in the name of other principles: their equality and their "needs." Our thinking is based on the assumption that work is always regulated by a plurality of principles connected to logical courses of action that take material shape in the work experience. The sphere of work is not subject to a single "court of justice." To workers, the plurality of principles within a single sphere constitutes a model of elementary criticism, should they unknowingly engage in philosophy by attempting to define the ways in which they are the victims of, or witnesses to, unfair inequalities.

Another issue arises from what Walzer calls domination when the inequalities in one sphere, however fair they may be, are imposed upon other spheres. The structures whereby inequality is transferred from one sphere to another pose fairly conventional sociological problems, and the oft-expressed condemnations of privilege and patronage, cheating and old boy networks, are simply variations on the theme of the illegitimate transfer of inequalities. From this point of view, the problem of domination defined by Walzer is an asset to the normative critique of work, for everyone questions the degree to which work-based inequalities are fair outside the workplace and, in particular, the degree to which justice at work is perverted by inequalities from outside the workplace.

If it is true that individuals behave "like philosophers," we can reverse the lens and observe that the philosophers' categories are not so far removed from those used by individuals. According to many philosophers of justice, modern societies are dominated by the plurality of conceptions of justice (Van Parijs 1991). In fact, awareness of the contradictory nature of the principles of justice is not new. Conservative thinkers have long been striving to show that the triumph of liberty and equality inevitably leads to the decline of solidarity, undermined by exacerbated self-interest. Tocqueville expressed fears that the passion for equality would pose a threat to liberty, and Nietzsche (1985) demonstrated that egalitarianism could destroy freedom since only the state can guarantee it and "the State is the coldest of all cold monsters. . . . Coldly, it tells lies, and this is the lie that comes out of its mouth: 'I, the State, am the People.'" Finally, Marxist criticism has long taught that freedom is potentially fatal to equality because it is also the fox's freedom to raid the henhouse.

Rawls's theory (1987) is the one that accounts best for the oppositions between principles of justice. It asserts that liberty does not take priority over equality, or vice versa, while emphasizing the contradictory consequences of these principles. In his estimation, inequalities are acceptable only insofar as individuals are free to compete on an equal footing in the tests that define their social positions; true merit therefore proceeds from equal opportunity. Free and equal individuals can set up hierarchies only on the basis of tests of merit that are open to all. However, because tests of merit in turn produce inequalities, it is important to limit their impact in two ways. First, by questioning the legitimacy and reality of merit in view of "natural" inequalities due to physical, intellectual, or social handicaps, which brings us back to the problem of hierarchical equality and primary goods, which are fundamental equalities. The second way to limit the impact of tests of merit is by examining the degree to which inequalities generated by equal opportunity are compatible with the social inequalities deemed to be acceptable, because the inequalities produced by merit must not be permitted either to exacerbate the plight of the most underprivileged or to affect a primary good like self-respect or autonomy, understood as the ability to take action. This requirement elicits what Rawls calls the difference principle, which entails limiting the effects of equality and liberty in order to guarantee a certain degree of equality and liberty for all. In simplistic terms, liberty, equality, and self-respect—which is the product of individual autonomy and the overall social cohesion attenuating glaring inequalities—form the fundamental framework for a theory of justice, the benefits of which are all equally desirable yet profoundly contradictory.

The workers who are the subject-matter of this book are not "Rawlsian" because they are not trying to establish an order of priority, a lexical order or a hierarchy of potential sacrifices, no more than they are seeking the conditions of an initial contract. Neither the "veil of ignorance" nor the "*minimax*" seems to be the surest means of arbitration. Instead, the agents find it preferable to seek a representation of merely bearable inequalities (Frohlich/Oppenheimer 1992). The fiction of the initial contract is more a philosophical necessity than a practical requirement imposed on the agents. In the "war" of the principles of justice, no deity overpowers the others; and as a result there is an ever-ongoing search for agreements and arrangements, on the one hand, and, on the other, an inextinguishable criticism, an eternal inability to reach a perfect agreement.

Critical Dynamics

The purpose of this book is to describe and analyze the normative and moral dimensions of the social experience. We endeavor to show that although social agents operate within moral frameworks, these frameworks are not the only factor determining their judgments. For one thing, their feelings of justice depend on the situations imposed on them, but these feelings also possess a dynamic of their own involving autonomous moral activity, obliging each individual to construct his or her moral experience, just as each individual constructs his or her social experience (Dubet 1994). The reference to three central yet contradictory principles of justice generates a critical dynamic in which all the agents participate, to some degree, and as a function of which they construct their normative experience.

Figure 0.1 The Realm of Principles of Justice

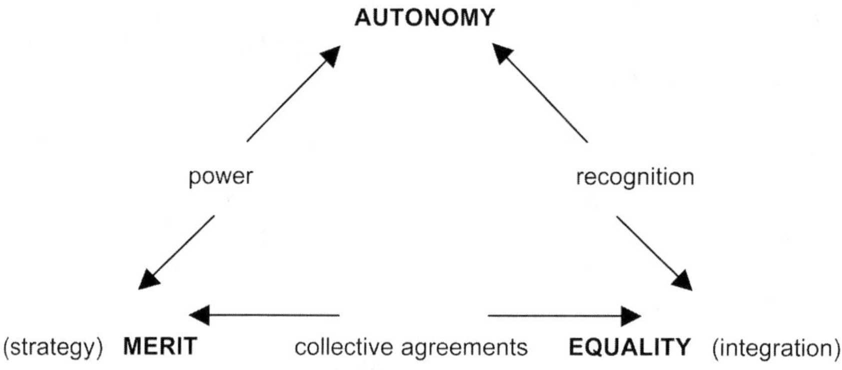

Table 0.1 Table of Criticisms

	Principles of Justice		
Principles Criticized	Equality	Merit	Autonomy
Equality	*excessive inequalities*	privileges	egalitarianism
Merit	selfishness	*exploitation*	domination
Autonomy	anomie	favoritism	*alienation*

The italicized words designate the criticism that arises when the principle itself is lacking: An absence of equality leads to complaints of unjust inequalities; lack of recognition for merit to complaints of exploitation; and absence of autonomy to alienation. The other words designate the criticism of one principle from the standpoint of another: the external critique.

1. The first of these mechanisms operates endogenously. Each subject criticizes his or her work situation based on each principle of justice: in the name of equality, in the name of merit, and in the name of autonomy. Problems arise because these criticisms are often contradictory. What is fair from the standpoint of equality may be unfair in terms of the other principles. Nevertheless, each of these criticisms has its own rationale.

2. Although they are simultaneously and necessarily interlinked yet mutually contradictory, the principles that structure the way workers evaluate justice do not necessarily result in fragmented or tragic experiences. Actually, these principles are rendered more or less compatible by intermediary constructs of justice, which are stabilized combinations rather than "pure" principles. These constructs are the framework for the daily routines and tradeoffs that enable the agents to overcome the fundamental "contradictions" of the principles.

Agreements mediate between equality and merit. How can merit, the result of each worker's activity, be reconciled with the equality of the individuals in a work collective? The answer is through labor law and collective agreements, which define a set of equivalencies between academic credentials and position occupied, between duties and qualifications, responsibilities and rewards, promotion by seniority and by selection. Individuals can thus refer to a whole set of relatively precise rules and frameworks enabling them to adjust their equality to their merit. Feelings of injustice are then based on failure to observe the rules, which are vigilantly upheld by union delegates, if there are any in the company in question, and which serve as the basis for the arbitration of labor disputes by the industrial tribunals. Labor laws and regulations are perceived by employees as constituting a happy medium, a system of checks and balances, rather than as literal embodiments of the principles of justice. The norms underlying collective agreements are less the expression of "values" than a means of readjusting the system. The rules are sound as long as they allow some leeway for maneuvering between opposing principles (Reynaud 1989).

Power mediates between merit and autonomy. Work takes place within an organized world that aims to achieve overall efficiency by assigning tasks and skills to a combination of machinery, techniques, and human beings (Dodier 1995). In practice, the organization of work combines the division of labor with the freedom of agents and allocates areas of autonomy—areas of uncertainty—and power relationships in which strategies are developed to test the individuals' merit and autonomy. In terms of principles of justice, the organization defines the merit attached to each job position and the autonomy granted to or earned by the individual. The concept of power is central here, in a field of tension between two poles: one being the authority attached to the positions and the other being the resources attained by the individuals (Crozier/Friedberg 1977). The various types of work organization breed feelings of injustice about anything that could be designated a problem of power or authority, such as authoritarianism, abuse of power, or exceeding one's authority. Conversely, power vacuums and failure to assume responsibilities destabilize the agents, accentuating tensions between them.

Recognition mediates between autonomy and equality. At work, as in social life on the whole, individuals perceive themselves as equals who cannot be reduced to their merits, but also as unique subjects who cannot be reduced to their equality either. In the following, for the sake of convenience and consistent terminology, we shall call the feelings of justice associated with the intersecting demands of equality and autonomy "recognition" (Honneth 2000). Workers desire personal recognition in the workplace, and this desire involves several dimensions. First, it is a matter of recognizing the dignity and utility of the work accomplished, especially what is commonly termed "dirty work," because people tend to associate the vileness of the work with the worker himself.[9] Second, the desire for recognition emerges as a claim to uniqueness: Workers want to have a name and face, regardless of their duties; they want their skills and needs to be recognized and their suggestions heard. Finally, recognition also designates recognition of the work itself, in particular its subjective toll on the individual: fatigue, stress, commitment, etc. The lack of recognition has been gaining ground as a criterion of injustice as new forms of labor organization increasingly mobilize workers' subjectivity, and cultural modernity has made fundamental values out of autonomy, authenticity, and self-fulfillment. A lack of recognition is experienced as an offense against the subject herself and the equality to which she is entitled, because as autonomous subjects we are all equal and unique.

3. Because the espousal of one principle will inevitably lead to criticism of the other two, the dynamics of the principles of justice move in an endless spiral. For example, from the viewpoint of equality, the rule of merit is that of self-interest, and the triumph of autonomy is perceived as the reign of anomie and moral mayhem. However, when the same individual judges on the basis of merit, the hierarchical order of equality appears to be a system of castes and privileges, whilst autonomy engenders an irrational disarray. Lastly, should the same individual adopt the principle of autonomy, merit becomes a form of domination, and equality a leveling egalitarianism. Thus, the object on which a moral judgment is passed may change shape completely depending on one's viewpoint. For example, though we may readily agree that the unemployed are victims of great social injustice in terms of equality, we cannot help suspecting that they are irresponsible, i.e., wanting in autonomy, and disapproving of the negligible disparity between unemployment benefits and the minimum wage. The same observer will often pass all three judgments, arriving at a paradoxical condemnation of both unemployment and its victims.

Many workers enter into a sort of critical spiral according to which the world has to be unfair and is always becoming even more unfair, because it is impossible to satisfy all the principles of justice simultaneously. The subject's relationship to the world is based less on belonging and belief than on criticism, on the rifts resulting from the very plurality of the principles of justice themselves. The only way for the worker to escape from the critical spiral is to detach himself from his own situation, broaden his field of comparison, and ask to what extent he himself and his "superiors" are responsible for the injustices that beset him. In short, the only way for him to temper the critical mechanisms is to gain some perspective on himself and his situation, and to gradually substitute questions of the good for questions of justice.

Our Focus

Rather than suggesting a new critical viewpoint or testing existing theories of justice, this book is an attempt to understand how social criticism is rooted in action and thereby takes part in forming subjects who are partially disembedded from the social mechanisms that structure their experience. We shall be taking up one of sociology's perennial questions: How can fully socialized agents also be the subjects of their own experience? How can they simultaneously be in the world and act upon it? How can they construct a meaningful world for themselves while at the same time opposing it? Our research necessarily focuses on the interaction between "universal" principles—universal in our type of society, in any case—and social situations. How do individuals experience and organize this interaction, of which they are necessarily a vector? The strongest critique is the one forged by society itself, which is far more trenchant than any "top-down" judgment; therein lie both the banality and grandeur of democratic societies. The purpose of this book is not to decry social injustices and the inequity of the world. The subjects do that forcefully enough themselves.

If it is true that the principles of justice are not ideologies, if they are neither sheer rationalizations nor the ultimate ruses of domination, the sociology of criticism must be substituted for critical sociology. Instead of judging in its entirety a social situation that is considered unjust, let us examine the agents' opinion of the justice of their situation and the world they live in. There is no need for us to substitute our critical faculties for those of our subjects, which are largely sufficient, nor should we assume that workers are misguided or alienated when they fail to meet our expectations. Without access to either the meaning of history or the secrets of the soul, we will simply have to observe what individuals think of their lot and their society. To be sure, we may be disappointed to find their indignation either insufficient or excessive by our standards, or their criticism of injustice somewhat imperfect and inexpert. Moreover, if it were simply a matter of saying what one thinks of the world's injustices, it would not be necessary to be a sociologist. We must therefore accept the fact that perceived inequalities are not "real" injustices, that certain real inequalities are not experienced as injustices, and that the only inequalities that are "really real" are those that are experienced as injustices.

By definition, injustice is a somber subject. Optimists will be dismayed by the gloominess of this book. They may find that workers are hypersensitive to petty injustices and that people are really not as wicked and resentful as our witnesses would have us believe. However, pessimists will also be dissatisfied because certain injustices they find appalling go largely ignored by workers, who endure many an inequity as the lesser of two evils. An individual can always build a good life despite the injustice of her society and the wickedness of others. Some will opine that human beings are not wise enough, others that they are too wise. The reader's critical judgment will perhaps make him or her react in the same way as the workers who speak in this book.

To document the normative activity of workers, we gathered three large sets of material from our subjects.

- We conducted a series of one-on-one interviews with 350 people, and analyzed 261 of these conversations. On the whole, this sample is a cross-section of the working population in France.
- The second type of data was derived from 11 focus-group interviews conducted with clusters of peers: farmers, laborers, nurse's aides, young managers, etc. We set up these groups with a view to discerning the lines of reasoning specific to various occupations. The choice of occupations was random, however, insofar as it depended on the research team's possibilities.
- Lastly, we submitted a questionnaire to 1,144 people. The questionnaire was designed to cull the respondents' judgments and opinions while controlling for variables defining their personal situation.[10]

In every case, we gave full credence to judgments and feelings of injustice, even when the grievances seemed "excessive" or "too diffident" in relation to the work situations described by the individual. A doctor who is paid six times more than a blue-collar worker may complain more than the worker, who finds his life acceptable as long as he has a job and can indulge in the leisure activities he enjoys. A college graduate may feel she is getting a "raw deal" although she earns more than a coworker who does exactly the same job but never finished college. The same boss is described by some as odious, by others as likeable, etc. This approach is not as naive as it seems. For when forming judgments and airing feelings, respondents are obliged to argue their case, to specify the principles and comparisons on which they are basing their judgments. Subjects will often express mixed and contradictory judgments because their angle, focus, and perspective are continually shifting. They may reel off a long list of injustices and conclude that, all in all, they are content with their lot in life. The sociologist, in turn, can build his or her own critique on the trivial criticisms, doubts, and queries any of us might come up with.

The first three chapters of this book treat the ways in which agents apply the three fundamental principles of justice: equality, merit, and autonomy. The fourth chapter deals with ways they express these principles in connection with problems of rights, power, and recognition. The fifth seeks to show how the clash between the principles of justice engenders an endless spiral of criticism, since each central principle militates against the others.

The next two chapters analyze feelings of injustice in the social contexts in which they arise. Based on responses to our questionnaire, Chapter 6 explains how conceptions of justice are more or less linked to social status and situations in the workplace. Régis Cortéséro wrote this chapter and, together with Benjamin Castets-Fontaine, did the statistical processing of the responses to the questionnaires. Chapter 7 examines the nexus between feelings of injustice and action, pointing out the gulf between action and judgments of injustice.

Notes

1. In the year 2000, for instance, although unemployment was down and economic growth robust, 79.8 percent of the French felt there was more and more inequality. (IFOP survey, French Ministry of Social Affairs).

2. From the translation by Weightman, John and Doreen, of *Tristes Tropiques*, p. 177.

3. This and the following figures are drawn from 1,144 responses to a questionnaire we distributed: cf. Chapter 6 and Appendix.

4. The industrial worker does not claim rights as a pauper, which would be charity, but as a citizen entitled to equality. Cf. on this head the analyses of G. Simmel (1998).

5. This is the reason why theorists bent on preserving the purity of equality confine it to a space that is not strictly social: that of human rights, democratic rights, or equal freedom (D. Miller 1999).

6. Rich and poor alike accept the fact that an executive earns four times as much as a cashier. There are some disparities in opinion, to be sure, but they are astonishingly slight: Five percent of the French poor are in favor of abolishing basic welfare as against 20 percent of the rich, while the majority approves of €615 welfare per month. Forty percent of left-wing voters are in favor of increasing the cashiers' pay as against 30 percent of right-wing voters. Forty-eight percent of the poor advocate taking money away from the "200 richest families" in the country, but so do 45 percent of the middle class and 34 percent of the rich. So there are differences of opinion, but they are not as profound as the consensus on what are considered just inequalities (Piketty 2003).

7. Article VI of the Declaration: "All citizens being equal (in the eyes of the Republic), they are all equally entitled to ranks, positions, and public appointments in accordance with their capacity and solely on the basis of their virtues and talents."

8. This Promethean conception of work and this faith in progress may seem outmoded now that progress has, on balance, caused so much damage, now that the dream of mastering history has become darkly comical, and now that leisure activities and private life have become so important. All the same, the communist Diego Rivera

painted monumental murals commissioned by Nelson Rockefeller, and his portrayals of work forged social movements and fueled revolutionary myths.

9. One cashier reported that, right in front of her, a mother admonished her daughter, "If you don't get good grades in school, you'll end up being a cashier like this lady!"

CHAPTER 1

Equality

E QUALITY IS AT ONCE the most self-evident and the most ambiguous of the principles of justice, for while it is taken for granted in democratic societies that we are all fundamentally equal, we nevertheless accept myriad social inequalities. What is worse, we find a great many inequalities perfectly legitimate—and any encroachment on those inequalities unjust. Pure egalitarianism hardly exists, if it all: not even 1 percent of the responses to our questionnaire might be termed egalitarian. The crux of the problem is that subjective equality is relative and based on comparing positions in the socioprofessional hierarchy. Gilles, a young engineer, quotes the adage, *"Quand je me regarde, je me désole, mais quand je me compare, je me console."* "It makes me sad to look at myself, but it makes me glad to compare myself to others."

Still, endless comparisons will not allay our sense of injustice if we compare our lot to everyone else's without any frame of reference. It appears that inequalities are truly deemed such only to the extent that they deviate, not from absolute equality, but from a representation of the inequalities we deem fair. Consequently, the principle of equality, which seems so simple and straightforward a priori, undergoes a transformation wrought by several sociological mechanisms. The fact is people fuse, and confuse, two overarching conceptions of equality. The first, *equality of position,* yields a whole set of critiques of hierarchies and "castes" that people find unacceptable because they are inimical to the standing and respect owed to individuals. The second conception is that of *equality of opportunity* to attain those positions. This conception denounces any form of discrimination impeding equal access to various and unequal positions to which everyone has a right to aspire in a democratic society. So the inequalities perceived through these two different prisms are not quite identical. But most people mix them up, and it is this mixture and its articulation that give rise to a basic and widely shared conception of equality.

Of "Castes" and Contempt

Although closed, "naturally" hierarchized social groups like castes and orders no longer wholly determine the social structure in our societies, and although institutional obstacles no longer bar passage from one group to another, the main criticism of inequalities concerns the social rifts, the "barriers," rather than the different "levels," that set individuals apart inside the workplace itself (Goblot 1967).

Why is it a matter of *castes* rather than *classes*? Because in the register of equality, agents are a priori less sensitive to exploitation and purely economic inequalities than to any form of social segregation. It is as though hard and fast dividing lines were drawn to set—and keep—social groups apart, as though the French Revolution had never been completed, as though social realms remained so remote from one another that their members don't even belong to the same human race. They feel subjected to an aristocratic order in a democratic world.

As these inequalities seldom have any formal or legal basis, they persist in our everyday attitudes and exchanges, in the very way we regard one another. What is most harrowing about feeling looked down upon is not so much *indignation* as *shame.* This is not shame at being exposed for all to see, but internalized shame, shame at being reduced to an ignominious—and, what's worse, invisible—condition (de Gauléjac 1996). Those who thought themselves equals are rudely awakened to the fact that they're not, and the sense of being an object of contempt is all the more acute in that it reveals an order of things so deeply internalized that the contempt isn't even intentional, isn't meant to be demeaning, for it is entirely a matter of course. This contempt affects the equality of conditions, equality between persons, or *fraternité* as the French revolutionaries would have put it.

"Treated Like a Dog"

The primary form of contempt is the elementary scorn for unskilled labor, which is often the most blatant. Yvan, a young blue-collar worker, discovered that his company parking lot was reserved for the engineers: *"It seems funny at first."* Daniele, a 22-year-old cashier, does not object to her bosses' authority or disparities in pay, but is appalled at the social chasm between the top and bottom echelons of the corporate pyramid.

"What really hits you is the difference between the top brass and us. You get the impression you're rank and file, see, like you're nobodies at certain times. In other words you get the impression there's a difference between the people at the top and the people at the bottom, as if there was nothing in-between.... You feel there's this gulf. And I'm not talking about the head honchos! Take the Christmas gifts, it's just incredible. When they ask you to take your pick, you get this dinky little catalog with a teeny-weeny assortment of really ordinary gifts, bottles of wine.... The floorwalkers, they get trips, appliances. You really feel there's this double standard." In the working world, hierarchical relations are not merely functional, but fundamentally inegalitarian, extending well beyond the company premises. Don't blue-collar workers need to park their cars as much as executives do? Don't cashiers need vacation travel as much as "floorwalkers" do? Why is what is offered to some denied to others? The workplace hierarchy is indeed pervaded by a wider-reaching inequality at odds with the fundamental equality of individuals.

A construction worker recalls how, during a heat wave, the technicians who came to the site complained about the inadequate air-conditioning in their offices—without saying a word about the working conditions for those toiling outdoors in the scorching sun! The assumption seems to be that men accustomed to strenuous labor are not made of exactly the same stuff as more delicately complexioned technicians. At base, as Halbwachs posited (1970), there is a fundamental inequality attaching to the very nature of work involving physical matter, to jobs that require neither training nor abstract knowledge. Because their work is simple, too simple, laborers see distinctions between "functional" levels and ranks turn into differences of "nature," and the gulf between the office and the shop floor comes to look unbridgeable. An assembly line worker gives a poignant rendering of this rift between two worlds. *"The big boss comes around from time to time, but we aren't allowed to see him because he doesn't like us, we're not from his world, we're the shop floor, see, we ain't skilled folks. Oh, yeah, he told us so: the white collars aren't to mix with the likes of us 'cause we're not from the same world. The boss is a scumbag. And that's the way management wants it. You gotta see it to believe it, that's really how it is. It's the company that creates this atmosphere: There's an upper crust and then there's us. Now there's two worlds: There's the blue collars and then there's the white collars, the supervisors. Those guys can't do a thing without us and we can't do without them either. There's no more respect. There are folks who sell out and others who grit their teeth and bear it, meaning me."*

The domination by management and the division of labor are not the only issues. There exists a far deeper inequality that strips certain workers of their dignity to the point of reducing them to "dogs." Louis works at a slaughterhouse: *"The little bosses always hollering, we don't know why. The ones who work in offices are respectable folk, whereas the others, well they're trash, lower class. The bosses talk to the workers like they're dogs.* " Indeed, the expression "treated like a dog" occurs in a great many interviews and says what it means: The inequality is so huge that it jeopardizes one's very membership in the same human species. Annick, a cleaning lady in a hospital, reports: *"Even though I'm older, if I say hi to a 30-year-old doctor he'll ignore me. A patient's about to arrive. If his daughter's a doctor, the supervisor warns us in advance: In other words we have to be careful and take good care of him, wait on him hand and foot. But why should we treat that person better than the guy in the next bed, who happens to be a simple worker? Poor stays poor, rich stays rich, and the gap's widening."*

The workaday world creates a tacit opposition between subtly hierarchized castes that circumscribe a multitude of personal destinies. *"The problem with castes,"* explains Cyril, a 24-year-old temp worker, *"is that everyone's more or less pigeonholed: Once you're poor you stay poor all your life. Every generation's like that."* When you're at the bottom, *"they can do just about anything they like with you"*—give you the dirty work, change your hours at the last minute. The whole chain of delegation of menial tasks engenders rifts that are all the more unbearable in that they separate people who should operate as a team.

There is a marked emphasis on the body in these accounts of workplace ordeals. Not only are workers "looked down on," they don't even get the same food. *"In the company lunchroom,"* says a sales manager, *"you've clearly got the managerial caste, the paper-pushers, and the workers. It's plain as day, we're not equals when it comes to grub. It's like water and oil: Shake it as you will, the oil stays on top, the water at the bottom."* Simon, a French rail employee, concurs: *"We don't get the same meal allowances—which means an exec can afford an appetizer, main dish, and dessert, and operatives only get the main dish or the dessert. I find that shocking!"*

Katia is temporarily employed at a school cafeteria. She is so enraged at the humiliation to which she is subjected that she wishes she were African, she wishes she were black, the better to dissociate herself from those who despise her. *"The schoolteachers really treat us differently because we're there to clean up. My father says, 'you know what, Katia, on the crapper we're all the same.' That's a pretty lame expression, but it's true. Now to them, the teachers, see, to them you're just a stand-in. I won't be able to go on like this, it's sickening. A teacher, say when she's working with little Amin, she won't be as conscientious as with a blond kid. You can feel it, you can tell someone who prefers the little blond kids to the little ethnics.... Some of my cousins live in a world I don't even know: the little habits, the little remarks, the little barbs that make you feel you're the black sheep of the family.... I'm in with the blacks, see, I don't hang with the whites, what with that mindset."* Katia feels so rejected by the white schoolteachers that, although white herself, she prefers to belong to the underclass of black outcasts.

The "Sneering System"

This perception of wrongful inequalities is not confined to the most flagrant scenes of class brutality in which the working class is patently plagued by the age-old curse attached to menial tasks. In a more ordinary way, it also concerns the long chain of prestige of the occupational hierarchy, as though the working world had preserved traces of an aristocratic hierarchy of respectability according to one's professional position. The display of courtesy between near equals in the workplace belies the rifts and latent disdain that persist in large bureaucratic organizations.

Although *conseillers d'éducation* (nonteaching disciplinary staff) in French schools have passed competitive exams and receive the same pay as teachers, Catherine complains that her peers on the teaching staff silently look down on her because her work is less dignified, for they are all very "touchy" on that point of honor. On the other hand, it goes without saying that the teachers can delegate to her all manner of unrewarding tasks. The "sneering system" is in fact rather subtle: Catherine belongs to the world of *school administration,* which is less noble than the world of *knowledge transmission.* Despite her official equality in statutory terms, she's not a "real" teacher and is consequently "looked down on."

Carole, teacher at a vocational school, denounces the caste spirit of her counterparts at the adjacent academic-track high school. *"I think it's a good thing we've got a single staffroom for the high school and vocational school because it allows us to mix with our colleagues at the high school and at the same time to see how teacher training can go to people's heads. There's this disparity between teachers of 'noble' subjects and the little vocational school instructors—or the 'lepers' as I call them. It's plain to see. There's this teeny-tiny area reserved for the vocational school teachers; we've got three armchairs and 65 square feet to cram all our stuff in. The rest is occupied by the rest of the teachers. It's pure racism. They must think vocational teachers are the same as vocational students, that is to say, the ones without much culture. Sure, I could very well have asked, why don't you say hello to me. But I don't feel like wasting my time, and that might've seemed a little aggressive."* This sort of treatment symbolically brings the oppressed and the new pariahs closer together. Carole has opted for the most radical form of labor unionism, which doesn't give an inch in the jockeying for position in the social stratification system, while fighting for a social revolution. So whereas Katia identifies with blacks because she feels rejected, Carole identifies with the working class because she feels despised, like the proletariat.

Sometimes, prejudice poses a threat to the elementary dignity of equal subjects. Michel, a young nurse's aide, explains that, to the nurses, *"We're nobodies. And as for the doctors, the first thing they look at is your rank. When they look at you, they duck to read the rank on your coat.... I'm 22, I'm not gonna stay a nurse's aide forever. I don't feel like putting up with that all my life."* The hospital world is particularly susceptible to this play of castes, these chains of contempt in which the dominant links consider themselves above the rules. Dominique, a nurse, recalls, *"There was this head doctor who used to smoke in my unit. He'd do his rounds smoking in the hallway, and before walking into a patient's room he'd ask the nurse to hold his ciggy for him. He wouldn't stoop to following the rules."* On the one hand, the hierarchy is rational and functional, and no one contests the doctors' authority. On the other hand, though, this hierarchy remains heavily symbolic and aristocratic, for the division of labor assigns a very precise degree of dignity to each and every activity: at the top, science and technology; at the bottom, the suffering and the "shit" (Douglas 2000).

Service or Servants?

In terms of equality, what is deplored is not so much power or domination as the chasms between—and the ignominy attached to—certain positions rather than specific persons. This is the reason why the issue of social contempt comes up systematically in every service activity. But how does one serve without being a servant? *"The customers know I'm in the position of a waiter and they're in the position of customers. They overrate themselves, they confuse serving with servile,"* says Damien, a bartender. *"I'm looked down on,"* relates a saleswoman at a bakery, *"because I'm in a fancy neighborhood where I count for less than nothing. There's way too many bourgeois moneybags 'round here and they sure as hell let you feel it."* A restaurant waitress doesn't wish to be a "maid" or a "slave." In the same vein, Linda, a cleaning lady, works for a family whose children won't straighten up their room because the maid will do it. It makes her feel "very small" to be beneath the children in the pecking order.

Tocqueville pointed out this problem long ago: The relations involved in the provision of personal services are hardly compatible with democratic equality, for although one may well be willing to obey a boss whose legitimacy is of a technical or political nature, it is nonetheless humiliating to obey a private person, even for remuneration. Money does not neutralize the humiliation; at best, it makes it bearable. Furthermore, the insuperable social divides in aristocratic societies permitted a certain personal closeness because they didn't jeopardize the pecking order. In the democratic world, however, though excessive aloofness is a form of contempt, so is excessive familiarity. Paul, a skilled confectioner, bemoans the *"contempt of those who take us for lollipop dispensers and don't stop their telephone conversations to order something from you. If a customer has to wait for three minutes in my store, they'll take the liberty of making a snide remark; three quarters of an hour at the doctor's, and they'll say hello to him cordially."* In the wake of the rapid spread of service jobs in sales, healthcare, and social work, the extreme sensitivity of person-to-person service providers about any signs of disrespect cannot be dismissed as merely anecdotal. Asked by whom they feel most ill-treated, service-sector employees put customers and users first, ahead of coworkers and management.[1] The fact that these employees are often school trained and qualified individuals, nurses and social workers, or college students working odd jobs, certainly heightens their sensitivity to this ill treatment.

Often enough all these petty humiliations prove all the more upsetting because they reopen old wounds: that embarrassment during recess when classmates made fun of one's bargain-basement outfit; that sense of shame at seeing one's parents derided; the wound that never healed at seeing one's mother step aside in the line at the store to let the wife of some minor local worthy go first; that ignominy of being looked down on by shopkeepers, neighbors, or civil servants. And yet, keener still is that abiding sense of shame at not having reacted, not having even responded because one felt so ashamed at the time.

The Just Order and Honor

The denunciation of injustice is more ambiguous than one would think, for the logic of castes is not binary: It is not confined to those on top versus those at the bottom, white-collar versus blue-collar staff, servers and served. In fact, the castes are diffracted along a long chain of ranks and positions, and maintaining one's position is a "matter of honor" (Iribarne 1989). Viewed from this angle, democratic equality in France is not so much absolute equality as a broadening of the aristocratic mindset, a democratization of the prestige attached to status in the sense in which Weber used the term.

Consequently, individuals are perfectly capable of deploring the contempt heaped upon them while jealously guarding their position in a matrix of microcastes that seems fair to them. Incidentally, this is why no one is truly egalitarian and why the flip side of the feeling of contempt is that of honor, the respect owed to each person's position, for honor and contempt are two sides of the same coin. In this sense, which does not detract from the foregoing analysis, I can feel despised while despising others—without, of course, admitting to myself that I despise them, for the prevailing order that establishes my position seems to me fundamentally just.

Demeaning Work and Defending One's Social Standing

Sandra, who is a secretary, does not complain much about her situation, but resents the fact that her boss continually requests her to empty his ashtray, thereby degrading her from coworker to servant. She defends her status because this demeaning task ought to be delegated to others: *"It's not really my role. There's a cleaning lady for that."* Hospitals, for example, are dominated by this dichotomy between honorable occupations and menial tasks (Hugues 1996). Recounts Therese: *"Us kitchen staff are considered the lowest link in the chain, we're looked down on.... One time, when a senior nurse dropped a glass, I handed her the broom and told her to sweep it up. She said, 'Hold up a sec, you see my rank?' I told her, 'My rank's kitchen staff, so you break a glass, you get a broom and sweep it up.' I don't know. They show up, they think they're royalty and we're there to wait on them."* Then there are hierarchies involving even more subtle distinctions, such as the bartender who won't wash glasses. If he does wash up, it is done as a favor—a gift beyond the normal call of duty, a friendly gesture transcending professional boundaries: He'll do a buddy a favor, but the decision is up to him.

In many cases academic qualifications are seen more as a mark of dignity and rank than as proof of skills. They permit the bearer to lay claim to a certain standing, and as such should keep him or her from having to do certain jobs that are deemed degrading. *"I didn't study all those years for this,"* was a recurrent phrase in the interviews: 41.1 percent of our respondents thought their jobs did not come up to their level of qualification. Such sentiments are all the more commonplace now that the devaluation of qualifications obliges job seekers to take up posts that fall short of the professional promise of their credentials (Passeron 1982). They have to lower their sights, while taking care not to demean themselves too far. In such cases, the feeling of debasement is not necessarily linked to a real decline in social standing: It ensues from the mismatch between hopes forged at school and positions offered in the employment market (Duru-Bellat 2006).

Benedicte, who was forced to give up her occupation as a hairdresser because she was allergic to hair products, has a hard time coming to terms with her job behind the counter at a bakery. She was accustomed to having a close rapport with her customers, including members of the *"bourgeoisie,"* who now treat her with disdain. She is also particularly hostile to "equality" for immigrants, which poses a threat to her social standing. *"When my mother asked welfare to help foot the bill for the school cafeteria, they told her: You have two grown-up children who are working. Ask them to help. Fatima and Mouloud behind her in line, they're gonna ask for the same thing, and welfare's gonna pay the cafeteria bill for their kids—and for all the others who ask too."* Sometimes the social decline is quite spectacular. *"I have the impression people think I'm an idiot,"* says Philippe, a 50-year-old alumnus of a good management school who used to hold an executive-level position. Now Philippe is reduced to selling carpets and doing the bidding of superiors who are much younger and far less qualified than he. With his wife, Philippe tries to maintain his self-esteem by continuing to cultivate middle-class tastes and leisure activities that are in line with his "real" social standing.

The same type of reaction often refers to age, sex, and ethnic origin. French workers are compelled to do what they call "beginner's work," "women's work," or "Arabs' work." Maïté believes cleaning staff are despised by *"paper pushers,"* though *"we're not the Arabs of society."* The conviction that they are doing a job they shouldn't have to be doing, work that is beneath them, is often expressed by trainees and temporary workers, who are treated like "gofers" by the permanent staff. *"The permanent staff think we're inferior because they're on the company payroll and we're just hired hands."*

There exists, in short, a panoply of more or less acute feelings of injustice based on a just order of inequalities according to age, academic and professional qualifications, and employment history. Some workers believe their standing has been eroded by technological developments that obviate the need for skilled labor. This conviction was expressed by construction workers we interviewed, who are currently reduced to assembling prefabricated parts, which puts them in direct competition with temp workers from Africa and Central Europe.

The Just Order of Institutions

When defending their position and the prestige associated with it, workers are often defending a more global interest, a just order of which their rank is the consequence and guarantee. In such cases, any encroachment on their dignity is tantamount to an encroachment on what they represent in terms of the symbolic dimension of their status, and what they embody is a higher good that is a fundamental element of social integration. It is in this sense that the republican model has to some degree supplanted the Roman Catholic model in France (Dubet 2002). We should note in passing that the association of prestige and rank with the function of promoting social integration is not confined to institutions that retain a bit of their "sacrosanct" and sanctuary status, such as hospitals, schools, and the military. For example, 73 percent of those who filled out our questionnaire find that there is too great a disparity between the salaries of managerial staff and cashiers, but only 32 percent feel the same way about the earnings disparity between doctors and cashiers. In the former case, "only" money and business are at issue, whereas a general and legitimate social function is ascribed to medical practitioners.

It is probably in the sphere of education that one finds the most patently manifest identification of status with the general function of promoting integration and justice. This is in any case the domain in which it is most clearly and blatantly expressed. Martine, a State-certified teacher,[2] explains: *"Agrégés are better paid. You might say that's unfair, but that's not the case. Their qualification stands for something, it's hard to obtain."* So it is reasonable for those who have passed a more difficult examination to enjoy higher pay and a less onerous workload. Martine concedes that *"equal opportunity doesn't really exist,"* but that does not prevent her from believing that hierarchies based on qualifications are morally justifiable and fair. In her view, what many might call privilege is a just reward, not only for greater merit, but also for greater value. For those who have passed their *Agrégation* have scaled the heights of culture and knowledge, which are a greater good. It is through them that schools can serve as true repositories of French culture and *"civilisation"*!

This reasoning serves to legitimize the inequality in question. Sylvain, an economics and social studies teacher, thinks the teachers' professional protectionism is perfectly justified because it is implicitly bound up with the role of schools and culture in society. Indeed, similar arguments are used to counter many a charge of injustice. Sylvain told us how *"the students were put in their place"* when they complained about a teacher who pulled his teaching material off the Web. He went on to laud the attitude of the school principal: *"The faculty held firm. We felt morally supported."* Sylvain did not find his colleague's conduct appropriate, but that was a minor consideration compared to the legitimacy of school authority, which would collapse if contested by the student body. In defending this just hierarchy, Sylvain does not feel he is defending merely his own interests, but those of an institution whose very existence guarantees a higher justice. For schools reproduce a just hierarchy, of which Sylvain's own career is a case in point: Schooling enabled him to rise to the position of teacher despite his modest background. Any perceived privilege or injustice can be justified if it plays a role in social integration.

Thus, interests that smack of professional protectionism are, as it were, transcended by the function of the institutions behind them. Any attempt to subvert the status of teachers is an attack on republican equality itself. Naturally, we can always question the good faith of such arguments. But regardless of our conclusions, the fact that the defense of social position draws its justification from this register is in and of itself of sociological value, because the just order of social stratification is founded on a principle of higher justice, on the definition of an ultimate good: the defense of equality, culture, or the nation. *"Today,"* points out one teacher, *"you have the impression society promotes mediocrity, and the star system is absolutely not our domain. We're about effort, about the long term, not the flash in the pan. The youths from the projects spend all their time dreaming of becoming soccer stars who make millions, or more or less mindless celebrities who make outrageous sums of money because they know how to talk on TV."*

Alain, a police officer and son of a police officer, puts forward similar arguments: The bureaucratic rationality of the police force is in itself a guarantee of fundamental equality before the law. When others on the force are upset because they fail to obtain an expected promotion or posting, it is simply because they do not know all the workings of the machine. *"It's not as unfair as all that because all grade-related and budgetary decisions are governed by a system of allocations. Only a certain quota of people can benefit from higher gradings. Those who feel wronged don't have all the facts, they don't know all the ins and outs of the matter."* This is a just world as long as people play by the rules. *"What really pisses me off is when one of my subordinates informs me of something. I'm an officer, so I like to be informed by my superiors."* A sense of injustice results from a flaw in an otherwise perfect institution in which everyone has to keep to his rank in order to safeguard universal equality within the nation and the Republic. Among other things, this hierarchical order is justified in that its rationality is the expression of a higher law without which *"man turns into a savage."*

Jeremie, a mailman, deplores the long *"downhill slide"* in the postal service—e.g., *"casual Friday wear"* and *"rampant commercialism,"* trends that he views as heralding the demise of a bastion of the French Republic. In defending his status, working conditions, and rank, he feels he is defending an ideal of public service, i.e., the unity of a nation sustained by standardized services. The theme of fair inequalities here implicitly involves notions of social integration and the community, or, to put it more simply, of the nation as a community of equals.

The Just Order of the Nation

At the outset, we are equals in the nation and in the community. Sometimes this framework is confined to a narrowly circumscribed community. For Vicente, a nurse, the chain of command in a hospital is based on a fair and functional division of labor, all the more so by dint of what Durkheim would have termed its "organic solidarity." *"There's no point having the best surgeon in the world if the operating room is dirty, if the nurses don't do the bandages right, if the patients aren't cleaned up right, if the rooms are disgusting. It's all a great chain.... They've never gone on strike because people just wouldn't understand. We're surrounded by craftsmen, farmers, and shopkeepers who're slaving away, who know we're not badly paid. So seeing us in the streets, they wouldn't understand. It would be like protesting against the steamroller that's leveling the country."* In other words, hierarchies are legitimate because they preserve and reflect the community.

"Natural" hierarchies are simply extensions of the "natural" community of the nation conceived of as a hierarchical organization that must be protected from danger and attack. Hierarchies within certain professions are justified to the extent that they are legitimated by the higher order of the nation, in much the same way that religious hierarchies were once justified by the need to preserve the community of the faithful. Fire department lieutenant Jean-Marie backs this theory of spontaneous organicism in associating the defense of gender inequalities and that of inequalities between French nationals and foreigners in the fire department. After pointing out that firefighting is a job involving plenty of risks and sacrifices, he assails the decision to admit women into the corps. *"Just go ahead and try freeing someone who weighs 280 pounds! If you're a woman, you won't be able to do it. Women don't have the same resistance to stress, they get all emotional when you need to keep a cool head. It's a biological fact: It weakens men a little to work with women."* He goes on to criticize the double standard of different physical tests for male and female recruits: *"It makes no sense because when you're out on a call, you ought to be able to do the same things. I admit women have certain abilities when it comes to being attentive to the needs of the elderly and stuff like that."* For Jean-Marie, this inequality of the sexes within the fire department corresponds to an inequality in society, which may call on its citizens—but not foreigners—to sacrifice themselves for their country. *"In recruitment we're going to favor people with a proper French background. I have a rather low view of Moroccans, Algerians, and other troublemakers. My priority is to give jobs to the French. The state should send the Arabs back to their countries.... These days the corner grocery stores are all kosher or nonkosher, which means pork or no pork. Me, I'm French, and if I want to buy ham or pork I can't 'cause I got a Muslim grocer who's opened up on my street."*

Military personnel we interviewed take the view that hierarchy in the army is likewise founded on shared values that guarantee the defense of the fundamental equality of French nationals. Foreigners, at all events those who do not "play by the rules," are a threat to the nation and, above all, to the institutions that embody it.[3] Julien associates the order of the barracks with the order of the nation. The military hierarchy is fair because it is based on physical and moral virtues revealed in the course of arduous ordeals, and in some cases that means hazing. *"That boosts morale. There's a little abuse involved, then again this is an elite regiment and me, personally, I don't find it shocking. Helps select the right recruits. We keep the best so as to stay a crack regiment in case one day we're needed. I think we're better off getting rid of ten jackoffs and keeping one straight shooter than keeping nine jackoffs and one straight shooter. Hazing's gone down because supposedly it shocked public opinion. Public opinion's a big word, but it did shock a lot of civilians."* Clearly, for Julien, rigorous military order guarantees national cohesion itself. He finds hierarchical inequalities to be just, moreover, and any criticism thereof profoundly unjust. *"We're often regarded as fascists. That's going a bit far, isn't it? And then with the remarks I was just making, that'll only go to confirm it!"*

When individuals reason in terms of equality of conditions and positions, hence in terms of a just hierarchical order, they tend to focus less on equality *sensu stricto* than on integration in a shared world to ensure a social cohesion that will accord everyone the place in society he or she deserves. This is why denunciations of social injustice draw chiefly on a morally charged vocabulary: contempt, humiliation, honor, respect, etc. Of course, the order in question varies from one profession to another: It is not the same for public school teachers defending the equality of citizens as it is for the armed forces defending the nation or workers defending the respect that is owed to them. But in any case it is the conception of a just order that will dictate the terms of the critique.

It follows that criticism of the "powers that be" will be chiefly along moral lines. Not only does the electorate hardly trust politicians, but many people actively mistrust them on the assumption that those in power must be rotten to the core. Politicians are not merely incompetent, they corrupt the community and undermine the shared values of the Republic, the nation, and the working class. This discourse presupposes two separate worlds: that of the powerful "fat cats," often identified with the encroaching outside forces of Europe and globalization, and that of the man in the street devoted to a just order (Birnbaum 1979). Though this discourse involves a wide array of different ideologies and values, its proponents concur in the conviction that we are "the people" and our enemies are either above or beyond "the people," outside of the elementary community that forges equality. The questions they pose point up this dichotomy: When so many people go hungry, how can we not be outraged by profligate government spending and presidential jaunts overseas? Why give so much money to foreign countries and so little to the poorest people in France?

Naturally, all the political scandals only serve to bolster this view. Henri, an IT engineer, told us the following story: *"A few years ago, there was this woman—we won't go into all the sordid details—who was on her own with two or three children. Anyway, she stole some meat from a supermarket around Christmas time, and she got arrested. She was unlucky to be that hard up, and unluckier still to get caught. Well, at the first trial they let her go, but then the decision was overturned and she was convicted. Then again, you got guys embezzling funds, you got a government minister on the take—it's outrageous—he sure as hell never goes hungry or worries about the cold. He's pleased as punch with himself. He sure as hell won't get bothered, he doesn't worry: 'How am I gonna feed my daughter, my wife, how am I gonna get by till payday'?"* Julien condemns the greed of management at the supermarket where he works: They are so "hard-hearted" they throw out expired items rather than giving them to the poor. In short, the "powers that be" are despicable because they betray republican virtues, sell the nation short, and ignore the suffering of the people. As David, a barman, puts it: *"Some people have millions, and some people have minimum wage to feed a whole family. They work their fingers to the bone. I find that beyond the pale, and it's getting worse and worse. In any case, France has been and gone, it's a rotten world, a fucked-up world, a world where you get crushed, it's sink or swim, no one bats an eye if you go down."*

Discrimination and Equal Opportunity

The main problem with the way people think about equality is that behind the same word, and often the same experience, lie significantly different, if not contradictory, interpretive frameworks. Most of our interviewees swung back and forth imperceptibly between equality defined as a position in an order and equality defined as a range of opportunities that should be accessible to everyone. In the former, the fundamental equality of individuals is an extension of the most minute "aristocratic" positions. In the latter, equality is conceived of as equal access for all to any and all equal or unequal positions. This is equality of opportunity, or liberal equality. To be clear about what we mean by the word "liberal," which often has a pejorative sense in public debate in France, it simply means that equality is considered a right of access to positions, a right that is the corollary of the fundamental equality of individuals. Equal opportunity is not so much a challenge to the social structure itself than the possibility of mobility within that structure. Critiques based on equal opportunity focus less on contempt and rank as such than on the fact that contempt and rank may block access to positions that are supposed to be accessible to everyone.

In these terms, all individuals are liberals and mix two critiques of social inequality. On the one hand, they feel that the social order of positions is not entirely just. On the other hand, they feel that inequalities impede individuals from attaining various positions. Condemnations of gender-based and "racial" inequalities underscore the shift from one register to another.[4] In the first approach, they are contesting a constituted representation of society; in the second, they focus on the social and subjective experience of individuals.

The Feminine Critique

Although "only" 28.8 percent of the respondents to our questionnaire stated that they had heard sexist remarks at work, the working conditions imposed on women were nonetheless deplored in all the interviews with women and most of the interviews with men.[5] The thrust of this critique goes to the heart of the conceptual shift from one notion of equality to the other, from considerations of castes and the naturalization of inequalities to the fight against discrimination.

Women are paid less, are less likely to be appointed to positions of responsibility, have greater difficulty proving their merit and securing permanent contracts, and are more often unemployed than men. Those who did not speak to us on their own behalf spoke on behalf of other women. Their inequality in the workplace is a direct consequence of a fundamental inequality, that of "castes," and of the naturalization of inequalities that women inherit as their birthright. Nadine explained that she wanted to become a pharmacist to prove to her parents that she was as capable as her brothers. All the women said that they continually had to overcome obstacles to their equality and that their careers are an ongoing struggle because, to be more or less on a par with their male counterparts, they have to do more and show they are doing more than men. To begin with, they have to work harder, as most of our female respondents affirmed. Linda, a cleaning woman, explained what her work meant to her. *"What I want is to have a job and get my paycheck at the end of the month. Then there's the benefits, you know, I get everything they do: I got my paid leave, got my paid vacations, I'm happy. I'd rather be a cleaning lady than stay at home on welfare. I don't like idlers."* But this relative liberty has its price: *"My husband is a bricklayer, I'm the one has to do all the housework. He hardly helps me with anything. He really could help me a little."* Fabienne is not a cleaning woman, in fact she might employ one herself: Both she and her husband are physiotherapists and relatively well-off. And yet her equality is by no means assured. *"My work's a little mixed with my family life, I juggle the two because I'm as much a mom as a physiotherapist. My husband can work seven days a week because I look after the children three days a week. I don't work on Wednesdays and weekends to be with my kids. As a result I do fewer sessions than he does, so I make less.... I wouldn't mind reversing the roles so I'd be free to organize my time, travel, get ahead in my career. If he feels like taking a course, he goes out in the evening. The reverse would be harder, not because he begrudges me that, but there are things at home I know how to do and he wouldn't.... I wish there were a way I could retire earlier. I mean it's more often us than the gentlemen who have health problems after pregnancies."* Neither Linda nor Fabienne could be described as angry feminists. Linda's husband is probably more "macho" than Fabienne's, who is willing enough but not very able; being domestically challenged is turned to their advantage by many a man (Kaufmann 1992). But both of these women pay dearly for their equality, which is never fully achieved. Absent the most strenuous exertions, the demands of work and family constitute a zero-sum game involving relative sacrifices in one sphere or the other. As Dominique, an office worker, sums it up, *"If you are a woman, you can't choose between a career and raising your children. If you put your career on hold, you can pretty much bet you won't get it back again when you return."*

Unequal treatment of women is not confined to the hearth and home: It is also endemic to the workplace, where male attitudes consign them to their sex. Elodie, a switchboard operator, describes the behavior of one of her coworkers. *"He comes in, acting like we're old friends right away, he asked for a kiss on the cheek, which I didn't like one bit. Then he just stands there in front of you looking at you. Or sometimes he come up behind you, touches your neck, touches your waist. He takes advantage of the fact that I'm younger than him."* Here again, it would be wrong to assume that such conduct is confined to the macho traditions ascribed to the working class. Therese, who gave up a "young exec" career to teach primary school so as to spend more time raising her own children, told us that when she was writing her thesis, *"There was this vile guy: When you walked by and you were wearing a skirt—I'm not talking about a mini-skirt, just an ordinary everyday skirt, nothing vampish—well, he'd turn around and you could see his eyes looking you over from the bottom up. That sort of thing is vile, I've never really been able to get over that. Most of the time, I dress in a blend-in-everywhere style so as to avoid being noticed because I just can't stand that really vulgar look from men."* Another student, Valerie, had to put up with even blunter advances, all the more unbearable as they came from one of her professors. During an out-of-town colloquium, the latter booked one hotel room for the two of them. *"It was 2 a.m., and I knew that making a scene wouldn't change anything. He insisted I was making a fuss about nothing, and I felt almost ridiculous, as though sleeping in the same room was completely normal. So I shared the room with the professor for four days. He didn't touch me, but if he had it would have come to blows. I spent four days with this guy. I slept and took baths in the company of this professor who talked dirty to me for four whole days. When I told my thesis supervisor about all this, I realized he was completely unaware of the situation. No one had told on the guy before, and that had been going on like that for five years. Most of the people I told, especially the men, said it's not a big deal, he didn't lay a hand on you. What's worse, I came out looking like I was uptight."*

Some time later, Valerie obtained a teaching post at another university. *"I found it very hard to find my place in this milieu. It's very hard to convince the professors you're up against that you're as good as they are. You have to do more to show them you're good in your field, that you're smart. The problem is the way they see me, as a girl who's nice and cute, as a good girl. They don't grab your ass because it's a university: It's an environment where people are very intelligent. It's quite perverse: You still have harassment, only it's intelligent, very intellectual harassment."* The equality of qualifications and diplomas has not kept women from being treated as inferiors because they are women and because a woman's body is deemed a handicap in and of itself. It is a handicap when they are "too good-looking," when they "get hit on," and when their beauty is associated with a dearth of other qualities. But it is also a handicap when women are not beautiful: They are still consigned to their bodies, though perhaps less eroticized and therefore less esteemed. Invariably, though, they are deemed incapable of hard work. Thérèse told us: *"Here in the kitchen we're in a man's domain, you know. We women are sent straight to the assembly line and that's where we stay. There's no chance of doing anything else. I passed my exam just like the men; I got a chef's certificate. If I passed the exam it's for the same reasons the men did. On that basis, I should be capable of something. We talk to the chefs about that. We ask them why we aren't allowed to cook.... They say we'd get burned, we aren't strong enough, they find pretexts that may be true, I don't know. But I used to work at an organization where I did the same job as the men."*

Our study yielded dozens of stories of this kind, and the prevalence of sexual inequality was confirmed by a number of male respondents who frankly assert their "superiority." In addition to Jean-Marie, the fireman we met earlier, there was Jean, a liquor salesman, irked by female coworkers who do not drink with customers: *"You have to drink. They don't accept women who turn up and don't drink. These women already have a lighter workload than we do, if they're not going to do the job right either.... Afterwards they take us to court. It's infuriating, it's maddening for someone who works really hard, who cancels his private life for his professional life."* Our male respondents by and large took more nuanced views than Jean, but basically owned up to these same obstacles facing women in the workforce. One male nurse stressed that it is much easier for men to pass the recruitment examination owing to the paucity of men in the profession. And once they make it onto the staff, male nurses are often excused from some of the more menial tasks—when patients aren't mistaking them for doctors, a confusion our respondent didn't mind and even found amusing. In another line of work, a warehouseman told us about the sarcastic remarks from his fellow workers, who treated him "like a woman" when he opted to work part-time so as to spend more time with his children.

Notwithstanding the diversity of situations and narratives it comprises, the feminine critique differs from the foregoing critiques on two specific points. First, the just order it presupposes is not a hierarchical order, but absolute equality between men and women. The order of professional hierarchies plays a secondary role, for women appeal to their fundamental equality to insist on their admission to professional hierarchies, hence the contention that the feminine critique precedes the class-based critique (Méda 2002). The second common attribute of feminine discourse is the virtual absence of the first-person plural. Women do not say "we" or "us" because the domination of women is almost always experienced in a personal, if not physical, manner. In the feminine experience, the perception of one's own body is far more central than it is for men. Consequently, the principle of liberal equality is invoked by individuals more than by groups. Finally, it appears that gender differences concern all women, regardless of their social condition.

Racism

Because they are set apart by skin color, accents, and racial stereotypes, the victims of racism are, like victims of sexism, prisoners, as it were, of their own bodies. Racist acts of aggression, like sexist assaults, are relatively rare: The majority of our respondents said they had never experienced any such attacks firsthand. However, 26 percent of those interviewed did say they had heard racist remarks in the workplace, and 11 percent felt they had been victims of racial discrimination at work. Again as with women, the tactics used to demean the victims are subtle and recurrent: disdainful looks, racist jokes that are supposed to be funny in the chummy workplace atmosphere, veiled discrimination at the recruitment stage, suspicions based on prejudice, etc. (Bataille 1998). Racism nevertheless differs markedly from sexism in that whereas women readily acknowledge their gender, the victims of racism have a harder time believing they are being discriminated against on the basis of the color of their skin until they eventually have to face the facts. For one thing, many do not wish to be different; that difference is imposed on them. For another, they have a hard time accepting the disconnect between the moral condemnation of racism and its widespread everyday practice. Though no one will own up to being a racist, a great many prejudices concerning "immigrants"[6] are blatantly expressed: They are accused of being welfare freeloaders, slackers (or, on the contrary, submissive drudges), criminals, and a threat to national culture. Most of them are confronted with these and similar prejudices rather than outright racist attacks. Notwithstanding their status as fundamentally equal subjects, the victims of racism are lumped together by others according to their appearance and ethnic origins.

Senam, a saleswoman of African descent, describes the experience quite well: *"No one ever comes out and says, 'I won't hire you because you're black.' They don't say that, but still it's there. You're gonna have to struggle at least ten times harder than the others, and people will try to sabotage you in little ways, it's very subtle. They're not gonna throw it in your teeth: 'Hey, I won't hire you 'cause I don't like your nationality.' Instead of putting it like that, they'll give you a whole bunch of reasons, but it all boils down to exactly the same thing, you know. I've been there, I could feel it. They keep coming at you, you can feel something's up. It's little things like that, it's in the nuances."*

Foreigners, moreover, face legal and regulatory hurdles. *"When I was in college, to work as a school monitor, they wouldn't take people who didn't have French nationality. Lots of my girlfriends got these monitor jobs: They worked three days a week, and at the end of the month they got a thousand euros. I had to work every day of the week, practically—housecleaning, babysitting, a little here and a little there. You can't help thinking it's unfair."* Now Senam has found work and everything is fine—were it not for the racism. *"I really got a lucky break. It's going great. We got a boss who's very kind, very obliging; she's someone who does her best to make everybody comfortable. As for the customers ... well, you can tell they'd rather it wasn't me taking care of them. Sometimes they're aggressive for no reason at all, just to be nasty. All it takes is for you to be having a bad day and you'll break out in tears.... French people are really careful, but there's one line that gets my goat: 'Don't you miss home? Don't you miss your family?' I interpret that as 'Get out!'"*

Sometimes, though, people are "much less careful," and the racism is point-blank. *"I had a racist teacher: 'I don't like blacks, I don't like Arabs.' He always said the same thing: 'If your parents can't face up to their responsibilities, then they shouldn't have so many kids.'"* Farida, now a hostess at French Rail (SNCF), recalls that when she was in school during the first Gulf War, *"one kid's parents refused to let their child take a history course with me in the class."* For Nordine, a housepainter, racism is a combination of a desire to humiliate and a direct insult. When he and his mother went to the bank where she has held an account for 25 years, *"the teller asked to see her ID. He wanted to do that to embarrass us in front of everybody, to humiliate us."* Once again, such incidents are all too familiar and we could cite plenty more, in varying shades of vicious, grotesque, and disgraceful treatment.

School

Sociology books are rarely bestsellers. But oddly enough, it seems as though everyone was familiar with their contents, and most of our respondents proved to be very able critics of the mechanisms that perpetuate social inequalities, condemning pell-mell, often justifiably, inherited wealth and cultural ease, social mores that are naturally antiegalitarian, the tacit complicity among the most privileged set, the stigma attached to growing up in a housing project, and so on—in short, everything that militates against equal opportunity. School serves as the pivoting point in the system of (in)equality. It is at once the principal means of perpetuating inequalities of opportunity and the principal means of redressing them. When we asked workers to identify the most effective means of fighting inequalities, school came first, at 34 percent, well ahead of trade unions (18 percent) and community organizations and political parties (8 percent). Moreover, the higher the respondents' level of education, the more social justice they expect from school. If the French place so much hope in the ability of schools to produce equality, it is perhaps chiefly because they believe strongly in the legitimacy of academic hierarchies. For public school laid the foundation for the French Republic and the modern nation in the late nineteenth century. Michèle Lamont (2002), comparing the attitudes of French and U.S. workers on the subject of schooling, comes to the same conclusion. Since its inception, a secular public school system open to everyone has been the cornerstone for hopes of social justice and national integration in a traditionally Roman Catholic country in which financial success was deemed much less commendable and honorable than academic achievement. So France has chosen an academic meritocracy over an economic meritocracy (Dubet 2004).

Criticism of unequal educational opportunities is extremely widespread. *"It's unfair to children, who cannot defend themselves, so it's unfair that everyone doesn't have the same resources at their disposal,"* says Claude, a corporate financial officer. Brigitte, a schoolteacher who likewise decries the inequalities she is up against in her primary school classroom, also blames the parents for failing to take an interest in their children's education. Schoolteachers are all familiar with the effects of a family's cultural capital on scholastic achievement, and parents are well aware that some schools are much better than others. One parent we spoke to found it extremely unjust that he could not afford to enroll his children in a private school. The cost of higher education is continually deplored by the less well-to-do, who resent *"moneyed kids goofing off at college."* Some of the poorest, moreover, retain painful memories of being humiliated at school. By and large, school, as it is in reality, is not considered a temple of justice in an unjust society. But the injustice seems to lie more in access to school than in the institution itself. Moreover, despite the reservations they express, our respondents are quite convinced that diplomas are justly deserved. In spite of a certain realism, workers have not lost all hope in schools as instruments of social justice.

Many who were flunked out of school accept the verdict. In interviews they often say things like *"I was a fool to quit school, I goofed off at school, I clowned around."* Katia, who, as we have seen, is angry about the way "society" treats her, accepts her father's verdict: *"If you had a diploma, you wouldn't be sweeping floors. Try that one on for size, Katia!"* François, a night watchman, believes that *"unequal wages are justified by the fact that some people have more qualifications than others."* To some degree, he grants, he has only himself to blame for where is now.

Henri, a 60-year-old laborer, agrees. In his day, working-class kids had to quit school and go to work at an early age. He became a laborer himself, owing more to social inequalities than to any lack of scholastic aptitude on his part. He notes, however, that young people nowadays can go to college more easily, and those who fail to seize this opportunity are partly responsible for their subsequent fate: *"I didn't have that chance."* Michel, quoted earlier complaining about the way nurses scorn their aides, nevertheless adds, *"Though it's true nurses are in charge of everything that has to do with administering drugs and injections and taking medical histories, you've got to admit they have more skills than we do. So it's normal: I goofed off at school, you can't expect to make 1,500 euros a month with a trade-school diploma."* Marc, a bank clerk and union activist, opines that, though it is terribly unfair that *"a garbage man's son is not going to make it into ENA,"*[7] it is perfectly fair that people with the most advanced degrees should hold top-echelon, high-paying positions.

If those who flunk out of school seem to deserve their lot in life because they "goofed off" there, it follows that the academic meritocracy engenders a just order. Nearly all the doctors we interviewed, for example, mentioned their long years of study for admission to the medical profession. An overwhelming majority of the teachers believe that, despite unequal educational opportunities, the "privileges" obtained by passing civil service exams are perfectly fair. Manuel, on the senior staff at the state-owned energy utility EDF, claims, *"Everything I achieved is thanks to my intellectual abilities that I developed."* However, even those who do not rank among the overachievers of the meritocracy think along these lines. Simon, who works for the state-owned French Rail (SNCF), is sometimes accused by private-sector employees of benefiting from certain "privileges." He retorts, *"I don't keep anyone from coming in and taking the same exams, so if I'm privileged, good!"* Despite all the criticism of the public education system, it is still perceived as the great distributor of legitimate inequalities. Social justice therefore consists in limiting the impact of social inequalities on scholastic selection, rather than mitigating the impact of academic achievement on social inequalities.

This conception of equality as a struggle against social discrimination seems to underpin the commitment of social democracy to reducing inequalities in the employment market. Public policies are now aimed at reinforcing the equity of education and training systems as a means of bolstering equal opportunity in the sphere of employment, while deregulating rigid labor laws that are deemed impediments to economic performance. In so doing, we are, imperceptibly, choosing equal opportunity over equal conditions. It should be noted that this is not necessarily the most realistic approach. For educational inequalities are largely the result of social inequalities in childhood, i.e., prior to school enrollment, and the reduction of educational inequalities alone has very little effect on social inequalities (Boudon 1973). Nevertheless, although equality of opportunity and equality of positions are closely interdependent, they are not necessarily compatible. Equal opportunity may produce inequalities that run counter to the relative equality of positions. It may even augment the disparities it was supposed to reduce.

"As for Me, I'm OK"

Workers elaborate a sort of synthesis between equality of position and equality of opportunity, a balanced view that emerged in all of our interviews. After reciting a litany of complaints and condemnations of lesser and greater injustices, those that permeate the workplace and those that make the world itself unjust and sometimes unbearable, our respondents often conclude by saying, *"As for me, I'm OK."* After recounting all their woes, almost all the respondents came to the surprisingly moderate verdict that, on the whole, they accept their social condition. This assertion prevails even among those one might expect to have grounds for feeling disadvantaged: A mere 8 percent of those surveyed said they feel mistreated. A full 65.7 percent of our respondents categorize themselves as middle class, 17 percent as working class, and another 17 percent as members of the lower class. The most outrageous injustices were ranked as follows: unemployment (40.6 percent), inequalities (30.9 percent), job insecurity (20.4 percent), and crime (5.2 percent). Furthermore, the inequalities in question, according to 47.1 percent, are between "the excessively rich" and "the excessively poor." Thus, the most shocking injustices were joblessness, job insecurity, and the excessive inequalities that exclude a person from a position considered normal or acceptable. In light of the acute sensitivity to injustice that emerged in the interviews, these weighted judgments merit further analysis.

We might interpret the complaints and remonstrations gathered in the interviews as a sort of social ritual: the presentation of oneself as compassionate and righteous, participating in a collective condemnation in the appropriate manner. This explication cannot be entirely ruled out, but we should be hard put to leave it at that, given the dreadful accounts our subjects gave of harrowing experiences past and all too present. Moreover, the fact that the interviews were conducted by young, and mostly shy, college students would not have induced the interviewees to go to extremes in overdramatizing their plight. I might add that the phenomenon is so common we can readily observe it in ourselves and our friends: we may have a thousand reasons to complain, even though, on the whole, we feel fairly well treated. The opposite attitude, which would consist in defining oneself as average and normal out of a wish to conform, is no more credible: For after all, there may be no little grandeur in portraying oneself as the heroic and worthy victim of social injustice. The phenomenon, then, cannot be dismissed as an artifact of the method, or a simple convention, of the presentation of the self.

Outrageous Injustices

Actually, "As for me, I'm OK" does not signify that the complaints and the suffering have been extinguished. They have simply been put in perspective because the subject has changed her viewpoint, her yardstick for gauging the magnitude and gravity of injustices and inequalities. Every interviewee was asked to name the inequalities and injustices they found most outrageous and intolerable in society in general and in the world as a whole. Howsoever these inequalities are described, they all have one thing in common: They are unacceptable because they exclude individuals from the community of relatively equal subjects, of those who share some basic measure of equality—specifically, the very fact of having a job and a home, the minimal social participation to which everyone is entitled.

The outrageous injustices are the ones that are spectacular enough to get picked up by television cameras and charity organizations: abject poverty, child labor, the ravages of war and natural disasters, third world slums and shantytowns, etc. We cannot gauge the intensity of the empathy aroused by this "remote suffering," even though some of our respondents are active in charities. However, it is clear that foregrounding these unbearable inequalities significantly alters our standards of comparison. Global television coverage has, as we all know, opened up the whole wide world (Boltanski 1993; Corteséro 2004).

In addition to outrages against the human condition itself, there are social inequalities that, according to the respondents to our questionnaire, go off the ten-point scale of "tolerable" injustices. They lie in the yawning chasm between immeasurably large and immeasurably small incomes. *"There are CEOs who get paid incredible salaries and manage to sink the company while remaining millionaires—they make astronomical sums, it blows your mind. The homeless, children dying in Africa, battered women, people who are willing to sell their children to make some money—it's like the end of the world,"* says Lucie. *"The megarich stuff themselves with caviar while the others are out there starving to death."*

The existence of an abjectly poor population of social outcasts seems to draw a lower boundary, above which any inequalities experienced become relative and, all things considered, bearable. With joblessness and homelessness becoming mass phenomena in France as in many rich countries, many of our respondents have known or narrowly escaped such a pass. And some have friends or relatives in this predicament. So the threat of exclusion is very real to them. Fabrice, a young hotel janitor, describes living in a suburban housing project: *"I find it unforgivable to pack people into the projects like rabbits and put stores around them so they won't leave the area, just because they're too dark-skinned or too light-skinned or too young or too pinko. It ends up turning them into savages. The youths who land there live like pigeons."* Jeanne, a mail carrier who does her rounds in one of these projects, adds, *"The youths in the slum are victims of terrible discrimination; they go through terrible experiences. They hole up there, and the violence in the projects, though I don't condone it, sometimes I can understand why they do it."* Serge, a building superintendent, has been on unemployment and knows what it means to be "beneath" equality: *"The unemployed, they'll hole up at home, stop going out, shut themselves up, turn in on themselves. They build up terrible feelings inside. I'm talking about feelings of hatred, resentment towards society, towards certain people, which eventually lead to despair, if not suicide. There you go. You can end up going to extremes. They're all saying, 'Just give me a job and I'll be okay!'"* Lucie, now a nurse, need only recall her stint at McDonald's to appreciate her present situation: *"I can't complain. Working at McDonald's was the worst work experience I've ever had. The pay is peanuts, you work long hours, it's awful. You won't have any trouble finding victims of injustice in there."* Jean-Luc, a skilled house painter, thinks of *"all the people who are out of work, all the ones making very little money, all the ones who are exploited, all the ones working absolutely insane hours in supermarkets, and the ones, especially women, working rotating shifts in the factory."*

Society could be graphed as a football or a bell curve whose tips and extremities represent inequalities beyond the bounds of "normalcy." *"Inequalities are relative to basic needs,"* notes Robert, a tax examiner. *"I'm shocked by extreme inequalities in standards of living and lifestyle."* François, a night watchman, adds: *"In any case, there's got to be bosses and workers, the haves and the have-nots. But what's unfair is that the haves crush the have-nots, the strong crush the weak."* Let us cut short this series of remarks, which could go on forever, with a comment by

Nadine, a nurse's aide: *"There's too much of a gap with the people who are too rich. There shouldn't be people who are too rich or too poor. There should be a happy medium. It's okay to have rich and poor, but they shouldn't be either too rich or too poor."*

I'm Part of Society

Anyone whose work involves daily contact with abject poverty feels privileged by contrast. *"The bums, you don't even see 'em. They're victims, people just walk on by, but I've been with those guys,"* says Philippe, a male nurse. *"The bums, they suffer terribly. Most of them are psychiatrically ill, and that's why they're alcoholics. I'm a man, I'm white, I'm from a French background, and I was taught to speak English, which enables me to communicate with people all over the world. I make a hell of a lot of dough, I have considerable purchasing power. As far as housing goes, I have a huge place compared to my personal position. So I'm extremely lucky, I'm privileged in every respect. I could be a billionaire, of course, but I'm in with the richest set, I'm part of a country that has just about the most welfare benefits, which allows me to get good health care and welfare support."*

Everyone draws the same comparison, regardless of their income bracket. Dominique, a surgeon, is in the top bracket. He bemoans the deterioration of hospital services and the want of recognition for his specialty, *"But I've always done what I felt like doing, despite all the day-to-day hassles. I've got no worries: I'm skilled, I'm solvent, I've got a steady job. I'm privileged, and that's one of the reasons why I have absolutely no right to complain. I'm a member of an elite. For instance, if I want to see a medical specialist anywhere in France, all I have to do is pick up the phone and I'll get an appointment."* Christiane, a banker, told us that when she sees homeless people, *"It's enough to make you want to shoot yourself. I don't think I have any right to complain. If you have a roof over your head and good health, the rest is a gift."*

Etienne, a 23-year-old sports counselor, is not nearly as well off as a surgeon or banker, and yet: *"I'm not one of those folks who make three bucks and spend four. I make three and spend two. So I'd say as for me, I'm OK."* Despite her low wages and status, Jeannine, who works at a university cafeteria, counts her blessings: *"I'm well aware that, compared to some people without jobs, the poor, they're just worse off. I got job security, I got huge vacations compared to some private companies."* Maïté, a nurse's aide, is in daily contact with the world of poverty. *"I've got a salary, I've got a job that's basically decent, I've got a husband with a decent salary. I figure I'm one of the privileged people. And I see patients who are underprivileged every day—people whose children get taken away because they don't have money to feed them. And me,*

I come in every day saying to myself how lucky I am, how happy I am. I've got a nice apartment, everything's just fine."

From the standpoint of pure equality—which is an honorable position, morally, but a difficult one politically and a risky one personally—it may seem obvious that our respondents' mantra, "As for me, I'm OK," is both a ruse and a consolation. Essentially, the wage slave accepts his fate, looking on the bright side of things or reflecting that there is always someone worse off than he is. To some extent, the individual's keen sensitivity to inequalities is cauterized by the prevailing ideology and the popular wisdom produced by centuries of submission. Then again, the accounts we collected are not those of people of modest means who are "naively" content with their lot, making a virtue of necessity. Most of our respondents express trenchant complaints about their work situation. When they change perspective, however, their feelings of injustice do not subside, but come to be measured on a different scale. They come to feel their situation is normal and adequate because, in their eyes, their primary needs are satisfied.

Multiple and Tolerable Inequalities

"As for me, I'm OK"—or "I'm doing well enough"—can be understood as a balanced position between inequalities experienced firsthand and the inequalities of the world. We might then posit a hierarchy of inequalities ranked in terms of relative acceptability. This assumption is borne out by a number of studies: Whether rich or poor, conservative or liberal, everyone seems to find income variance tolerable up to a fourfold disparity between rich and poor (Piketty 2003). A survey of European attitudes toward social justice showed that in every country except the Czech Republic, Europeans ranked the principles of justice in the following order: needs, merit, and equality (Forsé 2005). "Needs" were defined as the set of goods that must be provided regardless of merit or market-driven inequalities, in other words, the primary goods to which everyone is entitled, the *conditio sine qua non* of elementary equality.

The statement "As for me, I'm OK" is an indication that our subjects tend to look beyond the sphere of work. Their moderate verdict on overall inequalities suggests that they do not define themselves by their jobs alone, and their evaluation of the whole is a synthesis of judgments on multiple spheres of identity. Thus, the most ill-treated workers not infrequently consider themselves fairly satisfied consumers and that their "normal" standard of consumption "compensates" for the injustices to which they are subjected at work. This is the thesis elaborated by Hobsbawm (1989): American laborers perceive themselves as exploited, but also as middle class in terms of consumption and as "the people" in terms of their political clout. In fact, what makes inequalities bearable in many cases is that they are so manifold and various. They are not necessarily superimposed as one moves away from the summits of fame and fortune or from the abyss of the damned and doomed of the earth (Dubet 2000).

Now that social classes are no longer structured as "total" communities enclosed in their class-specific lifestyles, cultures, and destinies, individuals are confronted with a multiplicity of social statuses, positions, personal histories, and careers. The modern division of labor, the diversification of individual life histories, and the overwhelming influence of middle-class, mass-cultural models and values, do not in any way diminish inequalities or social domination; they simply *diffract* them, projecting fragments of them onto individual experiences and identities so varied that agents can no longer define themselves in one-dimensional terms. When social status alone determined the individual's identity, she viewed her situation from a single all-encompassing point of view. Today, however, she changes perspective easily: I may be mistreated as an immigrant, but not as an employee; I may be victimized as a civil servant, but not as a woman; I may be underpaid, but my work is rewarding in other ways; I may be exploited as a worker, but not as a consumer; as a mother, but not as a career woman, or vice-versa, and so on.

There are many drawbacks to being young, but there are some advantages, too (Galland 2004). By and large, individuals base their judgments on "potential." They feel they are being treated equally as long as they are able to lead a life worth living (Sen 2000). Though Eric is poorly paid as a young tree-pruner, he feels his situation is promising, simply because he is young, he's engaged to be married, he has his whole life ahead of him, and his parents are supporting him.

For the sake of intellectual or ideological convenience, we like to believe that all injustices cluster and crystallize around the same positions in society. Actually, that is true only of the extremes. When most people say they belong to the middle class, they may be referring not so much to their standard of living itself as to the sheer variety of ways of assessing that standard of living. However, lest we forget, this temperate judgment in no wise tempers the intensity of feelings of injustice.

* * *

The only way to grasp the principle of equality is in terms of the tension between fundamental equality and real social inequalities. This irreducible tension operates along two main axes that are inextricably merged in the agent's consciousness. From the "holistic" viewpoint, the condemnation of injustices trains its sights on illegitimate inequalities that are hurtful and humiliating insofar as they encroach on a system of castes or microcastes in which each individual's honor is bound up. But this unjust order is not indicted in the name of absolute equality because everyone deems it just and "egalitarian" to hold his position in a legitimate social hierarchy. This hierarchy is perceived as a sort of democratized aristocratic world, a world in which everyone is entitled to the inherent honor of her position. The legitimacy of this hierarchy is, of course, no longer based on royal or divine decree, but on a latent conception of social integration tending towards national cohesion. In short, equality is a just order.

Some individuals (often the same ones, in fact) develop an egalitarian critique of a far more individualistic nature based on markedly different assumptions. The equality in question here is that of opportunity. Social inequalities are not denounced as such from this perspective, but for constituting a mass of economic and social barriers that prevent individuals from obtaining access to positions to which they aspire. The inequalities denounced may be the same as those targeted from the "holistic" view, but the argument differs in its central axiom, which asserts an equal right to demonstrate one's value. In this sense, the liberal concept of equality appears to be the prerequisite for the elaboration of another principle of justice: merit.

Notes

1. The overall "index of injustice" we computed based on responses to the questionnaires averages out to 5.23. The indices are 5.67, 5.27, and 4.62 in incidents of friction with users, coworkers, and management, respectively.

2. In France, junior high school and high school teachers are recruited via two competitive examination programs, called CAPES and Agrégation. The former is easier. Graduates of both programs are qualified to teach in public schools, but those who pass the Agrégation exams (*agrégés*) are better paid and teach three hours less per week.

3. Initially, the nation was made up of a population of equals who took up arms to defend their liberty, a definition that did not exclude those of non-French origin. It evolved to become a nation of nationals, a community of citizens who share a set of rights and a national cultural identity. This is why the nation has long been deemed the only real repository of equality and democracy (Schnapper 1994).

4. I use the word "race," not because races exist, but because people (including victims of racism) speak in these terms to designate the racialization of social relations. The term "ethnic identity" is doubtless more accurate, but it fails to render the brutality of the facts.

5. Among the many pertinent studies we should cite: Blöss 2001; Fortino 2002; Laufer/ Marry/Maruani 2003; Maruani 2005.

6. That is, mostly (North) African ethnics, many of whom are (naturalized) French citizens—Translator's note.

7. Ecole Nationale d'Administration (National School of Administration), which trains the elite of the French political and business class.

CHAPTER 2

Merit

MOST OF THE RESEARCH into feelings of justice at work concerns distributive justice and merit (Deutsch 1985). Generally, this research is based on a utilitarian conception of justice in which the worker assesses the fairness of his lot by comparing his contributions to the compensation he receives for the same.[1] Because work is invariably regarded as a negative value, a sacrifice made by the worker in exchange for positive values—above all, money—the merit principle seems self-evident. So very self-evident, in fact, that it goes without saying in imagining a just world in which everyone would be rewarded according to their merits, efforts, and results. In this conception, merit also takes on a moral value inasmuch as it is a means of both exercising a freedom and repaying one's social debt to the extent that, "Thanks to my work, I don't owe anything to anyone and no one owes anything to me" (always provided I am paid fairly). However, like all the principles of justice, merit is less in evidence as a positive affirmation than in a host of condemnations of everything that obstructs or sabotages its recognition: favoritism, cronyism, nepotism, privilege, and the like. Recognition of merit is generally not gauged in terms of the bottom-line result of a balance sheet of contributions and rewards, but in specific contexts by means of a series of meticulous comparisons that yield a whole string of jealousies and frustrations. For any difference in treatment can be perceived as either a recognition or a denial of merit.

However, the dearth of due recognition for merit can breed more than mere frustration whenever a worker feels more than just poorly paid, but robbed of her just desserts, spoliated or, in simpler parlance, "exploited." Feelings of exploitation do not always stem from a particularly onerous or excruciating work experience; they may also derive from the worker's reckoning that he is being robbed of part of the fruit of his labor. Leaving aside obvious situations of flagrant exploitation, the concept of merit poses various quandaries for workers, problems akin to those addressed by justice theory. Fair assessment of merit depends on the tests used to measure it. But it also depends on the very nature of merit: Do I merit my merit? Is the equal opportunity system that confers merit fair? Is the assessment of merit based on my efforts, my objective results, or sheer chance?

Merit Is Just

The Place of Merit

Although individuals prize merit, philosophers tend to be much more circumspect. In 1875, when the German Social Democratic Workers Party adopted the slogan "Equal pay for equal labor," Marx retorted, "This equal right is an unequal right for unequal labor." At the other end of the ideological spectrum, Hayek (1976, chap. 9) points out that the market success of entrepreneurial efforts is not necessarily a vindication of individual merit, because it also depends crucially on luck, opportunity, the economic situation, and family background. Taken to an extreme, scrupulous recognition of everyone's merit would be at odds with a free and open society. As mutually opposed as they may be, Rawls (1987) and Nozick (1988) share the same doubts about merit. Rawls says, "The unequal inheritance of wealth is no more inherently unjust than the unequal inheritance of intelligence," while Amy Gutman illustrates Nozick's stance thus: "Courageous soldiers deserve Medals of Honor, even if they do not deserve their courage." Philosophers of justice all seem to agree that the merit principle would be just only if it validated pure freedom as well as pure equality by means of perfectly fair tests. Because these conditions are never entirely met, however, whether in the workplace, at school, or in competitive sports, merit cannot be deemed a primary principle of justice. These reservations are hard to refute. For example, sociologists of education have long since demonstrated that academic merit is not randomly distributed, but often simply the translation of favorable social determinants into individual talents. And yet agents still believe in merit, and to a certain degree they *have* to if they are to establish a connection between their efforts and rewards. All workers implement this principle of justice, if only in the act of "selling" their labor capacity. Belief in merit goes hand in hand with faith in freedom and equality, merit being a fair gauge of what an individual makes of his freedom and equality. This is why, despite all the criticism it draws, merit is inseparable from democratic freedom and equality.

Respondents to the 1999 European Values Survey conducted in 24 countries ranked merit as the second principle of justice, behind elementary needs and ahead of equality (Forsé 2005). Our own survey, using questionnaires, revealed a like attachment to the merit principle. To wit, 72.9 percent of our respondents think pay based on performance at work is fairer than seniority-based pay. Only 34.4 percent find it legitimate for positions of responsibility *"to be systematically reserved for holders of university degrees."* The vast majority believe one should be able to work one's way up to a responsible position by proving one's merit on the job. On the whole, they feel that workers' efforts should be systematically acknowledged, and 63.4 percent find it unfair that welfare recipients should be drawing an income *"almost equivalent"* to the minimum wage.

Of course, belief in the merit principle varies considerably as a function of social position and line of work, and those who benefit from the merit principle appear to be more attached to it than those who don't. Thus 91.7 percent of company heads and 76.4 percent of senior staff deem merit-based pay more just than a seniority system, as against 65 percent of laborers. But the fact remains that two-thirds of laborers favor the merit principle. Members of the left-wing electorate are only slightly less favorable to it than our sample as a whole: 66.2 percent versus 71.5 percent. True, employees with the least rewarding jobs are the least favorable to the merit system, but it is still preferred across the board to other ranking systems based on seniority or academic achievement when the latter criteria obstruct the proof of merit in the workplace. Indeed, purely meritocratic access to positions of responsibility seems to be a widespread demand among the most vulnerable elements of society: those who have known long-term unemployment or have felt handicapped or excluded owing to inferior scholastic qualifications. In the final analysis, the fact that belief in merit is not evenly spread throughout the various social groups does not necessarily mean that the merit principle is simply the way the ruling class rationalizes its hegemony, for even those who believe in merit a little less than the "winners" still believe in it a lot.

The Meritorious

Whereas 34.4 percent of our respondents feel that it is fair to require academic qualifications for positions of responsibility, the rate increases to 44.6 percent among respondents who hold graduate school degrees. In all likelihood, this trust in the merit conferred by academic credentials is strongest among those who have successfully completed their studies by dint of diligence and hard work.

Guy, a high school principal with university-teaching credentials, makes the point bluntly: *"Everyone has a chance, depending on his strengths and test scores. That's how it is. I think it's normal that those who busted their guts to pass difficult exams should earn more. Job difficulty is not a factor determining salary levels. How you scored on the exams is all that counts."* Thus, a teacher with an advanced teaching degree, a light course load, and gifted students justly deserves a higher salary than one with lesser credentials who spends more hours in the classroom teaching more difficult students, because the meritocratic scale established by the state teachers' exams is unassailable. Moreover, Guy stresses his own personal merit within the academic merit system: *"I had to leave school at 14 and work to support myself, so I did all my courses by correspondence and at night school."* Like "scholarship students," Guy is a sort of academic self-made man, convinced that he rightly deserves the position he has obtained under his own steam. Many respondents who assert their merit in no uncertain terms likewise advert to a humble family background, and the obstacles they had to overcome, by way of justification for the precious few "privileges" they have earned "the hard way." It may be noted that the autobiographies of leading French intellectuals often boast similar rags-to-riches stories. Then again, it all depends on what one means by a "humble background." Often as not, an insistence on the lowliness of one's family background gives the lie to that very claim: the lowly schoolteacher, the lowly country doctor, the lowly postal clerk are rather fortunate in the eyes of a lowly laborer.

Sonia struggled to become a librarian: *"I took the exams and battled for a position. I have a claim to be where I am. It's fair because not everyone has taken the exams."* She recalls how terribly unfair it was when, serving as a substitute teacher, she *"got paid half as much as the permanent teachers."* Having been a victim of the system of competitive examinations, she insists all the more on her own merit now that she has passed one, stridently affirming her faith in the merit principle: *"The first step towards reforming the civil service would be to fire all the people who don't do a stitch of work."* Sonia's ambivalent remarks are a good illustration of the power of the merit principle. Evidently, it is resilient enough to be reversible, enabling individuals both to justify holding a hard-earned position and to bemoan the privileges awarded to those who attain the same position through violations of the principle of "equal pay for equal labor." For the merit principle to be truly just, there must be absolute equality of opportunity.

Xavier is in charge of a winery. He worked his way up to that position on his merit alone. *"I got a terrific education. I taught myself both accounting and management, and did internships to learn wine tasting and selling. I did it all on my own. There are several ways to make it into management: Either you study to make the grade, or you work your way up from the lowest-level qualifications and get your own training on the job. Certain inequalities are just and justified. What do I think of financial inequalities? There are no inequalities as long as each salary bracket corresponds to work that doesn't have the same value. There may be financial inequalities, but not moral inequalities. That's entirely fair."* Xavier does add that, in his opinion, cellar workers deserve better pay. He challenges the base pay, however, not the disparities in wage levels.

Often enough, management and executive-level personnel insist that their merit consists merely of the number of hours they devote to their work, week in, week out. They don't even count, they routinely work more than 50 hours a week, they bring work home, etc. In their eyes, they are all the more deserving because the others wouldn't put in "more than the 35-hour week." Many senior staff also mention the risks involved in their work, whereas lower-tier, often lower-paid, employees are allegedly better protected from economic upheavals and the vicissitudes of the market. Joël is such a successful manager that he is now liable for wealth tax, of which he is neither ashamed nor boastful: *"My work's terrific, it's the fulfillment of my goals. Inequalities are fair when work is rewarded. I work 12 hours a day, and I'm better paid than those who put in 6 hours. I see no injustice in that. It would be a form of injustice to be treated exactly the same way. Managing a business with clear-cut, transparent rules is also a way of helping to get rid of injustice.... I'm pretty much a free-market liberal, and nowadays I have the impression everything is available to everyone. You simply have to implement a plan of action to attain it. I come from a very modest background— middle class, or lower middle."* Paul, a skilled confectioner, sums it up clearly: *"It's not that I have a lucky star. I've worked hard, devoted myself, given of myself to this. It's not necessarily an entitlement; it's an exchange: You give your working capacity and you get a certain lifestyle. It's not a privilege. As the boss, I see my privileges and I see my obligations. I don't belong to a caste that has unearned privileges. Everything I have, I deserve."*

Merit is earned. It is an asset individuals earn themselves. In both the academic and economic spheres, the statements made by the winners of "the meritocratic order" bear an odd mutual resemblance, even though the "values" of education and of business seem radically opposed. Teachers are inclined to dismiss business as "profiteering," whereas businessmen disparage teaching as a "cushy job." Yet their faith in merit is not undermined by such "minor details."

Is Merit Moral?

Assuming that merit is not merely an ex post justification for success, like equality it must be granted a moral dimension. After all, merit would suffice to define the set of qualities possessed by those who win out in the various competitions designed to detect it if those qualities had no moral dimension. Merit would then simply be what we "see" of the winners. And yet agents are not entirely satisfied with this definition. Sports commentators describing the victors of athletic competitions designed to establish the pure merit of the contestants usually don't confine their remarks to the luck, talent, and gifts of the champions. They also point out their courage, their tenacity in training for the event, their team spirit, etc. In an academic setting, evaluations usually take on a moral tinge, as though success depended more on hard work, constancy, and concentration rather than mere talent, for talent—presumably an accident of birth and genes—is not really a moral attribute. Consequently, for success to be morally just, the subjects, who are, a priori, equal, must have "decided" to succeed. In this vein, teachers are continually admonishing their pupils that they could do better if they worked harder. In this perspective, merit is presented as the realization of individual freedom, a manifestation, of sorts, of the salvation every individual is free to attain, as in the Protestant ethic: Although God decides who are the elect, it is up to each individual to seek out the signs of His blessing through hard work and sacrifice. Because merit is thus associated with a sense of accomplishment, failure is perceived as a loss of dignity, value, and self-esteem, losses that extend far beyond the practical consequences of the failure itself. People are ashamed of failing tests of merit, and the fairer those tests are, the greater the shame (Dubet/Martuccelli 1996).

Recognition of merit is not merely financial, but moral as well. Christiane, a 50-year-old schoolteacher, describes her discouragement and bitterness because her merit goes unrecognized by a school administration that *"doesn't give a hoot."* She works zealously, putting in long hours, devoting herself to the well-being of her pupils and the school, and yet, within the educational system, her merit is ignored. Not only does is she paid the same salary as those who make the least possible effort, but *"there's never a word,"* never a sign of acknowledgment of the merit she believes she has so amply demonstrated. Basically, agents interpret merit as a sign of a person's value and his devotion to the common weal. According to Henriette, a librarian, seniority-based pay raises are particularly unfair in failing to reward contributions to the collective effort: *"With seniority there's no emulation, no enrichment, no teamwork."* Cyril, a chef, is zealously devoted to his work, without which the restaurant he works for could not survive, make any money, or hire any staff. Yet no one acknowledges his pains: *"Never a word of thanks."* In the eyes of all these employees, teacher, librarian, and chef, their individual merit and zeal produce collective wealth. They would not be satisfied with simply earning more money, though they would not refuse it. But they believe their work has a moral value, too, because it demands such strictly moral qualities as professionalism, devotion, and skill, which should be rewarded accordingly.

Merit is moral because it requires personal commitment, says Marc, in charge of training at the state-owned gas company. *"What's unfair about day-to-day work is that the company operates according to civil service regulations, and I think the work people do isn't appreciated; seniority has too much pull, and people's commitment isn't appreciated enough. It's a shame because there are people whose work improves things, and others who are basically rewarded for not bothering anybody. The unions defend this system, and even though I was a shop steward for over 12 years, I'd say we gave too much too easily. So it's only natural that they feel unfairly treated now. They say, 'I deserve a reward,' but they forget they're getting paid for that."* In short, merit is moral because an absence of merit is demoralizing to those who work hard and deserve to be rewarded for it, and who see their peers, having shown no such merit, benefiting from their exertions. Although merit may not always be a virtue, there is no denying that the want of merit is nearly always a vice, for it allows "slackers" to protect themselves, keep a low profile, and, ultimately, shirk the collective work that produces the wealth of the staff, the community, the company, and the nation.

The insistence on the moral dimension of the merit principle is not confined to management and the middle class. Gilles is an assembly-line worker and father of six. His job consists in packaging lettuce, and in his opinion it is perfectly fair to be paid on a piecework basis, for this is the best means of accurately equating remuneration and results. Because Gilles has been at the job for several years, his employer offered to pay him a fixed salary privileging his seniority more than his output. Gilles declined the offer on the grounds that this type of salary is an unfair *"reward for deadbeats,"* who try to get away with doing as little as possible, forcing others to work harder to cover for them. He prefers a salary based on assembly line output, to which each is bound to contribute without either excessive energy or lethargy.

Michel, a hospital janitor, can no longer bear, in his capacity as shop steward, having to defend fellow staff who *"take advantage"* of the system: those who barely lift a finger when they show up for work, who repeatedly take sick leave during hunting or wild mushroom-picking season. Here again, though the merit principle does not necessarily reward virtue, its absence rewards vice. Delphine, a kitchen worker in the same hospital and another union representative, holds more radical views: *"What strikes me is that in the public sector there are lots of employees who do as they please, and in the private sector you'd get the boot; they wouldn't put up with a fraction of what goes on down here."* Often as not, employees do not consider themselves very deserving. They are less likely to assert their merit than to feel wronged when nothing sets them apart from those who patently lack merit.

The merit principle is therefore moral insofar as it applies a professional ethic of well-done work that has some collective utility. It is also moral in asserting the dignity and autonomy of the individual: *"I am a self-made person."* A person who can claim merit owes nothing to others and everything to himself: He is therefore respectable and autonomous. Merit is a form of currency with which to pay one's debts. In the economy of merit, even the boss is duty-bound to respect a worker who owes her position to her own hard work alone. *"I do a good job, so I don't owe anything to anyone, and everyone respects me."* This is doubtless the reason why lack of recognition causes so much pain and bitterness. Not everyone sees himself as the hero of his own tale of merit. However, many suffer because their merit is never fully recognized. They are victims, not only of an economic injustice, but of a moral injustice as well.

Unrecognized Merit

The strength of the merit principle resides less in the pride and dignity it confers on workers than in the intensity of the frustration and criticism caused by its absence. Although some agents are unable to display merits that shine brightly enough in their own eyes or in those of others, they all feel entitled to recognition for their work, their efforts, and their qualities and are forever comparing themselves to others and gauging their comparative merit. Merit thus becomes less an affirmation than a critical principle denouncing the injustice of workplace situations in which a wide range of factors distort or obstruct the recognition of personal merit. Regardless of position, we all measure the disparity between what we deserve and what we get, and between what we deserve and what others get.

The Arithmetic of Merit

The primary and most widespread injustice arises where workers opine, after painstaking comparisons, that they are not getting equal pay for equal work, for, as Paul, the confectioner, observed, merit is a stock in trade. But differences in job status sometimes interfere with merit's fair market value, and the condemnation thereof reflects and reinforces the condemnation of castes and privileges. Remi is an engineer in a medical clinic in charge of equipment, safety, and hygiene. When he compares his treatment to that of the doctors, he feels wronged because his higher-ups are *"administrators and docs who don't do a lick of work. They're civil servants who make four times what I do. That pisses me off a little. Doctors have always enjoyed a certain amount of respect, just for being doctors, and some use their natural authority to do as little work as possible. It's true the clinic wouldn't run without docs, but without maintenance personnel it wouldn't run either."* Remi finds his situation all the more unfair because he is paid far less than *"the fat cats who make four or five grand. I'd like to see someone hand them a broom for a week so they see what that's like."*

Some situations are even more explosive. Jacques-Henri is a computer programmer at a company formed out of the merger between two firms, each of which has maintained its collective agreement with its respective staff. While his employer pays by merit, the other one pays by seniority, so employees doing the same job may receive very different salaries. *"With seniority, even if you don't do your job, you're guaranteed a raise. The youngest staff"*—including Jacques-Henri—*"doing exactly the same work are paid 25 to 50 percent less."* Above and beyond this profoundly unjust system, there are "little arrangements" that add insult to injury. *"For example, certain people aren't asked to do too much because they're union reps you don't mess with. The labor courts and all that—they know the ins and outs of labor law, and if you fuck with them, they won't waste any time, whereas the new girl works till 8 o'clock every night."*

Criticisms in the name of merit feed on all sorts of grievances. Fabienne is an instructor at an organization that provides social services and job training for high school dropouts and juvenile delinquents. A radical leftist who has built up a whole critique based on the merit principle, she resents the faculty "privileges" of those who elude merit standards, those who are paid the same as she is, but for doing less. She feels awfully ill used, and above all underpaid, compared to "teachers" in the National Education corps who are exempt from standards of merit. *"I have more degrees than the teachers, and I work with youths who are known for being more difficult because they come from immigrant families in the projects. I specialize in working with youths after their release from prison. I don't get why, after 15 years, I make a quarter, or even a third, less than a National Education teacher, and I work a 35-hour week, whereas a teacher works only 15 to 24 hours a week. In junior high you'd see teachers using old notebooks with yellowed pages. Whether a teacher worked hard or not, he got paid the same."* But Fabienne's merit is not only up against the civil servants' higher status. It is even more categorically denied by the militant egalitarianism of the organization she works for, which treats all its employees the same. *"I'm not a clone of so-and-so, so-and-so, and so-and-so, because thanks to my commitment to the job I take care of all the formalities, I write applications for grants and bid on jobs; in other words my efforts get money for my organization. So I'm opposed to equal pay. I don't see why I should be paid the same as someone who works less, when I put so much more into my work. I'm committed to left-wing ideals, but seeing the working world the way it really is, I have a hard time. We are not identical, we haven't had the same experiences or the same training. Why should we get the same pay?"* Disheartened at her inability to exert any influence on her salary situation, Fabienne has decided to move to the country and "chill out," i.e., put in less effort from now on. If one can't get a raise, one need only work less to reestablish the balance of equity.

Criticism citing nonrecognition of merit as a factor is particularly complex and ambivalent because there is no single standard of measurement. For example, a university degree may seem a sign of merit to the holder, but it looks like a dividend and privilege to those who are paid less for the same work than those with the academic credentials. Hugues, an engineer, resents the advantages accorded to alumni of the elite *grandes écoles* in France: They land the best jobs and highest salaries despite the fact that this "old-boy network" of the nation's academic elect is no guarantee of on-the-job competence. In the job market, above all in career trajectories, everything depends on the prestige of one's academic credentials. Although equality of academic opportunity is deemed an essential aspect of equality, 65 percent of our respondents feel that it is wrong for positions of responsibility to be reserved for those with university degrees, for this monopoly thwarts the recognition of on-the-job merit. Basically, the problem of merit, academic qualifications, and work is reflected in what Walzer (1997) calls the "spheres of justice." Though we agree that a diploma certifies merit, is it fair for the hierarchies of the academic sphere to prevail over proven on-the-job merit?

The tension between scholastic merit and on-the-job merit gives rise to ambivalent judgments. Those with little or no academic training decry the excessive and unfair ascendancy of university degrees. Sylvie, who works in a daycare center, observes that *"those who've got nothing but a vocational school certificate are pretty much nobodies. We do the same work as the others and they treat us like shit."* Worse still, those without qualifications aren't even allowed to compete in merit assessments at work. Indeed, the more academically qualified the population, the more the want of a diploma becomes a stigma, a negative signal to public- and private-sector employers (Baudelot/Leclerc 2005). Those with the highest academic credentials form castes, keeping the best jobs for themselves, while those without a high school diploma are condemned to endless trials and tribulations: For how much merit can someone have if they haven't even made the grade at the most basic scholastic level?

Academic qualifications thus serve as *filters* and not as human capital (Bowles/Gintis 1976). Celine, age 25, lives on odd jobs for want of a high school diploma. *"These days you ain't got nothin' if you ain't got a high school diploma. Even if you got experience and no qualifications, believe it or not, that just doesn't count. You can apply for a job without qualifications but even if you got the skills it won't work. We're in France. I don't know if it's the same elsewhere, at any rate, that's the way it is in France."*

Aurore can't get away from temporary employment *"because I need a diploma for the job I've been doing for a year or two, but I can't be permanently employed because I haven't got the diploma. It's a bit much. I'm willing to believe there are so many people knocking at the door they have to set prerequisites for selection. All the same, when they've got a competent person right in front of them, but without the prerequisites, they won't take you."*

Maïté teaches music at various schools, but she doesn't have the academic qualifications required for a steadier position. She describes how she was humiliated by her peers at the music conservatory, who would acknowledge neither her talent nor her experience, although she's been teaching for years—on a temporary basis: *"It was awful, they gave me to understand I had no business being there. The person with the title has tenure, whereas my problem is living my passion."* After that episode, Maïté *"went into a depression."*

Generally speaking, the phenomenon known as "academic inflation" has diminished the value of academic qualifications, creating a widening chasm between qualifications and expectations on the one hand, and the positions available on the job market on the other. As a result, the spheres of scholastic and professional merit are drifting farther and farther apart. *"Fact is they were asking for at least two years of college,"* recounts Aurore, *"which I had. But the work didn't require two years of college; that was just a prerequisite to get your foot in the door, and it turned out to be a dumb, lousy job. It was closer to data entry clerk than insurance contract manager. What I've been doing for a year and a half, my dog could do. That kills me when they ask for two years of college. I teach my dog to read and there you go: He can do the job! That's what sucks, too—to realize you did two years of college and in the end they offer you a job your little 10-year-old brother could do. You're gonna tell me you learn for your own good, but c'mon."* Aurore is not alone here: Witness all those high school graduates working as cashiers or PhDs living on odd jobs. The gap between the hopes students harbor during their studies and the jobs they eventually hold exacerbates the endemic sense of having their merit scorned. The more academically qualified they are, the more employees feel underpaid: While 71 percent of high school graduates feel they're well paid in terms of their qualifications, only 44.6 percent of those with three years of higher education or more think so too.

But all these "minor" infringements of merit do not obscure the sense of outrage when, for instance, captains of industry receive "golden parachutes"—although they have failed. One owner of a company with a thousand employees fumes, *"It's shocking how much severance pay they're eligible for when they leave after bankrupting the company."* And it is all the more shocking in light of the fact that many top managers are forever urging the rule of merit, but will not submit to it themselves; in virtually all the interviews, this double standard was denounced as the ultimate scandal. Not only do the managers elude the common lot of their employees by dint of their extraordinary income, but they pervert the merit principle—out of which they have forged an ideology—inasmuch as they themselves evade assessment of their own merit. Those who preach hard-core neoliberalism and the need to outsource, those who inveigh against a "prohibitive" minimum wage, prepare golden parachutes for themselves. Thanks to them, the belief in merit will never be wholly naïve, for their self-serving double standard furnishes an all but irrefutable argument for those who eschew merit.

String Pulling

The hegemony of rank and entrenched positions is not the only impediment to the manifestation of merit. Merit is obstructed, perhaps more profoundly and more continually, by workplace relations, by judgments and procedures designed to define each person's merit. We enter here the inexhaustible universe of the critique of string pulling, favoritism, nepotism, and special privileges. A full 60.1 percent of those surveyed by questionnaire said they had observed favoritism at work: 43.4 percent of the respondents mentioned "networks," 46.7 percent alluded to "bootlicking," "brown nosing," "ass kissing" and the like, as well as string pulling by the trade unions.

Severine, a physical therapist, went into private practice because she couldn't stand the "brown nosing" at the hospital anymore. *"Brown nosing's something you're up against all the time, men, women, whatever your occupation. There'll always be the ones who manage to waffle through without working, without doing a thing, you know, the gifts to the department head, the dinners.... The girl who got the job despite her incompetence because her dad was head of the department. Merit! We're definitely not assessed in terms of merit."* Sometimes things go a little further with the so-called couch promotion, as some employees call it, in companies with a predominantly female workforce but in which men retain the positions of power: hospitals, supermarkets, insurance companies, etc. *"It's the couch promotion that shocks me,"* says one nurse, stressing the different forms of address (*vous/tu*) employed by doctors according to their degree of familiarity with the nurses. But "brown nosing" is also a means of self-defense and gaining recognition for one's merit, explains Didier, a computer industry executive. If you want your merit recognized, you've got to know how to make your merit known to others.

String pulling is most conspicuous when employers hire members of their own family and, as often as not, the beneficiary abuses his position. Aurelie recounts how the boss's daughter at the hotel where she worked made the most of her situation. *"She was better paid than me. Whenever her father showed up she'd start working as if she'd been at it all along. As soon as he left she'd sit down, have a smoke, and then do nothing."* Jean-Marc, who owns a shop and a restaurant, thinks this small-scale nepotism completely dominates the world of small businesses. *"It's the family members and the boss's girlfriend who are protected here. Take the case of the PA who's got a very special relationship with the boss. Even if her skills aren't all that hot, she's protected to the max. It's not about recognizing a person's qualities, it's the nonprofessional motives or situations that allow someone to arrive at a professional post."*

It is not entirely a matter of sentiments and family. Nor is it entirely clear that employers seek to reward merit, for when all is said and done, observes Laurie, a technician, *"They're not interested in what work you in particular are doing. The main thing is that the work gets done by the end of the week, and there are those who do more of it than others, and there are those who know that and shirk the work. In fact, you gotta keep your mouth shut and march along with the others, the way society marches. Then everything's fine."*

For Bernard, a welder, what's important to management is that the company functions, and if it functions *"because some poor suckers work harder, they don't give a shit."* He adds that *"career advancement is based on merit and the standards of merit aren't professional, they're standards based on people's opinions."* Bernard's skepticism about merit is based on his contention that it's not always easy to measure it objectively. Sandra, a secretary, notes that people tend to ask more of those who already work harder as it is. *"They know I'm nice, that I'm going to do it. The others pretend they don't have the time, they don't know how to do it. They don't want any hassle, so I do it. It's always the nicest, the most likeable, who get the least advantages, they're the ones people ask the most of. Then again, I'm paid to work and I like that. So there's really no problem."* Sandra is describing a fairly commonplace work situation in which it is neither rational nor easy to get people who lack energy and talent to do a job; you're better off asking the more efficient and amiable staff members. Paradoxically, a patent dearth of merit becomes a sort of privilege, as hardly anything is asked of those who are incapable; we're lucky they don't use their leisure to spoil the work the others have done. But when Sandra says that doesn't bother her, she may be lying to herself: There's no problem as long as the less deserving don't get promotions denied to the more deserving. What is more, an employee feels unfairly treated when someone obviously less deserving is granted the same promotion. The interviews we conducted abound in stories of pique and humiliation, such-and-such a worker feeling not only that her merit has not been duly rewarded, but that it hasn't even been noticed by her peers and superiors. The protagonists are then torn between rage, detachment, and depression.

Without glossing over the appalling immorality of string pulling, one might nonetheless consider it a form of social capital, a resource people avail themselves of without incurring much opprobrium. If string pulling is so widespread, it is because many benefit from it, beginning with those who, at times, condemn it. Sandra displays a great deal of savvy in this regard: *"Pulling strings isn't abnormal, seeing as someone who hasn't got any academic qualifications … , I mean you have to use all the resources you've got to get anywhere in life. It's very opportunistic, but I figure you've got to know how to be that way. There's no shame in using your connections, that's part of life. My father got me a job, which really helped me out, and then I got my parents' cleaning lady's son hired. I'm very glad I did."* She adds shrewdly that in her administration, the main reason employees join the union is to advance their own careers.

Jean-Marc displays the same acuity. How could personal relationships and personalities not affect the pure play of merit? *"At any rate, when you work with people you know, you're bound to favor those around you. It's not necessarily about inequalities, it's favoritism. If the person's competent, it's true you'll favor him over someone you don't know. You select from among dozens of applicants. What makes you pick one out of ten at any given moment? It's purely intuition. Assuming the same merit, same age, same sex, it's going to be the physical contact, it's going to be the gut reaction. But it's not justifiable either. It's a bit of a lottery. You choose in your soul and in good conscience, assuming you've got a conscience. And they're better off being tall and good-looking than short, fat, and ugly!"*

In other words, if merit is a primary principle of justice, the course of justice is perverted in the absence of purely objective and anonymous procedures such as competitive examinations. On the other hand, a meritocracy based solely on such selection criteria, which may fail to reveal certain types of merit, would also be unjust. That is the reason why meritocratic judgments are intrinsically unstable, and the agents vacillate between shrewd cynicism and petulant bitterness.

Petty Jealousies

Recognition of merit isn't only conditional on the personal preferences and arbitrary decisions of one's immediate superiors and company bosses. Merit is also subject to the judgments of one's peers, who regard the slightest difference in treatment as an injustice or, on the contrary, as recognition of special merit. The sense of justice is assailed by the opinions of others, jealousy, and envy. These petty resentments and minor infringements of merit are a source of mental torment, especially if the victim's anguish is mingled with guilt. After all, people are often inclined to ascribe to others the jealousy that is eating away at themselves.

Sylviane, a secretary, is tormented by the fact that one of the other secretaries seems to be specially "cosseted" by her boss. The boss's pet, who probably has higher qualifications and more "book knowledge" than Sylviane, talks down to her: *"I haven't got as many degrees as her, but I've got my skills, which ought to be taken into account. Her behavior is unbearable."* The problem of jealousy has far more to do with outward signs and symbols than objective facts. Didier talks about petty jealousies touched off by disparities in computer quality or office size or attributes. Everything counts: the distance from one's superiors' door; exposure to noise, heat, and light. One dressmaker we interviewed said the distribution of workstations at the tiny shop she works in gives rise to underhanded wrangling and enduring acrimony. In this register, everything is construed as a mark of each employee's merit and distinction. A friendly word, an omitted greeting: Anything and everything is fraught with meaning in such a microcosm, which bears a certain resemblance to a royal court whose courtiers spy on and envy one another. The obsession with merit makes the atmosphere insufferable.

Viewed through the prism of mutual jealousy, those who play the company game tend to be regarded by their peers as "collaborators." Renaud works at McDonald's and, unlike his staffmates, he'd like to stay on and move up in the ranks there. The others make him pay for that by calling him a "bootlicker," which reminds him of his school days when being first in class was frowned upon.

To avoid *"the gossip in the hallways, the wagging tongues,"* Monica, an assembly line worker, is forgoing a promotion she was of-fered *"although I think I earned it."* She adds that envy is particularly keen among women, who, in her estimation, are less capable of *"saying things to your face and having it out"*—a cliché spread by women themselves. Is this conflict avoidance a consequence of being in a sub-missive position that calls for a nonconfrontational approach, of being more dependent than men on the judgments and opinions of others? Hard to say, but the fact is, many of the woman surveyed complain of female jealousy. What Elodie refers to as *"heaps of rumors, heaps of hypocrisy when there are only women"* may have a simpler explana-tion: the key importance of the way the work is organized. As a rule, all the cashiers have the same standing, receive the same pay, and do the same work. And yet the management of the checkout system inevitably introduces differences in treatment, to which the cashiers are extremely sensitive: register location, working hours, rapport with the head ca-shier, the little exchanges of favors, such as working a Saturday to get some time off during the week, etc. Because cashiers are so dependent on management decisions, their merit always seems in jeopardy. Elodie tells how she made friends with a superior, and they had to stop seeing and talking to each other at work to scotch the spread of rumors. And what of special ties between a man and a woman, a male superior and female subordinate? The woman will always be suspected of exchanging sexual favors for professional ones.

Do the terms *jealousy* and *merit* apply in all these cases? It might be more accurate to speak of *envy,* the mimetic coveting of what another possesses, simply because he or she possesses it. Indeed, if *jealousy* consists in coveting what others have and what one does not have oneself, *envy* consists in coveting what others have *because* they have it. Whereas jealousy can be mitigated, envy cannot. As Freud put it, "Social justice means denying oneself many things so that others will be compelled to forgo them as well or, what amounts to the same thing, so that they can not demand them.[…] If one cannot be privileged oneself, at least no one else can either" (1981, 187). Consequently, as in Tocqueville and in Nietzsche, envy and resentment appear to be inexhaustible passions, born of our mutually incompatible attachments to equality for all and individual merit. It turns out that, despite a deep-seated faith in merit, many people, especially those subject to the greatest domination, are inclined to reject the merit principle on the grounds that it "spoils" relations at work by undermining the collective work ethos, setting everyone at odds. This sacrifice does not wholly allay their frustration, however, for one can never entirely do without recognition for one's own merit.

Exploitation

There are cases in which merit is not measured very precisely by comparisons with one's immediate superiors or close workmates, cases in which merit does not give rise to feelings of jealousy or envy. The absence of rewards, material and symbolic compensation for one's on-the-job exertions and sacrifices, engenders a sense of being exploited. In this case, the denial of merit simply means that the value produced by the worker is confiscated by his or her employers, that there is a fundamental non-equivalence between work done and remuneration for the same (Baudelot/ Gollac et al. 2003).

There is no need to share the Marxist conception of value and added value to appreciate the intensity of the feelings of exploitation in an industrial society in which labor is precisely gauged in terms of effort and output, and social inequalities plainly show that a large part of the wealth produced by workers is not returned to them. From this point of view, it is not Marxism that explains the force of the feeling of exploitation. It's the other way around: The experience of exploitation explains the success of Marxist interpretations of production relations, including those that are not of a strictly capitalist nature. Though our interviews rarely revealed any Marxist views of society, they nevertheless highlighted the ferocity of feelings of exploitation, perceived as a radical negation of merit.

Modern Slavery

Julien works as a gardener through a temporary employment agency and defines himself as a *"modern slave."* *"As far as I'm concerned, temping's awful. You can't plan anything from one day to the next. Not having any paid vacation, never being able to choose your firm, having to go back to a firm where things didn't go all that well—that's not overly motivating. Afterwards, in financial terms, temp work can be nicer than a fixed-term contract. That's why there's plenty of temp work. For me, it's a way out. You temp because there's nothing else to do. The way I see it, it's modern slavery, even if it can't compare to what went on a century or two ago. It's slavery to the extent that you've really gotta be available 24 hours a day and, at worst, you've got no private life anymore. I've seen the reality face to face and it's weird. That's why I split to temp it. I do physical work, but I can't take the slavedrivers anymore. Before, I was on the assembly line from six in the morning to two in the afternoon, I'd sleep from 2:30 to 5:30, eat and go back to sleep. Dreaming nights of the motion you've been making all day, thinking about nothing but that, obsessing with that motion. Teachers take home their students' work to grade; workers take home their backaches and pains. When you knock off and take a shower, it only removes the outward nastiness of this line of work."*

The strenuous, menial aspect of some types of work does not suffice to bring the merit principle into play. Merit emerges when the pains taken are not rewarded, when they are part of a system of exploitation. *"People tell me there's no working class left in France. That makes me laugh. Just take a look around. The way I see it, the working class are the ones who get stuck doing 90 percent of the work and only get 10 percent of the financial pickings. You see the dudes who don't do much of anything all day, but thanks to their connections or the 'fruits of their labor' they manage to clear 50 grand. Another guy is already sweating after 10 minutes, and he's got another 7 hours and 50 minutes to go. He's gonna slog away for 20 times less than the other guy. You ask me, that's the main inequality workwise.... As for overtime, it was shut your trap or get lost. The women who had kids to feed, they were 47 or 48 and they'd been at the firm getting exploited for 20 years."*

This exploitation involves a whole chain of domination, threats, pressures, and spinelessness. It is not mere theft, it is a morally intolerable perversion of all human relations. *"When I opened my trap, the boss said there's some 20-year-old youngsters waiting, open your trap and you'll see! They pressured me with their looks. They took away my coffee breaks. They saw me as an upstart. I was impressed at how long the other guys put up with the abuse.… Some folks won't have me doing hard work. I'm way less brawny than them and I manage to do the same work as them because for those guys, doing that work was all they had left to be proud of, sometimes at the age of 40; they couldn't understand how I could handle the same work. The foreman hasn't got much more to show for himself than me, but he abuses his power at work and generally doesn't have a life outside his job. It's his way to feel like a big shot. Some folks can't help criticizing because, to them, you're inferior. They love their job, not because they love lugging boxes around, but because they love insulting people. Outside of work, they're super-shy, you see them at the supermarket pushing shopping carts around with their heads tucked into their shoulders, kowtowing to their wives, but at work they let off steam with a bunch of 20-year-olds, they really let themselves go.… No such thing as a good boss. A boss is someone who runs your life. The one I have now does little things to try to sweeten the pill. He takes us out for a drink, lets us leave early. Those are things that make us a little tighter, I mean personally, but we'll never be that tight. Some bosses aren't as bad as others, but there's no such thing as a good boss."*

Julien's views are grounded on three fairly constant elements of the critique of exploitation as a denial of merit: First, the labor entails physical exhaustion, mind-numbing fatigue. Second, the labor is exploited, as though the vital substance the worker sacrifices served to nourish the others. Third, the workers end up acquiescing in this exploitation by taking pride in their pains and by making the most of their power to exploit, in turn, the weakest in their ranks. This much we have already gleaned from the sociology literature on industrial work, especially assembly line jobs. All these elements came up, to some extent, in many of the interviews we conducted. Bruno, a call center agent, describes a job paced by the second, employees who quit without having to be laid off, the girl crying at her workstation because at the last minute she has been refused a vacation to which she was entitled, and so on. And while all that is going on, "the company's making a killing."

A group of cashiers we brought together told us how the supermarket tries to boost margins by eating into the downtime between customers, a few seconds at a time. If each cashier checks out two more customers an hour, and this gain is multiplied by the number of cashiers and the number of stores in the chain, the sizeable profits wrung from their labor can be distributed to the stockholders.

Odile runs a gasoline station. Not only does she work 44 hours a week, though only 38 hours are remunerated, but *"they ask me to provide services that aren't in my contract. Fact is I have to do it, I don't do it for fun. I knew perfectly well if I didn't do it, I'd be out the door in no time."* Claudio, in the same line of work, is constantly comparing his salary to the profits of the oil company he works for and its managers' astronomical earnings.

Feelings of being exploited tend to be aggravated by grueling jobs that drain the workers' energy in order to profit their employers. Workers are all too keenly aware of the disproportions between their exhaustion, their pay, and their boss's income. David recounted his experience as a bartender: *"It's an unrewarding job, you've got to work endless hours. You've got to clown around with patrons and be cheery. They rail at closing time, whereas us, we're glad to knock off. There are so many people looking for work that if you're not tip-top, someone else'll come and take your place. Your health is on the line, you really take a beating, it wipes you out physically, sometimes brings you down, too. You're living in a world of oppression."*

In stark contrast to their exertions, workers see how their employers live: their houses, cars, extravagant purchases. To quote Cedric, a mechanic, *"Bosses: The more you give 'em, the more they want. Sometimes they ask us to knuckle down: 'Do more, it'll be rewarded one day or another.' Then two years go by, and no sign of a raise. I can't stand that anymore."*

Similar examples abound, especially in all the interviews touching on unpaid hours worked, a practice that undermines the fundamental concept of merit as a mechanism regulating the fair exchange of labor for money. Along these lines, criticism of employers, the rich and powerful, tends to be leveled, not so much at class differences and inherited privilege, but at an economic juggernaut, a machine designed to milk the workforce for all they are worth.

Even those with "nice" jobs, "nice" employers, too, sometimes have a lingering sense of being exploited. Nicolas, a tree pruner who *"loves his job,"* is a case in point: *"There's no way I earn as much as I deserve because basically my boss bills €400 for every day I work—that's how he does his estimates—and I get paid €600 a month. I'm pretty glad to have him for my training, though it's true he's not doing it for love. It's not as though he's going to give me a job at the end of my training. But I'm respected all the same. He's a nice guy. He lets me use the equipment on weekends so I can do odd jobs, so I can get by—else I couldn't, that's for sure. We've become friends: He took advantage of the friendship. We'd do overtime and then, since he was a friend, money was kind of a taboo subject, it was off-limits to talk about it. He used the friendship to make money a taboo subject."* In other words, bosses may be more or less likeable, but there is no such thing as a good boss.

Sweatshop Blues

Feelings of being exploited are particularly acute wherever substandard working conditions prevail. All told, 33.7 percent of our respondents feel exploited, but this figure doubles to 68.1 percent for those working in deplorable conditions. Subjective exploitation comes to 52.7 percent of those required to work overtime, 44.3 percent of those suffering from work-related stress, and 46.2 percent of factory workers. Perceived exploitation remains intimately associated with manual labor, and many of the interviews call to mind the sociology literature of the 1950s, 1960s, and 1970s documenting and deploring the physical exploitation of workers, their sweatshop existence and alienation. However, we mustn't lose sight of the fact that, at a fundamental level, the feeling of being exploited involves the application of standards of merit. A full 49.9 percent of those who think they are underpaid feel exploited, as against only 13.9 percent of those who feel their wages are fair. But what is a fair wage? The answer, for our purposes, is a matter of sociology rather than economic theory: A fair wage is what workers consider a fair wage.

Perceived exploitation is not confined to overtly capitalist-type employment relations. Even workers whose jobs are not the most arduous or underpaid can also feel exploited. Philippe, for example, a male nurse, thinks the pay disparities between doctors and nurses on night duty are blatantly exploitative. *"A doctor who does a night shift here gets paid €300. I get paid €10 a night for a shift on weekends. It's awfully unfair because the doctors sleep while they're on night duty. They only get woken up once every two weeks on average when there's a problem. That's something that really bugs the hell out of me. I talk about it to the other nurses. Sometimes, when a doctor comes late, we think about his €300, that's pretty heavy. From a legal standpoint, we don't have as much responsibility as they do. But we're closer to the patients, and that's why we say we're more deserving than they are."* The hospital is "exploiting" Philippe by paying him less than he deserves—and perhaps by compromising his professional conscience.

Although feelings of exploitation are most common among blue-collar workers, it plagues many other workers who apply merit standards to assess the disparity between what they give and what they get. That even includes owners of small companies, who don't count their hours, though they're "carrying the company," and feel exploited by their own employees, who get monthly paychecks and never have to worry about the future, even if their zeal leaves much to be desired. Yvon, another entrepreneur, basically reasons in terms of merit that he is not duly rewarded for creating jobs, seeing as he has to pay all the payroll taxes and *"in France the state milks private enterprise for all it's worth."* For all his pains, his lifestyle is no more lavish than his employees'. Christine, a primary school teacher, airs comparable complaints, even though no one is enriching himself on her exertions. Her view is that she is only paid to teach class, and all the other work, including meetings with peers and parents, is *"unpaid overtime, it's exploitation."* Her grievance is compounded by the heavy taxes on the middle class. Her income bracket is not eligible for benefits available to the poor, and at the age of 40 she is still borrowing money from her mother. All these cases lie somewhat outside the classic context of working-class exploitation, yet the sense of injustice here is no less acute.

For floorwalkers in supermarkets, their own exploitation is at once a matter of course and a sort of daily sport. Every morning they check their sales figures, product by product. They know exactly how much they've earned for the company—and how that compares to their salaries and their subordinates'. They are, as it were, archetypes of the capitalist, daily evaluating their merit and their operating result (or, more tellingly, *taux d'exploitation* in French). But unlike their own subordinates, they believe they can better that result, which proves alternately motivating and disheartening. Most of them are quite caught up in this game, which they find exciting, though they have no illusions as to the ultimate beneficiaries: the stockholders and the company's officers and directors, whose merit is hardly put to the test.

With the exception of company heads, senior staff, and "brain workers," over 25 percent of all the remaining respondents said they felt exploited, with the figure for manual laborers alone coming to nearly 47 percent. Though particularly prevalent among blue-collar workers, the equating of unrecognized merit with exploitation is not confined to manual labor. More generally, it is a consequence of being a wage earner, when work and wages do not add up.

What Does Merit Measure?

In *Principles of Social Justice* (1999) Miller introduces a distinction between *desert* and *merit*. He defines *desert* as the result of work, the objective performance, the value actually produced by the worker, akin to the "objective" performance of a student or athlete. *Merit* designates the effort made by the worker to achieve an objective, whether or not she succeeds. In general usage, however, *merit* tends to be used to cover both the objective result of an agent's action, or his performance, and the agent's commitment to said action. Every teacher knows there are two ways of grading their students: on the quality of their work or on their progress and efforts. Is there more merit in being a gifted but lazy student or a poor student who works hard? Most teachers apply both criteria (Merle 1996). This ambivalence between objective utility and effort is at the core of the doubts expressed by many theorists of justice who are reluctant to recognize merit as a primary principle of justice. Most of them see no necessary connection between *desert* and *merit.* On the one hand, success in a particular activity is not necessarily due to individual merit. Luck often plays a part, and ends are often achieved by immoral means. On the other hand, the very existence of merit is called into question if we admit that individuals are never wholly responsible for who they are, their individual talents and tastes, their vim and vigor, and indeed their handicaps.

The fact that agents themselves believe in merit, as they do in equality, does not keep them from harboring certain philosophical doubts as to the true nature of both principles. While the existence of merit is taken for granted, its makeup remains a subject of ongoing debate. Does merit lie in results or intentions?

Merit and Utility

Many workers assess their own merit in terms of participation in the collective pursuit of the department, factory, or company they work for. They know, or try to find out, what part their job plays in that pursuit and seek to define their merit in terms of utility and contribution to the functioning of the system. However, not everyone has the "good fortune" of the supermarket floorwalkers who can compare exactly what they earn for the company with what they earn themselves. In fact, it is often impossible to quantify what one produces or how much it is worth. Merit is then defined very generally as *utility,* meaning one's overall contribution to the harmonious functioning of society, a contribution gauged in terms of basic social values. This was how many of our respondents qualified the merit of doctors, especially surgeons, since the lives they save defy economic evaluation. Consequently, the assessment of utility hinges on an implicit hierarchy of values. Sandra, a secretary, told us: *"Doctors deserve their salaries, but what's really shocking is a reporter making €50,000 a month He may be good-looking and a good talker, but that's not right."* In terms of perceived utility, doctors are indispensable, but the same can hardly be said of journalists. Doctors are useful to everyone, journalism is a relatively futile activity.

Implicit in this line of reasoning is the notion of a just hierarchy of salaries based on the relative utility of professions, and many agents may, without knowing it, adhere to a functionalist view of society and the division of labor, allotting to everyone a place in the social hierarchy based on his or her contribution to collective utility. In this view of the industrious and the idle, every *desert* becomes *merit*: *"I should be paid,"* a busy mother told us, *"because society needs people to rear children."* Similarly, one proprietor of a tobacco/coffee shop argued that he was unfairly treated because his business, which plays a social role in the community, is being undermined by the extra tax on cigarettes. Dominique, an office worker, followed this line of reasoning to propose that the merit of a profession be determined according to its social utility: *"In a social classification, I don't see why a construction worker who builds bridges should make less than a doctor. If the worker does a bad job bolting the bridge together, it'll collapse. If you're a lawyer you earn more, but that's not necessarily more justified than the salaries of soccer players."* The astronomical earnings of soccer players and other stars seem particularly shocking because they are evocative of a world of glitz and glamour, a land of make-believe opposed to the serious world of serious work. In this artificial realm, moreover, there is no link between actual merit and the salaries, which are based on expectations and speculation. One of our respondents, a soccer fan, proposed bridging the gulf between his passion for the sport and his standards of merit by paying the players only when they win. One need only betake oneself to the stadium and hear the crowd booing the "overpaid idlers" on the field to appreciate the sway of utilitarian merit.

On closer consideration, however, workers face the same quandaries Parsons (1955) encountered in attempting to construct a functionalist theory of stratification. Merit can be measured in terms of functional utility only if we all share the same values, the same "private utility." But that is highly unlikely: The astral earnings of pop stars, for instance, are liable to seem less shocking to their fans than to detractors, let alone those who have never heard of them. Perhaps it is best to conclude that the merit-utility equation only works in industry, though even there the "pen pushers" are deemed overpaid "layabouts" by those on the shop floor. Our material shows that everyone believes his professional activity is fundamentally useful and indispensable, which is by no means absurd. But if we grant that claim, how do we get beyond purely localized comparisons to define merit?

To get round the impasse of defining merit in terms of functional utility, would objective success prove a sounder standard? Charles, an entrepreneur, finds that, capitalism being what it is, the only workable standard of merit is the market, a development he goes on to deplore: *"You're no longer recognized for what you do, but for what you yield. But that's the world we live in these days."* Like Hayek, albeit much to his regret, Charles believes the market does not reflect merit: *"I'm a selfish person living in a world of selfish people."* It follows that everyone had better be as rational and utilitarian as possible, that being the most effective strategy. Charles regrets the demise of a more humane capitalism that could reward *"real merit."* The market does not recompense effort, it crowns success, which does not necessarily depend on effort. So Charles understands why his workers do only the bare minimum, seeing as any extra effort will not be financially rewarded by the market. Though an employer himself, he believes a corporate CEO earning 100 times the minimum wage certainly cannot claim 100 times as much merit as a minimum-wage earner.

Some of the doctors in private practice we interviewed voiced similar doubts, pointing out that members of the profession who are making a fortune might be engaging in dubious practices: One need only keep consultations brief, see plenty of patients, and readily comply with all their requests for medication and sick leave. By choosing a field of medicine that does not involve life-or-death situations or emergency care, they can "get rich quick," provided they are not too conscientious about their Hippocratic oath. After all, popular wisdom does not equate the prosperity of medical practitioners with the triumph of altruism.

For those who feel exploited, it goes without saying that capitalism does not reward either merit or utility in a society in which the fruits of the workingman's labor go to finance shareholder dividends, mutual funds, stock market speculation—in short, all manner of "unearned" capital gains. They regard the winners of the economic contest as speculators, the great fortunes as built on the broken backs of the poor. The age-old Roman Catholic distrust of "filthy lucre," of the immoral practice of making money in one's sleep, is still very much alive in contemporary condemnations of injustice in the world.

Merit and Effort

If merit cannot be based on utility, which requires universal standards, or on the market, which proves amoral, if not immoral, it can be based only on subjective commitment, on the worker's own assessment of his efforts. Samira, a ticket clerk at French Rail, feels her efforts go unappreciated. *"We give a lot of ourselves in terms of morale, I mean psychologically. We give lots of things. There's inequality in our salaries compared to the work we do, compared to the emotional aspects that can be there, too. Because you have to have a very thick skin to work in a company like this that's open to the public. It's not always easy. We should be paid accordingly. Our managers get €3,000 a month, ticket clerks €1,200. When you compare the amount of work a ticket clerk does to what a manager does, it's outrageous, and all because the manager went to college. And he doesn't even know how to issue a train ticket!"* The salary does not reflect the subjective reality of work, which is far more complex and onerous than the work presumably corresponding to the figure on a paycheck. Claudio, a service station attendant, paid minimum wage for what is supposed to be a very simple job, points out all the expertise required in his line of work, all the merit his wages fail to take into account. *"It's not a factory job where you just do one simple thing. You've got responsibilities. There's bread you've got to keep track of in the cash register, there's this type of stuff doesn't show up on the paycheck. I don't work for fun—I work for the bread. My job's not mechanical, it's not just anyone who could do it. For example, this morning three drunks came into the station. If I'd let them walk all over me by showing I was afraid, or showing I was edgy, the situation could've turned ugly. I didn't do anything, that's exactly what you gotta do: nothing. You just show 'em you're doing nothing, you're just waiting there, everything's OK.... The head honchos at Total don't do a thing. They're the ones ought to be earning less, well, same as me. I'm closer to the gasoline than they are. I'm fed up hearing customers say 'have a nice weekend' 300 times a day. I don't have any nice weekends 'cause I work all weekend."*

This argument was aired at length by all the respondents whose work involves person-to-person service—teachers, nurses, social workers, ticket clerks, etc. They all stressed that their work is far more complicated and, above all, far more onerous than their employers presume. It is not only a question of the physical exertions involved, for the psychological strain on service workers can take an even heavier toll. Maintaining discipline in the classroom, holding hands with sick patients, coping with the often aggressive demands of customers are tasks that service employees consider every bit as draining as manual labor. Now, this strain is unique to each worker, and invisible to others because it usually manifests itself in anxiety, fear, and doubts about one's own worth. In any case, individual merit is by nature so subjective, so dependent on personal standards and experiences, that it cannot be measured by any common standards and therefore cannot be rated a true principle of justice. As Rawls pointed out (1987), moral merit can be defined as "to each according to his own effort," or better yet, as "to each according to his conscientious effort." But how can we objectivize that effort and, what is more, its conscientiousness if the individual in question is the sole judge thereof?

Keeping Merit at Arm's Length

Agents believe in merit even though they share the philosophers' doubts as to how to establish true merit. An initial response and an initial critique might focus on the rules used to establish merit and fair competition. The self-employed—for example, the groups of small farmers we interviewed— spoke at length about the administrative regulations that undermine the manifestation of their merit because the markets in which they operate are not entirely transparent. Due to agricultural policies and the clout of supermarket chains, say the farmers, the winners are not the most deserving, but the shrewdest, the craftiest, the best protected. Land left to lie fallow is more profitable than cultivated land, investments reach full yield at the very moment that market prices collapse, quality produce is taken off the supermarket shelves to make way for cheap standardized mass produce, and so on. Some of the farmers added that international competition favors intensive farming in countries with unlimited land resources and underpaid labor. Under the circumstances, merit is not crowned with success.

It follows that equitable rules and equal opportunity are essential for the realization of merit. If merit is to be just and recognized, resources and opportunity must be fairly distributed from the outset so that all entrants in the meritocratic competition start out on a perfectly equal footing. But such absolutely equitable starting rules are wishful thinking. Guy, the high school principal we quoted earlier, developed this argument to its logical conclusion. Prior to merit assessment, *"to prove that all pupils are equal, we would have to take them away from their social and family environment"* (as they did in Sparta) *"and put them in the same conditions. And then we'd see in the end whether they all have the same level of achievement."* Cut off from all sources of social conditioning, merit could be realized in all its purity and cruelty, for *"there is no such thing as a completely egalitarian society. Let's say we were to give €1,000 to everyone. At the end of a year some would have increased that capital tenfold and others would have squandered it all. It's the same in the education system and in society. Injustices related to remuneration levels, I'd say they exist, and they're not injustices. In a totally egalitarian system, individual initiative is snuffed out, society goes into decline. When pay disparities range from 1 to 10, or 1 to 15, I'd say that could be considered all right. From 1 to 500 is a different matter."* In other words, even if the initial distribution is fair, and assuming agents are free to use that equality as they see fit, vast inequalities will still ensue, inequalities so excessive that they could jeopardize the fundamental equality of individuals. Pushed to the limit, merit would come to resemble a form of brutal Darwinism, as Didier pointed out: *"We're well aware that in animal species it's survival of the fittest. And even with laws, it's the fittest who remain the fittest."*

It is, in all likelihood, the severity of the merit principle that puts workers off. This may be why the dominant, for our present purposes the winners of the competition, tend to draw attention to the role of chance in their success, the good fortune of having been born where they were born, of having had the chance to go to college, of having been helped by others, etc. It is as though they were bringing up chance to counterbalance their pride in victory, to prevent one man's merit from swelling to the point of crushing those around him. For the underdogs, attachment to merit is invariably tempered by a deep-seated mistrust of a principle that has the potential to shatter any working community, any equality. Not only can merit be perceived as a trick used by employers to step up competitive productivity, but it is also a potential threat to the basic equality, autonomy, and self-respect to which everyone is entitled. Though merit may be a universally acknowledged principle of justice, it must be held in check by equality and respect for human dignity, lest we be left at the mercy of merit.

Moral reasoning grounded in the merit principle is used to justify success, to point out the unjust causes of failure, to question judgments and rewards, and to provide a basis for feelings of exploitation. Merit is an active principle of justice in that everyone is continually evaluating his or her own merit and that of others, in that it triggers a critique that is uninterrupted and of variable geometry, and because it enables us to define just inequalities. Winners believe in merit, and losers believe their merit is ignored by those who dominate them, who are often blinkered by their own merit. While equality is an ontological principle implying a definition of human nature that is forever undermined by the existence of real social inequalities, merit is an arithmetical principle equating the cost of work with its remuneration. If we agree that individuals are free and equal, merit furnishes the only means of constructing just inequalities based on each person's contribution to the collective weal and on the use he makes of his freedom. It is, of course, always possible to argue that equality and freedom are fictions and that, in consequence, merit is also a fiction. The philosophers mentioned at the beginning of this chapter are right about this point, and social agents—whether or not they've read the philosophers' works—may well share their doubts. This is why universal adherence to the merit principle is constantly attended by doubts about its foundational criteria. And this is why many people keep this principle at arm's length, though without ever being able to dispense with it entirely, as evidenced by the sheer prevalence of suspicions and jealousies based on merit and the nonrecognition thereof. But the theorists have failed to grasp one essential point: This fiction is necessary for the establishment of a just hierarchy, which, we may recall, is the crux of the philosophy of justice. Merit may be an illusion, but it is an illusion necessary for the moral aspects of action. Hence, merit derives its strength more from sociology than from philosophy. Its theoretical definition remains problematic and vague. And yet it is a standard to which we all refer whenever we compare our lot to others' and whenever we address the question of just compensation for our work. Like equality, merit is involved in forming a just order, over which, however, it can never exercise complete control. Individuals are therefore ambivalent, at once attached to the merit principle and wary of its application.

Note

1. For Aristotle, merit is the founding principle of distributive justice (Adams 1965; Homans 1974; Kellerhals/J. Coenen-Huter/M. Modak 1988).

CHAPTER 3

Autonomy

INDIVIDUALS APPLY THE PRINCIPLE of equality to evaluate the fairness of their *position* both in society and the workplace. With the principle of merit, they measure the *equity* of the reward for their labor. Work cannot be reduced, however, either to the status it confers or to the exchange of effort, utility, and good will for a pecuniary consideration. Work is also a subject's involvement in an activity that intrinsically gives pleasure, happiness, fulfillment, and a sense of freedom. At the other extreme, work can create a sense of alienation, of being crushed and worn out, even if it is well paid and confers a position the worker deems appropriate. In evaluating this aspect of work, subjects employ a subjective standard related to the traditional notion of job satisfaction. But satisfaction is too vague a concept. Being satisfied with one's salary and status is not the same as being satisfied with one's profession and one's on-the-job activity "in and of itself." Hence the need for a separate examination of workers' judgments of jobs they find fulfilling or frustrating in their quest for self-realization in the workplace. Here, workers are *subjects,* for the agents who make these judgments cannot be reduced to their social status or financial interests; here, it is the individual's perception of her self-realization and creativity on which her feelings of justice or injustice will be based.

These judgments are subsumed under a principle of justice we can call *autonomy.* In abstract terms, the sense of autonomy is the subjective and social manifestation of the postulate of freedom. But on-the-job autonomy is also linked to the strictly anthropological dimension of work as the realization of human creativity. In weighing up the satisfactions obtained and sufferings sustained in his occupation itself, the individual is assessing the justice of his lot and engaging in a social critique. The desire to be one's own master and achieve self-fulfillment falls within the province of justice if we acknowledge that, in democratic societies, the fact that we are all equally free prompts us to behave as subjects (MacIntyre 1994; 1997). If equality is an ontological postulate and merit an arithmetical rule, autonomy is by nature an ethical principle. It is not based on a postulate concerning human nature or on a calculation of utility, but on the relation of the self to the self.

The standard of autonomy, as the practical realization of freedom in the workplace, is eminently subjective. Hence the prevailing *ambivalence* about autonomy, since every occupation can be easily construed as a test of autonomy, as either fulfilling or obstructing it. Whereas subjects readily bring up the topics of equality and merit, they rarely explicitly advert to autonomy, whose manifestations involve various registers—the self-fulfillment of a vocation, self-expression in one's work, a sense of mastering a trade. These are all variations on one and the same principle of justice, that of the human need to be an autonomous subject. Like all principles of justice, however, autonomy is a hidden god, a principle whose absence is more clearly and deeply felt than its realization. Just as agents critique and construct their experience around an equality and merit that can never be fully realized, they affirm their attachment to autonomy when they are most deprived of it.

"But I Love My Job"

Labor Is a "Value"

Proclamations of "the end of work" should not be taken seriously. At any rate, they tend to be vague, confusing the decline of the Protestant work ethic, of the labor movement, and of the ideologies of "Adam's curse," or work *as* suffering, with the trend toward subjective detachment from work. In France, the end of work has hardly withstood the advent of mass unemployment; the evils of unemployment are by no means confined to poverty and exclusion, and they clearly demonstrate that the anthropological function of work did not die out in the wake of the gradual transition from industrial society (Schnapper 1997). To many of us, work is preferable to unemployment, even if it isn't necessarily more profitable. Witness Henri, a maintenance man: *"I love working with my hands, so instead of doing nothing.... Honestly, at the time, I could have stayed on unemployment for two years with a better salary than the one I had when I started working."*[1] The fact that jobs are now scarce in France does not mean work has lost its meaning. What appears to have declined is the sociological conviction that work is the hub of social existence to which everything is attached: income, identity, culture, political affinities, etc. Industrial society had, in large measure, grounded this work-centered model on a conception of social class as a "total" entity that explains the whole of social existence. In this historical context, moreover, most sociologists thought they could explain social behavior by tracing the chains of cause and effect between different positions in the workplace and different behaviors. This representation has now given way to far more complex models of causality, but that does not imply either the end of work or the end of social classes. It simply means neither work nor social class is considered the sole core of social existence.

We may no longer believe that mankind is nothing without work or that radical emancipation has to be the ultimate aim of the labor movement, but we still attach considerable value to work. In France, the percentage of the population that agreed to the statement "work is very important" rose from 60 percent to 68 percent from 1990 to 1999 (Riffault/Tchernia 2000). After family, work is considered to be the most fundamental aspect of life, and 39 percent like their work for its own sake, regardless of the income and social position it confers. The inherent interest of one's job, the responsibility involved, and the working atmosphere topped the list of criteria for this preference. When asked to evaluate their work on a scale of 1 to 10, 50 percent of those surveyed rated their jobs above a 7, the average rating was 6.8, and only 10 percent gave it under a 4 (Riffault 1994).

Virulent criticisms of their jobs notwithstanding, virtually everyone finds sources of satisfaction (Baudelot/Gollac et al. 2003). The most important is a sense of personal fulfillment, selected by 41.5 percent of the respondents, ahead of money (36.9 percent) and social integration (21.1 percent). Our survey likewise showed that sources of job satisfaction are both more numerous and more frequently cited than sources of dissatisfaction. The four leading sources of job satisfaction are human relations in the workplace (53.5 percent), variety (45.5 percent), scope for initiative (35.2 percent), and responsibility (34.5 percent). The four main sources of job dissatisfaction are that it is fatiguing (51.2 percent), monotonous (23.4 percent), stressful (22.3 percent), and dirty (17.7 percent). All things considered, work seems more of a blessing than a curse. But that does not mean that only a minority complain of injustices, that we could divide the workforce into two groups—those who like their jobs and those who don't—because often enough the same individual will pronounce both positive and negative judgments. What is more, it is not hard to imagine that workers tend to be more critical when they like their jobs and have a lower tolerance for its attendant hardships and injustices, for those who like their work are also likely to be more demanding of it. All told, 82.25 percent expressed ambivalence, both favorable and adverse assessments of their work. This ambivalence is confirmed by the indices of job satisfaction and dissatisfaction we computed from the aggregate results of 1,144 questionnaires.

Table 3.1 Effect of Working Conditions on Satisfaction Levels

Working Conditions	Satisfaction Index	Dissatisfaction Index
Very Good	2.94	0.89
Good	2.62	1.47
Bad	2.07	2.22
Very Bad	2.00	2.29
Average	2.55	1.54

This index is the average of the sum of the responses to questions regarding reasons for liking or disliking one's job.

Although it is obvious, even reassuring, that job satisfaction should reflect the quality of working conditions, it should be noted that this satisfaction index is consistently high, even when working conditions are bad. We found that ambivalence persists when we correlate the satisfaction index with qualification or income levels: It is obviously better to have a high-paid, highly qualified job than the opposite, but workers still find reason for satisfaction in less favorable working situations. It follows that work has a value "in and of itself." Having noted that 98 percent of their respondents have a generally positive attitude toward their work, Baudelot and Gollac (2003) concluded, "It is work as an accomplished act in and of itself and for its own sake that is the source of happiness." Work *qua* work retains value, now as in the past, and perhaps even more than in the past, now that it is less of a necessity for survival and more of a demand for subjective fulfillment (Herzberg 1966).

The ambivalence of our work-related judgments is nothing new and probably a reflection of the nature of what we understand by work, since we use the same term to encompass what the Romans called *opus,* or work done, *operae,* the activity itself, and *labor,* the suffering of peasants and of women giving birth. Between salvation and damnation, ambivalence about work profoundly informed the medieval worldview and religious thought, and the Protestant valorization of work may not have been as radically new as is often claimed (Le Goff 1977). So there is nothing surprising about our ability to love and loathe work *at the same time,* to feel that it is simultaneously building us up and tearing us down.

Kako and *Kalo*

In *The Human Condition,* a book that is now a classic, Hannah Arendt (1983) takes up the ancient Greek distinction between *labor* and *work.* Labor is mechanical, a necessity for survival, excluding man from society to situate him in nature. Greek philosophers called it *kako,* and considered it less than human, delegating it to women and slaves. *Work,* on the other hand, is truly human, dignified, and autonomous, and the worker is acknowledged as the creator of a work. Work of this kind was called *kalo*. *Kako* was held to be vulgar and exhausting, *kalo* aristocratic and fully human. While this distinction worked in societies built on slavery, bondage, and abject exploitation, its legacy lives on in the hierarchy of respectable occupations and menial tasks. For Alain, a laborer, work is sheer drudgery: *"You have to get up in the morning and go bust your butt because, in spite of all, you get a paycheck, health insurance, a couple perks. I think work is like modern slavery. You need to work to live, otherwise you're a total nobody."* Suchlike sentiments are relatively rare, however, because *kako* and *kalo* do not make for two distinct worlds, but are mixed together in most professional activities. There may be some creativity and autonomy in what are presumably the most menial occupations, as evidenced by a few of our interviews of workers who complain bitterly about their jobs.

Let us come back to Katia, the school cafeteria worker who felt she was the object of the teachers' vitriolic scorn: *"I'm the cafeteria lady. I'm the one who forces you to eat when you're not hungry anymore. When you don't like your spinach, I'm the one who says, 'Eat your spinach, it's good.' I don't want to spend my life sweeping floors. I don't want to be a secretary, pushing paper and gabbing all day to the other girls about my weekend. My thing is to be a dancer. I want to go to another country, make myself useful. I'm nothing here."* And yet Katia likes her *"shitty job"* too: *"I can't complain. I've got a great team. I'm happy to go to work in the morning. Every evening at five o'clock, I stand at the door, and that's when I see all the parents. It's great because I can communicate with them. I'm on friendly terms with one of the moms, you know, she's from Cameroon. The parents think we take a lot better care of the kids than the teachers do. We teach them to talk, we teach them a lot of stuff in fact. We practically educate them. We tell them not to say bad words, not to hit each other. The teachers don't do that. Who are the ones who help them? We do. Who are the ones who put their shoes on? We do."* There is something good, worthy, creative, a bit of *kalo*, in the job that Katia dislikes.

David, the bartender mentioned earlier who described his excruciating exploitation, also told us: *"What I like is relating to people. It's one of the rare jobs where you get a chance to work while having fun. So it's fulfilling. You don't notice the time go by."* Sophie, a head waitress, who describes her work in entirely negative terms, saying she is exploited, stressed out, worn out, and looked down on by managers and patrons, nonetheless does not regret having taken the job: *"I believe in myself. I've learned more here than I did in five years of college."* She feels she has grown by coping with real-life ordeals, which make her erstwhile academic adversities seem utterly artificial. Having overcome her timidity, she now envisages opening her own restaurant. She likes the atmosphere and the work, a reality that gives her a sense of existing and living more intensely than in the hollow world of college. Catherine, a checkout clerk, went through a nightmare when her company was taken over and her new employers demoted her, which felt demeaning, and yet: *"I always say I love sales, and I always will. That's all there is to it. It's a job I like. I could have gone into civil service like my husband, but I didn't because I'd miss the contact with customers."*

At the other end of the spectrum, activities that are presumably creative, or *kalo*, can also become mired in *kako*, the constraints of necessity and alienation. Aurelie's adventures in the world of hairdressing began like a fairy tale, only to end like Maupassant's short story, *A Woman's Life*, whose heroine discovers the vile reality of a married life she had so craved. At the outset, everything was wonderful, everything was *kalo*. *"My mom bought me electric clippers and I started cutting my brother's hair, and everyone else's, some styling and doing my friends' hair. I could feel that I really liked what I was doing, that I enjoyed doing it."* So she got a job in an upmarket chain of hair salons. *"It's really great. We greet our customers with a smile. That's something that comes naturally to us. It isn't hypocritical either, it's really sincere. We all have sincere smiles."* But then the mood darkens. *"The boss is always making snide remarks. He thinks it's funny, but we don't. He throws his weight around because he wants to show he's in charge.... I do a lot of the dirty work, straightening up, have to clean more brushes than the others, more robes, more towels, order supplies, stuff like that. That isn't really my job, but if there's a slip-up, I'm the one who gets bawled out."* Aurelie ended up feeling threatened. *"It's true that when you tell someone you're a hairdresser, people immediately think you dropped out of school and that you're a little thick in the head. And I forgot to tell you I'm stressed out all the time, I'm always scared of getting a reprimand. I'm always afraid I did something wrong. Where I work, they pay pretty much attention to the way you speak, the way you hold yourself, and those are really things that totally stress me out. I'm always afraid of getting criticized, I'm always afraid of being watched. Even when you're just answering the phone. In the salon, I have the impression I'm somebody else. There are things you can say, and things you can't. When I smile at customers I'm being myself. But from then on, I'm not entirely me, I don't use my own words, just these stock phrases."* Aurelie feels that her vocation has been ruined, and that her autonomy, her very identity, are in jeopardy. She has even been told to lose her southern French accent because it's out of place in the salon.

It is plain to see in the foregoing cases that autonomy, whether partially realized or largely undermined, is a principle used to assess one's situation in the workplace—even in settings where we would hardly expect to find it. Skeptics will argue that any expression of affinity for a job which is presumably arduous, poorly paid, and generally despised is but a defense mechanism, a means of salvaging some self-esteem. Given the vital importance of self-respect, we are compelled to find some saving grace in our work, even if it means inventing it as a last consolation, even if it means magnifying our tribulations. If that is the case, the sense of autonomy and self-realization is one of the tricks of domination, of the prevailing ideology that impels everyone to find a little grandeur in the most thankless and menial tasks. Exploiting the pride of the subjugated, it persuades them of the dignity of their trials, thereby inducing them to accept their subservience.

But there is a *kalo* component of these judgments based on the notion that work should have an all-encompassing scope, like a total artwork, or like the work of a philosopher or sociologist who can hardly imagine any other professional pride than his own, never stopping to think that there is as much intelligence and human creativity in a diesel engine as in a Kantian critique. This position is all the more contestable, and, frankly, untenable, in that the valorization of the creativity and autonomy attaching to most jobs does not preclude even the most virulent criticism. It is to refute this naively aristocratic view that the examples adduced in the following pages are expressly drawn from among what are, *prima facie*, the least *kalo* of work experiences.

Independence and Autonomy

The principle of autonomy is based on the subject's feeling and conviction that she has a value of her own and a freedom that are threatened by working conditions and must be defended at all costs. Beyond certain heroic stories that are always somewhat suspect because they smack of attempts to build a monument to one's own achievements, we see that autonomy manifests itself in putting up a resistance to destiny, an opposition to forces that erode the worker's sense of being—and will to be—a fully fledged subject. The principle of autonomy is best grasped by focusing on details and, above all, on the scope for initiative and freedom that enables agents to create, if not all of their work, at least a significant portion of it. For some, it is a matter of independence; for others, of struggling to attain some measure of autonomy within the workplace system. Though autonomy is never absolute freedom, for we are always dependent on others, it does mean that the subject is not entirely dependent on his "superiors" and that it is the subject himself who forges his ties to others (Renaut 1989).

Eschewing Victimhood

In its most clear-cut form, the desire for autonomy takes the form of plans to escape salaried employment and strike out on one's own. Every year in France, tens of thousands of people start up their own companies, most of which are one-person businesses. Not all these startups prove successful.

Some are last-ditch efforts to escape long-term unemployment, but most are buoyed up by the aspiring entrepreneur's resolve not to take orders from anyone anymore: The dream of being one's own boss is less about being the boss than being rid of one. For Djamel, who works at a gas station, the dream of being self-employed one day is the only thing that makes his job bearable: *"Let's say that in the workaday world there's a bunch of sharks and all the little fish. It's up to us to decide if we want to be the little fish or the shark.... If you want something, if you do what's necessary to get it, you can do it. All you need is to really want it. As I was saying, you can do anything, even move mountains.... You hear there's three million unemployed, you say to yourself, there's no jobs in France. But that's not true, it's not true! Get motivated, get some get-up-and-go, get up early in the morning and go look for a job. You'll see, you'll find one. I feel like being my own boss. I'm going to work for a few years and put some money aside to start up my own business."* We could easily puncture Djamel's dreams and delusions by citing the daunting statistics on small business bankruptcies. But at the same time we should note that he has found therein a spur to action, a plan for autonomy. And then again, is it really all that misguided to want to set up on one's own, especially seeing as certain groups of immigrants have found more work in "ethnic business" that in the industries to which they were hitherto confined? For Florent, a youth counselor, it is a matter of realizing his vocation as a musician, both for the love of his art and the desire to be his own boss. He turns down other job offers: *"They're no better than assembly line work in a factory. The monotony drains your brain."* So he is "sweating blood" to make it as a musician. *"I haul ass to do what I feel like doing. I can make it. If you're motivated and put in the time and effort, you can do it. So if you don't, you've only yourself to blame. It's not going to be someone else who's going to wreck my life."*

Though they may not dream of being their own boss, others approach their jobs as an adventure, a challenge they have to overcome. What we are inclined to call careerism and ambition may also be a resolute and sometimes ruthless quest for autonomy. Serge, the manager of a cell phone sales outlet, is determined to get ahead. *"My goal is a good position—his position. My boss plays games with me: I do him favors, I put in double the usual workweek, for no extra pay or extra credit. I don't have the diplomas to make a bid for his job right now, which is something I really regret, but it's a bit late for that. So I'm learning on the job. That's working out fine, but if it doesn't, I'll take a year off. I'm not married to this job.... I work more than I have to because I enjoy it, because I want to get ahead, because I want my agency to make a good showing, a better showing than the others. I want to go all the way, as high as I possibly can. Me, I was the little newcomer trainee who didn't know his ass from his elbow, had to start from scratch. I had to bust a gut to get the skills, it was quite a fight. I enjoy what I do and anyway, that's the shape of my life."* This may be an odd expression of autonomy, but it is autonomy nonetheless, for Serge has made up his mind not to give in, but to take his life in hand and turn his career into a kind of performance, a sort of heroic athletic achievement. There are various subjective ingredients in his brand of ambition: a desire for self-assertion and self-reliance, a desire to compel respect and to refuse submission.

Sylvie, an engineer, won't "submit" either: *"Anything but being a civil servant. You have to show you can deliver on performance, and for me, that's not a drawback.... The men tend to treat the women like secretaries; we're only good for making coffee, typing, but they'd never give us any credit for technical abilities.... We constantly have to prove we're as good as they are. It's a choice I made. I'm treated right because I make sure they treat me right. It isn't only true at work, it's true everywhere. If you let people walk all over you, they will. If you go on the principle that people should respect you, well then they'll respect you."* So she decided to fight her way up through the ranks in her company. Readers may be more indulgent toward Sylvie's desire to succeed by showing that women can also earn their autonomy than toward Serge's trivial self-seeking careerism. Their motives, however, may not be all that different.

But Djamel's daydreams and Serge's ambition are not the only avenues to autonomy. Jeremie told us he was willing to accept the job insecurity of temp work in return for a relative degree of autonomy. What he found most unbearable about his previous job was being watched all the time. *"Right from the start, they told us there were cameras in every aisle, that you could get a reward if you saw someone stealing and told on him. Imagine the vibe! And then the guys always breathing down your back. They would time us, and we had to write down the exact time when we knocked off.... You weren't allowed to talk because we weren't there for that, we were there to work."* So Jeremie chose to hire on at a temp agency as a means of gaining a modicum of autonomy, if not on the job, at least in the choice of jobs. *"Temp workers feel they've got a certain amount of freedom. They can quit their job when they like and take a two-week vacation, even if it's not paid. I know people who were offered permanent contracts that paid less who preferred to go on temping because they felt freer. They didn't feel like getting tied down to one company."* In other words, after a stint in a universe reminiscent of Charlie Chaplin's *Modern Times,* Jeremie elected to trade financial security for freedom. In so doing, he was adopting a resistance strategy that can be traced back to the late nineteenth century, when French laborers who were unwilling to sell themselves wholly to their employers would roam the country without ever settling down, under the mistrustful gaze of the bourgeoisie—and of their fellow laborers.

Luc, a temporary construction worker, adopts a like strategy, a similar trade-off between freedom and security. He begins with a radical critique of on-the-job injustices: *"Racist prejudice: The blacks don't get permanent contracts. Sexist prejudice: Girls can't get jobs in construction. I find it shocking. The ones there get paid less than the men. If you're young, you keep your trap shut. And I'm short, too! I come from a working-class family, so I didn't have the same exposure to culture as everyone else, though if I had, if I'd happened to be in a higher class, I would have gone to college. The bosses really feel like big shots, but they got no reason to because I've seen bosses who've never poured concrete and have the nerve to walk around giving orders. They pay the workers peanuts and expect gigantic results. The boss sits around at his desk all day and gets paid twice as much as the workers, though they're the ones breaking their backs. A guy on the site may be about to keel over, but he'll keep his mouth shut.... The unions are useful, but they're too busy trying to calm down angry workers. There's too much bargaining these days between the unions and employers, too much siding with employers."* Assessed in terms of equality and merit, construction work, as Luc describes it, is exploitative, backbreaking, and wholly unjust. To escape this ruinous element, Luc has opted for agency work. *"I like temping a lot because it has advantages paywise. The other advantage is that if you don't get along with the boss, you can just walk off the job. You're pretty free to choose where you work, you can quit whenever you want. That means you can move around, you don't get stuck in one place. That's just it: different settings, getting to know new things.... Me, a victim? I can't call myself a victim. I've never claimed to be a victim. I feel like I'm above all the discrimination."*

More often than not, of course, temporary work is something people accept for lack of a better offer; they don't usually trade job security for freedom. Nevertheless, the arrangement enables young, unskilled workers who are condemned to backbreaking labor anyway to retain some autonomy, some control over their own lives. Luc's remarks clearly illustrate the importance of autonomy as an individual attribute and possession. In addition to threatening equality and merit, work encroaches on the allotment of freedom or autonomy with which everyone feels he is endowed as a fundamental asset, a primary virtue, a treasure that must be preserved. Hence the paradox of workers' saying they are victims of execrable working conditions while stubbornly refusing to define themselves as victims. Because autonomy is axiomatically a subjective principle of justice, acknowledging victimhood amounts to surrendering to an unjust fate and subjectively renouncing ownership of oneself.

A Space of One's Own

In most cases, the appeal of autonomy lies neither in dreams of success, career ambitions, nor in the perilous adventure of job insecurity. Asked in the questionnaire what they liked about their jobs, 35.2 percent of our respondents cited scope for initiative and 34.5 percent responsibility. In more modest terms, the desire for autonomy is manifest in attempts to construct an area of freedom, what organizational sociologists term a "gray zone" (Crozier/Friedberg 1977). Usually this zone is not freely granted by employers, but staked out by employees. Most workers presumably enjoy such a gray zone, an autonomous space conferred by the organization of workplace operations, which can never be absolute or hermetically sealed. Furthermore, the delegation of work necessarily entails the creation of gray zones inasmuch as a job assignment can never spell out every single task involved, so the operational organization cannot wholly forego some measure of personal initiative and adaptability on the workers' part. Instead of attempting an exhaustive list of all the gray zones expressly granted or spontaneously arising out of functional exigencies, let us merely describe a few of the ways in which employees tweak or twist their daily job routines to give themselves a little leeway at work.

Yvon likes working night shifts because he doesn't have any superiors breathing down his back. He resents the way the forewoman pressures the day-shift crews, whereas at night, *"We can relax: there's no boss around. We can chill out together seeing as we're amongst ourselves. Since we don't see anybody during the day, we're sleeping. The night shift's laid back. Sometimes the day shifts who relieve us already have their overalls on. That must be stressful all day, what with the bosses at their backs barking at them to get a move-on."* Apparently, the night time is the right time, at work as at play, for social norms and inhibitions to ease up, breeding a sense of complicity and security. Véga has already presented similar findings in her study of the nursing profession (2000). The night offers protection, partially eclipsing the "pecking order," shielding the complicity of the team and, in the amicable give-and-take that ensues, affording each member a bit of autonomy. Yvon pays a high price for this small difference, this marginal latitude, but he feels it is essential in order to protect himself from his *"Gestapo-brand"* boss.

Celine has taken a more comfortable strategy. After having spent a long time searching for the position that suited her best, she found her niche at the intersection of several different hospital units, where she does not entirely belong to any of them. She explains her "marginal secant" position in terms that sound straight out of a sociology textbook: *"My job is also an opportunity for me to be creative. It's also a creative space. I've always occupied whatever space of autonomy I was given, and now that space is immense. I can do a great deal. I can do as I please, while realizing of course that there are boundaries not to be overstepped. I have supervisors and coworkers. Those are the tacit rules and we know them well."*

Sometimes autonomy is forged by the nature of the work itself. Let's return to Nicolas, the young tree trimmer who made such a precise calculation of the "exploitation rate" to which he was subjected. He likes working in the trees because, up there, he doesn't have a boss nagging him or giving orders. *"I like climbing trees. It's a kid thing to be way up there, the adrenalin and all that. I definitely enjoy it. I don't like jobs where you sit around getting bored to death, and it's really a profession where you learn a lot about trees—compared to forestry, where they teach you to manage trees so they can become lumber, to turn them into money, it's mainly for production. Whereas pruning is really for the person, it's ornamental, it's really for making a pretty tree. It's more creative than forestry. That's definitely something that turned me on.... Let's put it this way: When you're up in a tree, you're the boss, no two ways about it. It's an occupation with safety risks, so everybody has to listen to us; the guys on the ground don't have our experience. When it comes to pruning, we call the shots. The boss is still the boss, but he doesn't know how the pruning has to be done, so we run the show ourselves. The boss writes up the estimate, but he doesn't climb. When he shows up, he's under our orders."* This depiction of a quasi-artistic profession is all the more striking in view of Nicolas's outright condemnation (cited in the previous chapter) of his own exploitation.

Autonomy can be procured by more resolute means. Unable to bear a senior staff position in the private sector any longer, Estelle opted to teach school instead. *"Inside the company it was total madness. We were stressed out and unhappy. If they don't like somebody, they'll do everything to make him go in the end. It's sickening to watch. I've never had to put up with that kind of pressure. I was always able to draw the line and command respect. The sickening thing is seeing people knuckle under. I don't mind being told off if I've done a bad job, but if it's just because they don't like me, I give 'em hell.... So, after three years, I quit. I figured that wasn't what I wanted to be doing all my life. I took the schoolteachers' exam and passed—and thank God. I like it. What I like is that children are filled with wonder, and they're not mean. Whereas with adults, what's unbearable is that nobody ever marvels, they act like everyday life is sheer drudgery, and everyone takes it out on everyone else by being mean, by making petty remarks. Being with children is like a breath of fresh air for me, but with the other faculty it's the same old moaning and groaning: 'This year's class sucks; I've never had such lousy kids....' If this doesn't work out for me, I'll set up a business where I'll be my own boss."* In discussing her job, Estelle does not bring up money or equality; the only thing that interests her is finding a job that suits her, a job in which she won't have to put up with what she calls the "meanness" of her superiors and coworkers.

From Vocation to Self-Realization

The epitome of professional autonomy is a vocation or calling, defined as total personal involvement in one's work. A vocation was long held to be the exclusive domain of the noblest pursuits, as prayer, art, politics, or war.

According to Weber, however, the advent of Protestantism led to a sort of popularization and democratization of this vocational model. A thoroughgoing subjective commitment to one's occupation became an ethical imperative, and one was to seek signs of belonging to the elect in professional success. As a result, even the most trivial pursuits came to be shorn of their age-old stigma, and even they could satisfy the imperative of achievement. Although the religious significance of work has dwindled over the centuries, the desire for professional engagement and fulfillment is so deeply ingrained that it has survived as an ethical imperative, conferring on work a special significance that goes beyond its economic utility and its function as a means of social integration. Although work is no longer a form of prayer for inner assurance of otherworldly salvation, it is still attached to a form of worldly salvation whenever people expect it to provide personal fulfillment, the realization of their particular talents, predilections, and personality. Whilst work is no longer a curse, nor a means of salvation (if it ever was one for that many people), it is still conceived of as one of the core experiences of personal fulfillment. Professional activity is still subject to the ethical demands of a subject seeking fulfillment on autonomous terms.

Vocation

"I am delighted, delighted," Marie, the nurse, told us. *"A personal approach to caring for a patient covers everything from technical procedures to moral and overall support. It's a little embarrassing, but I feel incredibly privileged to be in contact with people who are so enriching in whatever way—it may be their disease or their pretty complicated stories. That's why I wouldn't change jobs for anything in the world. The rest depends on working conditions, but it's wonderful."* Marie's enthusiasm does not keep her from faulting the lack of manpower or the hospital management: *"We get the impression we're big nobodies."* But she derives personal gratification from answering her calling. Michel is *"overjoyed to be a doctor."* Dominique always felt a calling to become a surgeon: *"When I was a little boy, I wanted to be Dr. Barnard."* Sometimes, the vocation comes with experience. *"I felt drawn to it a little,"* says Lucie, a nurse. *"So I figured: I'll try to pass the nursing exam, might as well. Then I didn't find it half bad and, partly out of laziness, I stuck with it. In the beginning, maybe it wasn't really a calling, but now I like it. I'm delighted, no doubt about it. I love taking care of people.... Sometimes it's really tiresome, I get sick of it, I'm wiped out. I tell myself I ought to quit, go back to school, get a BA in literature, do something else, something easygoing where I could take my vacations, kick back, and enjoy life with my boyfriend and all that. But I'd rather be a nurse. It's hard work, but I love it."*

Surveys of teachers conducted several years ago showed that the model of "the vocation" was alive and well, still a powerful element in the way teachers described their work. Many said they had "always wanted" to be teachers or professors (Dubet/Martuccelli 1996). *"Take away the parents and the school administration,"* Brigitte, a schoolteacher, reflected, *"and children are extraordinary creatures, with their spontaneity, their innocence, their eagerness to learn. You can't be stingy with your time. I never have been, and I've never regretted it either, because it's definitely rewarding. It's an opportunity, a delight, and I wouldn't know how to do my job any other way. I don't count the hours, I don't count the dough."*

The same types of discourse prevail in the arts. Sebastien says he deliberately chose not to make much money in order to work in the music business, selling records. *"I'm in a professional situation that could be considered unstable. That aside, I have no complaints because I've got a fulfilling job, even though it's not going to make me a millionaire. It's a way for me to get involved in music. I have more to learn from my bosses than they have to learn from me. That pretty much sums it up."* Actors and musicians invariably take up this discourse about their vocation, self-fulfillment providing ample justification for any personal sacrifices. Elodie is an actress in a small company, performing *"for peanuts. There's plenty of municipal funding to set up a soccer team, but zilch for the little community theater, and lots of people think we're just freeloaders. They think drama's boring, doesn't interest them, it's worthless…. For me, it's mainly a way to feel I'm in the right place."*

Occupations in healthcare, education, social work, and the arts are directly descended from the concept of the vocation and its attendant sacrifices, so the aforecited sentiments should come as no surprise. After all, training for these professions is designed to make sure the aspirants are cut out for their chosen vocation, even if the original religious context is now so remote. Naturally, we can always dismiss the talk of a calling as a canonical structure of discourse employed to justify the choice of a profession ex post facto, seeing as career choices owe as much to chance and necessity as to a genuine vocation. But, even if vocation is a conventional autobiographical trope, the very fact that these professional histories are ranged under vocation goes to show the sway of autonomy in the construction of experience and self-image. We might also note that the delight these individuals take in what they do for a living is not simple-minded: They persistently inveigh against the forces, the penury, and the bureaucracies that prevent them from accomplishing what can rightly be termed their vocation.

Interaction

In a previous book we described the long process whereby the ideal of a sacred calling evolved into a quest for personal fulfillment (Dubet 2002).

The "caring professions," such as education, healthcare, social work, etc., once emblematic of sacrifice and devotion to higher principles, are now perceived as paths to personal fulfillment. They now require devotion to an inner, immanent divinity instead of an outer transcendent one. The religious model constructed by the Roman Catholic Church has shifted to a secular one, rational and republican, but the concept of vocation has not been entirely purged from the caring professions. French schoolteachers used to feel they were obeying a calling because one of their duties was to personify the Republic and its values, just as the priest personified the Church and the faith. Doctors and nurses personified the marriage of science and compassion. Social workers personified the social values of the Republic, the labor movement, and the Church. This vocational model, which is intrinsically "Catholic" in that it involves a form of transubstantiation in the human *incarnation* of higher, sacred values, has found sanctuary in institutions like School and the Hospital, which preserve Reason as the Church once protected the Faith. This model is now in turn undergoing a process of decline and disenchantment. But the disenchantment is only partial, for the essence of one's occupation now appears to be the personal gratification derived from the bonds forged with others on a basis of empathy and authenticity. We no longer expect our occupation to sanctify universal values, but to enable us to experience our uniqueness and authenticity through interaction with others.

As the model changed, becoming secularized and "routinized," it seems to have spread far beyond the professional domains traditionally associated with religious and then republican institutions. The individual now sees his work as rewarding if it offers him the opportunity to find fulfillment in his interaction with others. In *Le Nouvel esprit du capitalisme* (1999), Boltanski and Chiappello are reasoning along parallel lines in showing that the new management theories draw on an aspiration to freedom and self-fulfillment that is derived from artistic inspiration.

Jean-Luc "ditched" banking and realty to set up his own business as a painting contractor. In addition to being his own boss now, he is especially gratified by his *"excellent rapport with customers. Generally, they're either people I know or people I've been recommended to."* He approaches each job as a sort of adventure with his customers. He and his customers "co-opt" each other, whereas in banking or real estate, the client is forced upon you, as he puts it, and so becomes more of an *"enemy."* Terry, another independent contractor, sees the commercial relationship primarily as a human one: *"I'm coming to your house to re-do your bedroom. We're the best of friends. You contacted me for this, and I said great, I'll be glad to. At the outset, you're in love with your client. And your vision of their finished bedroom is that of a master painter. Only, when you're about two-thirds done, a huge amount of stress sets in. You have a love relationship at the beginning, then a stressful relationship:*

You don't hate each other, but.... At the end, we're relieved: You give me the check and we go our separate ways. It's great. That's the way it goes. In the end you part amicably."

François is a night watchman. Not only does his job leave him time to read at night and do sports during the day, but he also sees himself as a kind of social worker, *"a blend of Mother Teresa and complaint desk."* What makes his job rewarding is the interaction with others, where the playing field is level. In the realm of human interaction, we're all equals, at least we interact there as unique human beings whose academic credentials and qualifications, among other things, are wholly immaterial in the immediate context. Besides, in any occupation, our relations to others belong exclusively to ourselves because what is at stake or on stage is our selves. Georges, a bank executive, perceives his work as being, above all, *"human." "It's contact with people who really have very different horizons. They're all professionals with small firms, there's always something new. It's thrilling—we end up knowing each other well—it's rich in human contact. I couldn't work all day staring at a computer screen. It's really, really pleasant."*

As a bus driver, John has no say in choosing his routes, no control over speed limits, traffic jams, or red lights, for that matter. But: *"What I enjoy is relating to customers. People ask the driver for directions, lots of tourists, too, there's just plenty of interaction."* Human interaction even spices up jobs that presumably involve stricter supervision and greater submission. A number of cashiers told us that customer relations are essential to them because they get personally involved in each interaction. Estelle: *"It's great, it's something I enjoy. We're constantly interacting with our customers. I'm eager to start management training, my life's good."* Nurses' aides frequently claim that sharing the patients' social background means they have better relations to them than nurses and physicians do. In human interaction, at any rate, they are on a par with the medical staff because "human" skills are required, not medical acumen. A mail carrier resumes, *"I've been delivering to the same route for 25 years. I've watched the kids grow up, and that's what's interesting."*

An appreciation for human relations, or the assertion thereof, is not only the result of the trend toward a service-based culture in which we deal more with people than with things—though it would be a mistake to underestimate the extent to which technical and industrial jobs involve far more in the way of direct customer relations in our day than they used to (Goux/Maurin 1998). More to the point is probably that human relations permit a unique form of equality in that I can relate to others only on the basis of who I am; at the same time, my uniqueness is on a par with everyone else's. Because its cardinal virtue is its "authenticity," it defies hierarchy. This largely explains why the fight for recognition is particularly keen in service-sector businesses based on human interaction. When businesses strive to standardize and control human relations, interaction becomes an utterly alienating experience, to which Aurelie bore witness: She never felt like herself at work when her smile and accent were being monitored.

The Manual Trades

One of the most compelling demonstrations of labor pride and awareness was its defense of the manual trades against the "scientific organization of labor" (Touraine 1964; Touraine/Wieviorka/Dubet 1984). Workers defended the notion of their "trade" or "craft" so tenaciously because it is the backbone of what we are calling autonomy. As master of her trade, the worker also holds the ability to organize her work, to control her performance and working pace. She owns something in addition to her mere physical strength, and this ability is the basis for part of her pride, dignity, and autonomy. So the skilled worker is not, strictly speaking, a proletarian, because he owns something, as a farmer owns his land or a craftsman his tools. In selling his labor to an employer, the skilled worker is actually selling the product of his labor, not his skill or his "soul." He doesn't sell himself. Since the golden age of revolutionary unionism, when workers were akin to craftspersons, the concept of having a trade has changed profoundly. Yet, whether a person's trade is something acquired through qualifications, recognized by the organization of labor, or obtained in the face of opposition from the latter, it remains pivotal to the sense of autonomy. To hold a trade is to possess freedom of action.

"The Worker Is King of His Craft"

Our housepainter friend Terry paints a clear-cut picture of what a real craft is: *"The worker is the master of his craft. It's not quite the same as an apprentice. The boss has a job to do, too. He may have more responsibilities, he may get paid more, and he may have to pay more costs and social security charges. He's got his job as boss. He's not superior to the worker, because the worker also lives in the element of his job. The worker owns his qualification, and the boss shouldn't interfere with that too much. If I'm a good boss, my authority comes from doing my job right, being efficient and fair. The worker is king of his craft, that's a wonderful thing. Work isn't drudgery: It's a diamond in society. I think a craft should be treasured as a natural value."* At times, agents speak more eloquently than social scientists, particularly when Terry explains that a good boss looks for business and organizes jobs, but mustn't interfere with the craft itself, which belongs to the worker.

Cyril says he is *"completely fulfilled"* by his job as chef, *"even if I don't get paid enough in relation to the energy and hours I put in."* In fact, he has a hard time putting up with being treated like a regular employee. He doesn't like it at all when the boss walks into his domain, the kitchen, to watch him work. *"It's a matter of pride. Sometimes it's a little hard to have someone come in to take a look at your work when you've been handling it from A to Z. Sometimes, it's hard for me to realize I'm not the boss. It's hard for me to put up with somebody walking into the shop and inspecting me from head to toe, as though I was an apprentice."* Cyril knows he mustn't take his professional pride too far, though: *"Some chefs are idols of a personality cult, the kind that are full of themselves and horrible to their staff."* But he does see it as his duty to impose his *"conscientiousness, the devotion you can have to your work. Anyway, that's how I interpret it. In other words, I won't quit trying till I've come up with the dish I'm after."* Fabien, another cook, *"loves"* his work, the *"fantastic"* atmosphere in the kitchen, and the *"good stress." "How can you make something excellent out of very little? You have to be creative. You ask yourself: Will that work? Will they like it? My pleasure's in pleasing the customer—making good food and satisfying the customer. I'm happy when I hear the customer sent his compliments to the chef."* Indeed, some trades become passionate pursuits: *"Cellarmaster: That's the top of this profession. You're working with something that's alive, and besides it's a pleasure to the palate, it's one of life's pleasures you can share,"* says Gerard. Paul, the confectioner we have already met, explains that *"the work involves recipes that are slightly secret, that are passed around confidentially. So there's automatically a privileged side to it, you feel a bit unique."*

Painters and cooks are craftsmen, quasi artists. The consciousness of practicing a craft, however, may evolve in activities that would seem, at first glance, less "inspired." Laurent, a shopkeeper, cultivates a similar professional pride in his work because, in his eyes, asserting oneself in one's trade is a means of self-defense. *"I've always been lucky enough to work without anyone peering over my shoulder. As long as my work was well done, they couldn't find fault with me. So I never had to justify myself at work, I was always free."* This pride consists in owing nothing to others, it is the "workers' dignity" (Lamont 2002). Laurent adds: *"I don't go for make-believe, I don't like hot air. I like what's tangible. I don't like boats bound for nowhere, I like destinations. The one thing that counts in life is the sweat running down my brow to earn money, and I want to pass on that view of things."* Mastering a craft means gaining autonomy, and therefore respect; if you want to be respected, you have to make yourself respectable and prove your mettle.

Guillaume, a crane operator, describes the system of exploitation in which he is trapped. *"No unions, a breakneck pace, unpaid overtime. You only wear your hard hat the day the safety inspector comes around…. The bosses are like: 'Safety man's coming round today, put on the harnesses, the other gear, put on this, put on that.' The problem with safety is it's every day.… You go to work, it's dark out; come home, it's dark out. I'd get home just in time to say goodnight to my son, who was going to bed. In the morning when I left, he'd still be sleeping."* Despite these working conditions, Guillaume thinks a person can still assert a certain degree of autonomy and thereby preserve a vital measure of liberty and dignity. *"It's up to you to defend yourself. Those who don't sound off get passed over.… A greenhorn has to prove himself. It's not so much that there are inequalities, differences. When you start, you have to prove yourself, even if you see guys next to you who are moving up in the ranks even though they don't do jack shit at work. You gotta prove yourself, gotta sound off, gotta put up a fight."* The way to prove yourself is to refrain from *"borderline crooked"* schemes that involve "borrowing" the company truck, cement, equipment, etc. for your own home improvements or moonlighting jobs. Furthermore, you need to be professionally above reproach, for the entire construction site depends on the crane operator, who must be precise, careful, fast, and, like Guillaume, assertive, instead of *"spending his life complaining."*

If you have a trade you can have "character" (Sennett 2002). You can resist the pressure from management and peers, you can stake out your own sphere of action because you know you're indispensable, because you're irreproachable, whereas you are witness to others' shortcomings and errors. Many people we interviewed explained that they succeeded in asserting themselves, in running the show, and their bosses do not deny them any of the little liberties they require—leaving work early, taking half a day off—because everyone knows they are "irreplaceable."

But this sort of "character" should not be mistaken for a simple matter of personality, or even obduracy, for it requires a commitment to one's profession and an ability to hold one's own. In many a hospital unit, nurses make themselves so indispensable that, for all intents and purposes, they "run the ward," just as some secretaries "keep the firm running." Some teachers get such remarkable results and have such a good rapport with their students that they become "untouchable."

It is not only at the top of the professional pyramid that one can make something, create something, asserting the autonomy to which everyone is entitled. The problem is, then, one's ability to objectify and gain recognition for the results of one's work. Fifty percent of the workers we interviewed like what they do because they can identify the results of their work, because they can say: Here's what I've done.

Occupation vs. Interaction:
A Matter of Gender or Sector?

Generally speaking, our interviews revealed a certain gender divide over the expressions of autonomy advanced by respondents. Women seem to value human interaction more than the occupation itself, whereas men more clearly show their attachment to their occupations. Among the reasons for liking their work, human relations are cited by 59 percent of the women surveyed and 40 percent of the men, while the fact of "seeing the results" of their work is cited by 63.1 percent of the men versus 36.6 percent of the women. How should we interpret this discrepancy? It may be due to the fact that women are vastly overrepresented in the so-called caring professions like education, healthcare, and social work: Four out of five women work in services, compared to one out of two men. Conversely, men are far more present in the manufacturing sector and in traditional trades. So the difference appears to be less between the sexes than between the types of occupation to which each gender gravitates.

Carol Gilligan (1986) is among the feminists who interpret this disparity differently. On the one hand, she posits, women's psychological development is radically different from men's, emphasizing continuity and reconfiguration of the mother-daughter relationship rather than displacement and separation. Women are less concerned with universal principles of justice than men are, and more drawn to an ethics of solicitude, an awareness of people's needs and of people themselves. One of the consequences of their early socialization is that women are more "dependent on the environment," more sensitive to others' opinions of them. On the other hand, they have a prolonged experience of the private sphere in which they have heavier responsibilities and commitments, so they are more inclined to project these private norms onto the professional arena. They are more responsive to the needs and feelings of others than men, who are traditionally more involved in production, politics, and warfare. It is true that classical modernity, that of the Enlightenment and industrial society, long confined women to the status of minors and to the domains of the family and charity, "abandoning" to men the "weightier affairs" of industry, politics, war, science, and philosophy.

Which of these two explanations shall we pick? They're not necessarily incompatible and may even be mutually reinforcing. Arguing *ceteris paribus,* Baudelot and Gollac (2003) show that women take a more immediate interest in their work where interpersonal relations play the preeminent role, attaching more importance than men to listening to others and feeling that others are listening to them. Our own inquiry yielded similar findings.

It should come as no surprise that autonomy is based at once on prior social identity and on the type of work one does. These two explanations show that the principle of autonomy involves deep-seated identities, the subject's most profound inner convictions, those that are both materialized and threatened by a person's career, through the tension between fulfillment and alienation.

Alienation

Alienation is one of those concepts we can't manage to do without, despite—or perhaps because of—their ambiguities. A concept of variable geometry, alienation may mean the very fact of selling one's labor power, but that would be more aptly termed an unfair exchange or exploitation. It can also signify the agents' submission to categories of the dominant ideology. But here we come up against the difficulties of defining ideology and the risk of ascribing alienation to everything and everyone, save those who proclaim themselves nonalienated by denouncing the alienation of others—which may, in fact, be interpreted as a subtle form of alienation, blindness, and vanity. The agents could also be said to be alienated in terms of objective truth, reason, or the meaning of history. But the argument can easily be turned around, for isn't a naïve faith in one or another of these verities yet another form of alienation (Israël 1972)?

And yet, if the notion of alienation keeps coming back in through the window every time theoretical rigor prompts us to usher it out the door, this is because we need a concept to describe a phenomenon of social experience that can be reduced neither to submission to the prevailing order or authority (against which agents pit their equality), nor to economic exploitation. That experience is the destruction of autonomy, an inability to develop as an agent in one's social experience; it is the feeling of being trapped inside social categories and frameworks that preclude the experience of one's autonomy (Seeman 1967). Alienation consists in having your identity and action wholly determined by others, to a point where you see yourself solely in terms of the action and the opinion of those who dominate you. What generally ensues is a feeling of impotence, a total loss of autonomy, and a conscience writhing in the conviction that you are responsible for your own unhappiness. Thus, women who are treated only as women at work, and not as workers, may feel unable to break out of the categories causing their alienation, just as students who are flunking out of school find themselves unable to shed the "dropout" label and end up blaming themselves for their own failure.

When workers regard their work in terms of autonomy, they develop a specific critique, distinct from those based on merit and exploitation or on their fundamental equality. Salary and social inequalities are irrelevant; instead, individuals resent the domination inherent in the work itself, that which bars them from becoming subjects in their work; worse yet, that which destroys them as autonomous subjects. At this juncture, two main critical strands intertwine. The first concerns the control over work itself, the destruction of all personal initiative. The second expresses the destructive effects of work, particularly fatigue and stress, that threaten the subject's integrity. In other words, discourse about autonomy and self-realization at work cannot be dismissed as mere sentimental fantasies when the work is essentially uncreative *labor,* for these same fantasies generate critiques that are every bit as radical as those stemming from equality and merit.

Of Control and Constraints

Contrary to popular belief, assembly line work has not yet faded away in France; in fact, it went from 8 percent of jobs in 1984 to 10 percent in 1998. During that same period, hourly work quotas shot up from 7 percent to 23 percent. Outside rush orders went from 28 percent to 54 percent, and penalizable errors increased from 46 percent in 1991 to 60 percent in 1998. Just-in-time pacing and planning has steadily spread in the manufacturing industries—and now in the service sector, too (Durand 2004). Though we seem to be progressively moving out of the industrial society, away from its representations and structures, work is still as tightly controlled as ever.

Indeed, many of the interviewees already quoted in this study forcefully condemn the tight control exercised over workers, eroding their autonomy. Joëlle describes her work on the assembly line thus: *"I take a tube, screw three nuts onto the plastic parts, and stick it into a machine that welds it together. While that piece is welding, I start another one. What's more, it's everyone for herself, it's a team working but it's not teamwork. Nobody helps anybody else. I don't like the kind of work I do. I know that in the working world you have to go so fast, you end up missing out on a lot of things."* Agnes works the packaging line: *"The thing is, it's so boring. Even if they change your workstation, you're still doing the same thing. It's been eight years now, and I'm beginning to get seriously tired of it."*

Sometimes office work resembles factory work. *"First I do the capture on the sorter reader, then I enter the checks on the computer, till I get all the checks for the accounting day right. Unfortunately, I would've liked to be doing tasks that give me some professional satisfaction. It's routine. There's no meaningful result that makes you happy to have put in a day, to have accomplished something. A teacher, for instance, when he's got a pupil, in the end there's a result, there's something. So that might be fulfilling, he's happy to see this kid who wasn't doing much at school getting better grades and all. Me and my workmates, we enter the checks, and after that, it's none of our business. When I shut that door, I'm elsewhere, waiting for retirement."* This job is so *"idiotic,"* adds Elisabeth, a financial services clerk at the French Banque Postale, that it wouldn't even justify a raise. *"If they wanted to give us a raise, I'd say no, this job I'm doing doesn't deserve pay. What I mean is that if I were to ask for a raise, I ought to have an argument and show I've earned it, but I have nothing to show. When I delivered the mail, at least I was someone: I got some respect, I was the mailwoman. People were happy to see me; they treated me to little things like a piece of candy or a cup of coffee, and I felt like I was doing something useful, too."*

Not only is the work monotonous, it is high pressure and fast paced. *"'What was that, which city?'"* Thierry works at a call center. *"You enter the name of the city. 'Your name?' You type it in. 'Spell your name.' You type it in. If you've got it, there you go: The machine spits it out. What bothers you isn't so much the customers, it's the pressure you're under."* Boris is another call center operator. *"When you leave work, you're completely drained. Between each call you get a 7-second break. But when traffic peaks and you've got 30 calls waiting, you're really in for a bruising. You get it from the customers complaining about poor service, and you also get it from the supervisor. He's the one who gives you permission to take a break, plus you have to beg him for it. It's really the working world, because you can't do what you want."*

Setting the pace and intensity of work is not the only way for management to control work and workers. Employees want to be *involved* in their work, to make it "intelligent" and important in their own eyes. But not only does management control them, it opposes their developing a personal interest in the job, as though the employer were simply purchasing labor power devoid of intelligence and initiative. *"We're just numbers,"* says Fabrice, a hotel maintenance man. *"They've already told us they could replace us just like that.... They don't necessarily ask us to be totally committed, they simply ask us to do our job, and that's all. But you know, I don't want to work like a machine, with my eyes closed. I've got to get into it, get involved, and that means when the alarm clock goes off in the morning, I've got to get up thinking that that's one reason to go to work, to learn something. I've got a brain, and my brain needs exercise. I'm no genius as it is, so I wouldn't want to sink any lower."*

Some ostensibly more autonomous activities are closely supervised. Karine, a hairdresser, has an artistic, creative vision of her profession, but has to subordinate her talent to her boss's demands and give up her autonomy. *"My employer kind of keeps an eye on me. I mean, I couldn't do something I like if she didn't like it. I'm satisfied with my work in that I'm not treated like a dog, though it is true that it's frustrating in my line of work. I can't give expression to all the things I feel like doing. There's always this opposition from the boss. Even if the obstacles to my creativity are indirect, there are definitely limits. For example, I can't try this tint on a customer's hair if my employer doesn't like it. The whole time, it's like there are two eyes on you, watching what you're doing.... There's the employer and then there's the employee. You are treated like a human being, compared to the assembly line where you haven't got any rights. Here, at least, you're somebody. But you've got to bring in profits, whether you do a good job of it or not. You've got to put in the hours, can't ever say a thing, got to toe the line, and you have no right to be heard there, you've got no opinion, no say."* Although she's not working on an assembly line, Karine is nonetheless engaged in a silent struggle to appropriate a modicum of autonomy at work, to defend her *métier.* In any case, individual resistance at the workplace is not resistance to work per se, the manifestation of a latent urge to curb exploitation. On the contrary, it is subjective involvement as a defense against such stringent management control that employees feel they will never be able to identify with their work and make it their own. From their point of view, it is their very personality that is at stake. As Boris puts it, *"I don't want to join the herd."*

Even the most ostensibly independent workers like Michel, a physician in private practice, feel the screws tightening on them and strive to defend their profession. *"A doctor doesn't have a boss, he has hundreds of bosses because in a certain way the patient is the doctor's boss. Whenever a patient calls, I have to respond; my freedom of movement is at the mercy of emergencies. I have another constraint imposed on me by society and the healthcare system: I'm tied to the national health insurance organization. I'm accountable to them, and my fees are not up to me. If I want to keep seeing patients, I have to enter this organization."*

Claude is also a general practitioner. *"I find in my profession everything I wanted to find in it: communication, passion for the work, self-fulfillment, because your patients trust you so much. I earn more than you may have heard tell."* But the profession is "spoiled" by the commercial relationship with some "customers": *"They think they've got everything coming to them, you try to control yourself so as not to throw them out."* For that reason, Claude is in favor of state control of healthcare and wants to become a *"civil servant."* The erosion of autonomy, then, is not due solely to bureaucracy, the more or less rational organization of work, or the employers' will to control. It can also stem from the mere play of interests that an individual cannot break away from; and it turns out that submitting to customers is hardly more "fulfilling" than submitting to one's boss.

Terry, a skilled painter, who, as we have seen, cherishes his customer relations, thinks the magic triangle formed by employer, worker, and customer is *"eaten into by what I call the economic termites, because you're always thinking about the economy, you don't think about the nature of the work you're doing. And the only little shops left on the streets are the banks. Customers don't want to pay what the goods are worth, so product quality goes down the tubes: The fruits don't have any flavor anymore. The boss wants to make too much dough and buys himself a BMW and swimming pools, the worker's forced to do slipshod work, the customer always wants to cut corners. You can't do this job without cutting corners."*

Stress and Fatigue

Since autonomy thoroughly engages the subject himself, unjust working conditions strike to the core of subjectivity, the worker's body itself, producing fatigue and stress—the physical symptoms of alienation, as it were. The incidence of on-the-job accidents and health-related absenteeism in France is ever on the rise (Askenazy 2004). In all likelihood, this increase is due to the accelerated work pace, the quality requirements, and the pressure to perform (Aubert/de Gauléjac 1991). But it may also be owing to a change in workers themselves who, desirous of self-fulfillment, are less and less willing to bear the burden of a job they find disappointing. Consequently, the tendency to complain of fatigue and stress appears to be more legitimate than in the days when suffering at work may have seemed part of the order of things. The more a person sees himself as a subject entitled to seek fulfillment in her work, the more repugnant she finds working conditions that obstruct that fulfillment, and the more exhausted and agonized she will be by mindless and over-controlled work.

Should we really draw a distinction between stress, a managerial malady, and fatigue, a workingman's affliction? Nothing is less certain, even if some do not call their sufferings by the same name as others (Loriol 2004). Among the respondents to our questionnaire, 72.2 percent said they were fatigued and 45.7 percent stressed by their work. These percentages do not vary significantly as a function of occupation, although more blue-collar (79.8 percent) than white-collar workers complain of fatigue, and women (50.7 percent) speak of work-related stress more than men do. And how does one tell stress apart from fatigue, tension from exhaustion?

In the words of Sophie, a head waitress: *"I'm worn out, I'm tense, on edge. There are times when I need a breather and they don't realize it, they don't care if you're tired. Comes a time you just can't go on, you could cry, you could be awful to everyone, you look like a walking corpse.... One of these days there's gonna be a wave of walkouts. I think some day that'll happen to them, the way they treat people. The customers are monsters. You take a customer who gives a waitress a pat on the ass, he's still welcome as a customer, but if I owned the restaurant, he wouldn't get past the door. I tell them a waiter is not a servant. I'm not your dog."* Sophie has backaches, which the doctor ascribes to fatigue. Her psychologist says her sleep disorders are due to stress. Either way, Sophie is *"fed up."*

Autonomy rests on the principle of the subject's involvement in his work. Not surprisingly, the responses to our questionnaires recurrently and emphatically showed that the feeling of being scorned and unfulfilled at work ends up making people sick. Controlling for profession, gender, and age, feeling scorned at work multiplies by 2.5 the probability of health problems warranting sick leave for two weeks or more. In other words, the denial of autonomy and dignity is more damaging to one's health than the physical working conditions.

* * *

Despite its profoundly subjective nature, for the individual alone is the only judge of his autonomy, the principle of autonomy forms the basis of a specific critique of the work experience. Whatever gives a person a sense of self-fulfillment at work is just, whatever prevents him from feeling that way, and whatever might eventually destroy him, is unjust. This principle cannot be confused with equality, which would be readily amenable to a military order, for example, or with merit, which demands no subjective satisfaction from work. Autonomy is, therefore, a distinct principle of justice—and one that is all the more active in the construction and critique of social experience insofar as almost everyone seems to apply this principle, to the extent that they expect to be *subjects* in relation to their work. Work may be regarded as an encounter between an a priori autonomous individual and a situation made up of constraints, rules, and controls. That is why judgments concerning work are almost systematically ambivalent, why the discourse of self-fulfillment and that of alienation mingle and reinforce each other. What builds a person up at work is also what can break her down.

The force and constancy of the principle of autonomy may well stem less from the changing nature of work than from the transformations within workers themselves (Lallement 2001). Our modern age, that of the triumph of equality and rationalization, is also ruled by ethical individualism, by the call for a free and sovereign subject capable of taking charge of his own life and of actually feeling fulfilled (Taylor 1998; Touraine 1992). Thus, many seemingly tolerable situations at work are no longer bearable, on the grounds that everyone has the right to be a *subject* in respect of her own work. In the same way that democratization is, in a certain sense, the mass spread of aristocratic pretensions, individualism is a democratization of *kalo,* the right to self-fulfillment and autonomy in one's work. And although new management methods do tap into individual creativity and autonomy, these principles are not reducible to modes of domination. Individuals are hostile to these "free-market" management methods anyway—in the very name of their autonomy.

Note

1.   In a previous survey, we estimated that about 20 percent of those who stopped claiming minimum unemployment benefits lost money by accepting employment (Dubet/ Vérétout 2001).

CHAPTER 4

Law, Power, and Recognition

NOT ALL FEELINGS of injustice stem directly from equality, merit, or autonomy. Some workers feel deeply wronged when their employers or workmates do not abide by the rules of labor law. The abuse of power, harassment, and threats are considered serious injustices. Many, moreover, have a sense of being wronged in a more personal way when they feel "invisible," ignored, mistreated, humiliated, or when they suffer from a lack of recognition. And yet, should we consider that the principles of justice that are negated by infringements of the law, the abuse of power, and the denial of recognition are of the same nature and consequence as the principles covered in the preceding chapters?

We don't think so, despite their prevalence and prominence in the criticisms expressed by our respondents. They are not fundamental principles of justice, or principles of the first order, because they are constituted as intermediary areas of criticism, as combinations of elementary principles. Indeed, if we accept the idea that equality, merit, and autonomy are fundamental and, in large measure, mutually conflicting principles, each of which, pushed to its logical conclusion, negates the others, intermediate areas of justice must form in between them, areas that are more ambiguous and often closer to the agents' immediate experience. It is only natural that agents should combine and associate the "pure" and mutually conflicting principles in these intermediate areas.

To wit, the sphere of law and rules stabilizes and organizes the tension between the fact that we are equals and the fact that work categorizes and ranks us according to our merits. For are not labor laws and agreements ways of combining the fundamental equality of individuals with the relations of subordination that are generated by every attempt to organize workplace operations and that define each worker's merit according to his skills (Supiot 1994)? As to power, it is the medium of all organization designed to combine a form of general rationality with individual autonomy. Power operates—unequally, to be sure—between the collective constraints objectifying merit and positions, and the autonomy of each worker (Friedberg 1993). And the realm of recognition lies in the field of tension between autonomy and equality: We want to be recognized, both because we are all free and because we are all equal, because we are different and yet similar.

Thus, law, power, and recognition form normative principles, or vectors of criticism, structured by more fundamental principles, which they combine and seek to harmonize. In the intricate "wiring" of assessments of justice, they function at once as rectifiers that convert alternating into direct current and as fuses that short-circuit when the tension mounts too high. But this logic of composition and mediation by no means detracts from the acute feelings of injustice triggered by the infringement of laws, the abuse of power, and the denial of recognition. On the contrary, these feelings may be even more immediately discernible, and more to be expected, than the fundamental underlying principles of justice.

Defending One's Rights

When contracts of employment, whether they are known to employees or more or less tacit, are not respected or deliberately flouted, employees experience a profound sense of injustice. This sense is widely shared, for 45.3 percent of those we surveyed said the companies they work for did not always abide by labor laws. In many cases, the employees' resultant sense of injustice is aggravated by the impression that their trust has been betrayed. Bitterness mixes with anger because this breach or betrayal is an outright challenge to the fundamental equality and respect owed to workers, who get the impression they are being manipulated or reduced to the state of an object. Perceived exploitation may be the predominant grievance in complaints about unpaid overtime, illegal working hours, disregard for safety regulations, unlawfully prolonged job insecurity, and the like.

Law or Rules of the Game

Not only is the denial of legal rights an injustice, but the observance of labor law will not suffice to satisfy workers' sense of justice, for the manner in which one employer or another uses or abuses the law may exacerbate the workers' impression of being victims of an even greater injustice. Employees have the impression they are being manipulated by those who make deft use of the labor code to their own advantage. Hence, application of the law does not necessarily satisfy the individuals' "axiological rationality," or moral expectations. The question of rights and rightfulness underlies feelings of injustice that cannot be allayed by the mere application of rules. Unless we hold that the law is the expression of a unique and transcendent value, and that legal rules derive directly from a basic law (Legendre 1999), procedural justice is not, in and of itself, a central principle of justice. Despite the traditional state domination of the system of professional relations in France, which hardly favors contractual and collective agreements, it seems that labor regulations are increasingly instrumentalized and adapted to the "needs" of the company (Lallement 1997). Supiot (2005) arrives at this conclusion much to his regret, observing that "negotiated" or local law is expanding its reign at the expense of a more basic law capable of anthropologically grounding the identity, equality, and responsibility of subjects.

It is the very nature of labor law to be a law of compromises and negotiation (Saglio 2001). The labor code is the product of the power relations between management and labor. It is a set of rules that makes the game possible, rather than the direct transcription of a system of principles. Furthermore, the agents' conflicts and interests can transform the law, progressively adapting and fine-tuning it to meet the most punctilious of demands by means of collective agreements that are directly negotiated and therefore directly malleable. In this sense, the right rules permit the players to play and, if need be, alter the game. One might even say these laws and agreements are the traces of a social conflict that is momentarily frozen by more or less stable compromises (Schelling 1960). In terms of the principles of justice, rules and agreements are intended to reduce the tension between equality and merit, between the equality of citizens and the inegalitarian, hierarchical exigencies of production. Like the definition of fair pay, they are an effect of arrangements or "Rawlsian" compromise between equality and the market (Rainwater 1974). This law is a collective agreement, as the concept is defined by certain economists, who show that no pure market can create the moral obligation, trust, and solidity needed to stabilize and predict the conduct required for the market itself to function. The collective agreements lay down general rules based on the equality of citizen workers, with specific provisions concerning working hours, occupational hazards, duties, professional codes of conduct, etc. In France, everyone is supposed to work 35 hours a week, remunerated according to a set pay scale—except in cases where any of the thousands of special exceptions may apply. These special provisions are so vast and complex that strict application thereof is known as "work-to-rule."

Ever since the 1930s, the collective agreements in the various branches of French industry have established a system of equivalences and correspondences between scholastic and professional hierarchies (Desrosières 1997). On this head, despite the widespread admission of the inequity of scholastic inequalities, France seems to persist in taking an "adequationist" rather than "constructivist" approach, allotting jobs on the basis of academic qualifications. It is true that the dominion of qualifications over the employment market seems to have been reinforced by the burgeoning of skilled jobs on the one hand and academic qualifications on the other. In 1954, four out of five gainfully employed people in France had no high school diploma; whereas from 1994 to 2002, 1,300,000 skilled jobs were created as against 400,000 unskilled jobs (Marchand/Thélot 1998; Méda/Vernant 2004).

It goes without saying that these collective agreements pose problems of justice. For example, Harry, a young plumber, concedes that qualifications give rise to just inequalities: *"People who've got heaps of diplomas, who get company jobs for the same pay as a regular worker who doesn't have any diplomas, now I find that unfair. You do all you can to get diplomas, to get good pay later on, and it turns out all that gets you nowhere."* On the other hand, he adds, qualifications are unfair in respect of real working conditions: *"To be a surgeon you gotta take a bunch of tests. But when you work in construction, you work out in the cold, it's pretty physical, it's rough conditions. Now you take a surgeon or a doctor working in heated rooms all the time, I don't see why he should get higher pay than me."* Depending on the chosen criterion, merit at school or merit at work, the collective agreements can look fair or unfair.

Trust Betrayed

Every relation at work, like every social relationship, is based on what Durkheim called a "tacit contract" more fundamental than any legal contracts: a set of shared unwritten expectations that allow trust to be established between agents, since the law cannot cover all possible situations and relations—unless one attempts to "live by the book," constantly consulting the labor code. Hence, one needn't be especially litigious to feel wronged when the trust presupposed by this type of contract is betrayed.

Other things being equal, flouting the rules is, along with a lack of recognition, the factor most heavily associated with the total index of injustice that we have formulated. It is, moreover, a feeling far more common among blue-collar workers (62.8 percent) and in the working class in general (49.2 percent) than in other social categories. This distribution suggests a close link between the flouting of rules and the sense of being exploited. Bruno, for instance, a supermarket employee, has to put up with working conditions that fly in the face of labor law regulations—or lose his job. *"Sometimes I finish work Friday evening at 7, then start again Saturday at 5 in the morning. That's not legal because there has to be an 11-hour interval. The floorwalkers get fringe benefits, though that's prohibited. If you join the union, you're gonna get fired, because with the union you come under labor law, and that's not good for management. They don't take to that when it comes to working hours, overtime. Nobody wants to take risks, everybody wants their little job."* When workers describe the ways in which they are exploited, they mention compulsory unpaid overtime (of which 23.9 percent of those interviewed complained), disregard for mandatory breaks, imposed vacation dates, infringements of safety regulations, etc.

It is all the easier to break the rules, explains Jacques-Henri, a computer scientist, seeing as *"it's astounding how many people work in a company and don't know what they're entitled to, because they don't know the union agreements, they think their superiors have all the rights."* Serge, a unionized building superintendent, explains that his role consists in ensuring compliance with the legal texts of which workers are ignorant—*"though we're not in the Middle Ages anymore!"*

In other cases, breaking the rules directly infringes on the equality of individuals. François, a night watchman, recounts: *"My wife got laid off because she was pregnant. Soon as he found out, her boss fired her.... I also saw a woman on the staff get sexually harassed by the boss and fired because she turned down his advances. She gave notice after the umpteenth advance, he sent her a dismissal letter, their letters crossed, and she never set foot in the company again."* It also happens that pledges and promises are not kept, thus undermining the equality between the parties. *"When I was hired,"* says a telecom employee, *"we were promised regular promotions. After three or four years nothing came."* In other cases, the actual job doesn't match the job description, a job-market variant of bait-and-switch. According to Luc, a salesman: *"You're going to do a job that's different from the one you were recruited for, whether you like it or not. Take me, for instance: I'm a salesman, and to this day I spend seven out of nine hours a day doing things that have nothing to do with the job I was hired for. I find that wrong.... It's exploitation really, I perform a job I'm not paid for."* All that is often experienced as betrayal, deception, as a trap from which employees cannot extricate themselves without taking formidable risks, specifically that of losing their job.

Arbitrary Application of the Rules

The nefarious ways in which legal rules and regulations are misused, twisted, and instrumentalized by those who organize workplace operations are no less shocking to workers than the ways in which they are directly contravened. In other words, rules are not just rules, they are also versatile implements of action in an ongoing power struggle. The law then serves to formalize fundamental inequalities between those who enjoy its full protection, and those accorded little, if any, protection. There is, moreover, a yawning abyss between the rules of law and the practices that remain subject to the sway of organizations and employers: Being right is not enough to be treated right. Furthermore, workers' ability to avail themselves of the law is unevenly distributed, depending on the extent to which the workforce is unionized and informed, and on the state of the job market. We might even, at the risk of exaggeration, compare labor law to a penal law that prohibits stealing while nonetheless tolerating it according to the circumstances, victims, and perpetrators of the crime.

Even when the letter of the law is scrupulously observed, workers may have a sense their employers and superiors are not respecting its spirit. Jerome, who works at a supermarket, describes one breach of the tacit contract: *"This guy who's supposed to leave Saturday on vacation, they told him he couldn't take his vacation. He'd booked to go skiing with his kids. When he heard the news, he said I've got no choice. They told him: You know what you can do with your vacation! He was sick that morning, wouldn't you know it, his head was spinning."* Salaried employees like Jerome without job security feel particularly vulnerable and unprotected; what is the use of labor law if your employers can break the contract and impose their own terms? Temporary employees often have the impression they work longer hours than the others and do the most menial tasks, because they are like "Kleenexes" that are thrown away after use, while it remains complicated and costly to dismiss an employee with a solid contract. From this point of view, the least stable believe they have no rights, while others seem to have all the rights.

And then, many workers say, the law is one thing in theory, quite another in practice. Resuming the story of his wife who was fired because she was pregnant, François says she sued in the labor court and won: Her employer was ordered to take her on again. But *"you wouldn't have believed the atmosphere there."* She was *"sidelined,"* nobody talked to her, she got depressed, and finally decided to quit, thereby forgoing severance pay. Ultimately, she lost out, for even though the law upheld her rights, she paid dearly for her victory.

Nicole, a secretary, had a similar experience. Wrongly accused of theft a few years ago, she was dismissed. The labor court cleared her and ordered her boss to reinstate her. Her working life has been hell ever since. She is assigned impossible tasks with a view to tripping her up, her peers are under pressure not to talk to her, she communicates with her superior via memos. But she hasn't given in yet.

Tarik, a real estate agent, has. After he had an accident while climbing onto a rooftop, his employer got rid of him by systematically assigning him to inspect the roofs of their buildings. In all these cases, the feeling of injustice arises when individuals come up against an overwhelming power that twists the rules to its own advantage. They are manipulated and treated as second-class citizens.

Of course, admit the employees we interviewed, labor law does protect us, but employers know the law and how to use it far better than we do.[1] After all, isn't it said that a good manager is one who knows how to shed labor at no expense? That's what Thierry, an assembly-line worker, thinks. He told us how his company used the pretext of a union representative's back trouble to dismiss him without compensation. His workmates went on strike in protest, but the company's case was well put together and it won in court. What Thierry finds all the more galling is that the man's backaches were work related.

What's worse, some employees opine, is the fact that in big companies the unions are recognized and fairly powerful, so unionists are accorded special protection. First of all, management will not risk any clashes or lawsuits with union representatives, so they are hardly ever threatened. The few organized hospital staff we met, for example, readily admit that they are "untouchable." And we may remember that one of them, Michel, bitterly disparaged all his staffmates who "hid" behind their rights.

One temporary employee in a highly unionized enterprise reviles the "union clan" thus: *"The unionized people, I mean the union representatives, form a little cocoon with their mates, which makes for lots of inequalities with regard to others. 'Us, we're the union reps, not you.' If you don't join the union, you're wrong. You get plenty of lip, and you get treated differently by the bosses and the other employees. So I'd say the unions are a source of inequality."* While Roger thinks he wasn't promoted because he's a union representative, Gilles admits that *"being a union representative, I'm not treated like the others. I obtain in one week what it takes others several years to get."* All things considered, workers find labor law extremely malleable; it does more to buttress established power relations than to combat them. Where the unions are weak, their members are at risk; where strong, their members are protected.

From Injustice to Formal Complaint

Every year, tens of thousands of cases are settled by the *prud'hommes,* the French labor courts.[2] This institution is particularly interesting for our purposes because the judges are representatives of both sides of industry. To the extent that they embody opposed interests, they neutralize this intrinsic opposition by rigorously applying the letter of the law—and often refraining from ruling on the deeper issues at stake (Cam 1981; Delamotte 1983; Hunout 1987). Their judgments do not really touch on intentions or context, and although they may quell a dispute, they will seldom fully satisfy the plaintiffs' desire for justice.

The labor disputes brought before the *prud'hommes* are often not about breach of employment contract *sensu stricto,* but about moral issues that come up in workplace relations. In other words, it seems that the complainants do not sue because labor laws have been infringed, but because there is a moral issue in dispute: a sense of betrayal, manipulation, contempt, deception, etc. Behind an effective claim for damages that may be awarded by the court lies a latent demand for justice, for reparation of a wrong. A moral breach is settled in legal terms in order to show that a relation of trust has been abused. Complaints are lodged, not because the law has been violated, but because relations in the workplace have deteriorated.

One supermarket employee said he accepted illegal working conditions in exchange for a promise of promotion. When he realized the promise would not be kept, he filed a complaint. *"I was willing to go along with it as long as there was some trust between us, but since there were no rewards behind it, no job improvements, no give-and-take, I put in a complaint."* One sales manager explained: *"They wouldn't give me what I needed to do the job, so I got fed up. It was a whole heap of things: I was baited, I was harassed. I went ballistic, so now I'm getting even."* These two accounts, like so many others collected by Elodie Rotenberg (2005), show that complaints serve to referee a prolonged dispute far more than to reprove noncompliance with the labor code. Often enough, claimants explain they had willingly accepted illegal working conditions for a long time until they realized they were being hoodwinked. Then, as in couples that are breaking up, one of the parties calls on the court to give legal form to a conflict that, at base, hinges less on compliance with a contract than on the deterioration of relations and trust. The cases are put together like indictments recounting the entire story of a breach of trust. The mismatch between the court ruling and the nature of the complaint is such that at least one party will be convinced justice has not been served, since the court ruling does not address the real issue of the dispute.

In certain cases, each party simply wants to get even with the other, and the court finds for the more adept, not to say cynical, of the two. Indeed, many a verdict smacks of deceit rewarded. One employee, for example, made cunning use of a legal loophole to sue for damages: After a day's work, he would withhold the documents needed to legally declare him (he had "forgotten" them at home), which meant he'd worked illegally that day, whereupon he would quit his job and file a complaint for illegal employment. The scam worked several times: In each case, the employer was reprimanded and had to pay damages to its "employee." Another ploy, apparently far more common, involves methodically building a fraudulent case for grave negligence so as to dispose of an employee without incurring any expense (Chateauraynaud 1991). Martine told us her husband, a truck driver, had not been paid for overtime but couldn't prove it, because his employer had doctored the on-board recorders in the trucks and procured false statements from other truckers. It goes without saying that, there again, the victims feel that by confining their ruling to observance of the letter of the law, the courts are not doing justice to the victims' moral grievances. Linda, a nurse's aide, described how her boss turned an absence into a resignation in order to get rid of her. She won in court and was awarded compensation. But that does not fully remedy the wrong she suffered. *"In human terms, the depression I went into after this whole business, it's really tough. The boss can get people to self-destruct little by little, morally and physically. It still eats me up inside."*

In fact, the *prud'hommes* do not operate like courts of justice that address intentions and circumstances beyond mere adherence to the rules, but like arbitrators seeking to resolve a conflict by reaching agreement solely on the technical merits of the case. Whereas a classic court hearing has a symbolic dimension, a legal ceremony, opening and closing statements, an audience, a dramatization designed to bring out the intentions of the guilty parties and the suffering of the victims, in other words the moral dimension of the parties' conduct, labor court hearings resemble summary proceedings for parking violations. As they are elected on union tickets, the judges can reach a consensus only by scrupulously adhering to the letter of the law and refraining from passing judgment on the real issues involved and the intentions of the parties concerned (Linhart 2000). There is doubtless a need for rules, to which agents are attached; but above and beyond infractions of the rules, workers feel that what is chiefly at stake is their equality, their merit, and their dignity. It is not because a rule has been broken that a wrong has been committed: It is because a wrong has been committed in the first place that one seeks actionable evidence thereof in the form of a violation of the rules.

Power

Like labor law, power is ambivalent and ambiguous because it is at once a constraint and a resource, because, as Parsons theorized it, it is a medium. Power circulates between two poles in the organization of the workaday world: at one pole, the ability of management to impose its choices in the name of rationality and economic imperatives; at the other, each worker's ability to construct the realm of his autonomy. Clearly, the field of tension between these two poles is highly unbalanced, and workers criticize first and foremost these imbalances rather than the exercise of power as such.

Tyranny

When the imbalance becomes intolerable, workers revile the tyranny of their overreaching superiors and employers, who seek to extend their power beyond the sphere of the mere organization of work operations. To quote Blaise Pascal, "Tyranny consists in the desire of universal power beyond its scope"[3] (*Pensées*, §92).

Yvan, an assembly-line worker, borrows from the vocabulary of soldiers, crime novels, and fairy tales to describe the corporate cast of characters: *"There's the bosses, the brass, they do the raids—we call that raids. We act nice, but there's stoolies who're there to nail the temps. For example, eat potato chips and you're as good as fired. They're little rats, assholes who want to shine for an extra 15 bucks a month. And then there's the company ogre. He's very scary. He really scares the shit out of the temps, eats 'em alive. There's a mess of problems on account of him 'cause he's in the know: So you'd better not goof off, better not kick back; the heat's always on. Even the engineers feel the heat."* Alain, also a factory worker, depicts a similarly oppressive atmosphere: *"They talk to us like we're dogs, scumbags, brainless pieces of shit. Therefore, you feel you've got to shut up and do the damn dirty work."* It's no exaggeration to speak of violence: In fact, certain employees *"go apeshit and start whacking the supervisors, even if they're gonna get the boot after that."* Jerome recounts how his supermarket manager shoved an employee, and then sued him for assault: *"Everyone's keeping mum 'cause we're all scared."* The tyrant in question also happens to be a crook. Jerome is a mute witness to his regular scam, which consists in demanding reimbursement from wholesalers for allegedly inferior unsold produce, while he resells to local farmers for use as animal feed.

Remi, an engineer, describes his boss as *"a big jackass, a shithead who can blow his top and say some disgusting shit. He won't exactly mince his words, it's idiotic. I don't think it's our job to put the other guys down, but to make it clear they screwed up, they can make it up. We ought to readjust, not bawl them out."* Monique, a cleaning woman in a college dormitory, feels she is at the mercy of her sadistic superior. *"If you have a run-in with her in the morning, she'll harass you. For example, she'll say: 'I'm not giving you any gloves this week.' That's harassment, punishment, really, kindergarten-style."* Tyranny breeds on fear, explains Maryse, a cleaning woman at the university. *"Last year, the boss was a woman, and it was really tough. She was always telling me, 'If you don't do it, I can get you fired.' Basically, it was blackmail, and I was scared seeing as I needed work so bad, and since I was scared, I'd go do it. I was terribly exhausted because psychologically, physically, it's hard. Coming to work in the morning, you don't know what she'll be like. So, if she's having a good day, it'll be all right. If not, she'll always find something to pick at. And another reason I was scared was that in an atmosphere like that, you don't want to make things any worse, so I didn't dare say a word. You never know what'll come into their heads. It really is scary.... The only thing we think about's our job. What work can do to you, it's incredible. It's tiring, and sometimes the kids'll be talking to us, but you're so upset about what happened at work that sometimes you don't even listen."*

Florence, a waitress, described how her boss tyrannized the staff not so much by insulting them, but by constantly changing their hours at the last minute, making it impossible for them to plan ahead and organize their private lives. His control over the schedule gave him enormous power. *"My boss, I see him as a boss from the 1900s or 1930s,"* an accountant told us. *"I mean he likes to see his staff work late. He's not afraid to make us come in on weekends or work unpaid overtime either. The receptionists and secretaries have to wait till Friday for Monday's schedule."* His boss is crooked, Florent adds, and he forces his employees to cover up his *"scams."* *"It's just like on* Dallas*!"* Benedicte's boss is also moody, and *"takes it out on the boys. Some days, she always picks on the same guy; the next day's different. It's pretty much the luck of the draw. Sometimes she's nice; other times we're not so lucky!"*

The sheer quantity of these accounts carries conviction. Nearly 40 percent of our respondents complained of friction with their supervisors. In all likelihood, bosses who are nasty and a bit unhinged do not outnumber employees with the same character flaws. But their ability to do harm obviously far outweighs their employees'. In other words, managerial inconstancy appears to be a consequence of their autocracy and moodiness: Spitefulness does not necessarily enter into the equation. Some of our interviewees mentioned their bosses' quirks and obsessions, their propensity for changing everything overnight, even if it meant going back to the old system again the day after. In such instances of arbitrary inconstancy, as in cases of physical or verbal abuse, power becomes perverted in the sense that it is neither rational—i.e., predictable enough for others to behave rationally in return—nor respectful of others' autonomy and power. Annie, a receptionist, says her supervisor is likeable, but *"she's a walking whirlwind and that sure stirs up an awful lot of dust! She's someone who's always bustling around, stirring things up, talking up a storm, always in a rush, running all over the place, expending a huge amount of energy for results that sometimes aren't even worth it. They fall flat ... and then we move on to something else. Two months ago, 'We gotta do this, this is the solution to all our problems,' and then all of a sudden not another word about it."*

Coercion

Normally, the object of power and sound management is to obtain consent. However, it is not unusual for the veil of consent to tear, revealing one of the hidden but essential resources of power: blackmail. On this matter, our observations largely coincide with those of Courpasson (2000). Talcott Parsons's analysis of power as "currency," a resource that is shared unequally, but at any rate shared, proves too pacified to account for the the ice-cold ultimatum with which workers are all too often faced: submit or quit. Plainly, widespread unemployment in France has given more teeth to the threat.

A hairdresser describes his dealings with his boss as being perfectly correct, except *"if you start making demands.... Then you're out on the street, you're in for daily harassment. That's what happened to me."* A sort of covert war ensues, in which the employee uses the only weapons at his disposal: retreat or work-to-rule. *"I said to myself, if that's the way it's going to be, if he isn't going to give an inch, neither am I. He paid the consequences, but he made my life hell afterwards: He'd knock me in front of the others, it was indirect harassment. I was the ugly duckling, and I ended up quitting."*

Another bout, this one pitting Jocelyne against her supervisor: *"I went up to her and said, 'I wanted to tell you that I'm pregnant.' So she pulls out my file and says, 'But you already have a child." I say, 'Yes, this is my second.' I was so proud! She goes on, 'But he's only a year and a half?' I say, 'Yes, that's right.' She says, 'You people breed like rabbits!' When it was time for my maternity leave I went to see her, and she basically told me if I left I'd forfeit my rights."* When Jocelyne returned after maternity leave, she was assigned to a new position far beneath her qualifications, and then her supervisor made every effort to lure her into professional misconduct in order to get her fired.

In some cases, coercion is an integral part of management style. Louis compares the fast-food restaurant where he works to a soccer team: As long as they're winning, everything's hunky-dory, the coach is nice, the players are stars, and everybody feels good. But the pressure to perform never lets up, for the manager will be in serious trouble in the event of a losing streak. *"The manager doesn't try to be liked. It's sales he's after. If you're holding things up, he won't beat around the bush, he'll tell you to your face. He won't be gentle to you to find out what's wrong. We realize it's clear that we're pretty much just human cattle to them.*

I get along with them all right. They're polite to me, yeah, sympathetic, as long as I hold up my end!"

Bruno works in a supermarket in which far less effort is made to conceal the use of coercion as a means of staff management. Just as unemployment and exclusion form the "lower" limits of the realm of acceptable inequalities, coercion abolishes any give-and-take of power. *"The director doesn't talk. He barely says hello. I don't worry about it. I don't know how they evaluate me, I don't know what they think of me. He makes sure the manager makes sure the employees are doing their job, and in the end it's the employees who're in for it, it's always the employees' fault. They make you feel you're a nobody, like you're a total nobody, you're just a cog in the machine, and you do as you're told, you obey. You got a job, you want to keep it, so you stick with the herd.... No one wants to risk his paycheck, it's every man for himself, and that's something the management knows full well. Everyone hunkers down, and then they all turn on each other. If you can badmouth a coworker, you do it for the brownie points. If you sound off, they'll make you pay for it right away. They say, 'Look: there's ten guys out there waiting for your job. You don't like it, hit the road, Jack.' They say, 'You're unhappy, you can quit.' Or, if they really want to push you to the wall, they change your hours one day to the next. They want you to be scared of the manager. No, I don't feel like being part of that system, it's psychological harassment. They keep saying, 'If you don't like it, get lost!'"*

Sometimes it is the customer who embodies the threat of power. Laurent, a young technician, works for a subcontractor that is wholly dependent on its main customer: *"As subcontractors, we have no say. At certain times you've just got to take what they dish out. The guy will call you up sometimes, like snapping his fingers, he says: 'Get over here!' You know, the ways customers do, and if you make the mistake of talking back, you're sacked. They beckon you over like this . . . , they say 'tu' to you though you're not friends. One time the client came to the shop and told everyone to get the hell out! See, they can do that to the little guy, the low man on the totem pole. You've got to knuckle under. You don't feel good about yourself."*

Coercion destroys normal work relations, and workers come to feel the boss's "humane" style was sheer hypocrisy, just a way of lulling "suckers" into submission. Power is unmasked as a blackmailer threatening to take away your job, your career hopes, your social position. Like love affairs, stories of power relations in the workplace often start off in the enchantment of courtship and consent and end in vicious threats. As a result, many of the workers we interviewed deem it wise to mistrust the boss, even if she seems friendly—in fact, especially if she seems friendly—for she has a card up her sleeve that the ordinary employee hasn't got: the power to say take it or leave it.

Manipulation

Power appears particularly unjust when it is *perverse*: when it is used, not only tyrannically or coercively, but to manipulate individual employees or the whole staff, to fan rivalries and petty jealousies, to divide and conquer. Power can sunder a collective, or a group striving to function as a collective. This is how Monique describes one such insidious strategy: *"The boss tends to isolate us and pit us against each other. She knows she doesn't stand a chance if we're united, so she does her best to divide and conquer. We figure we have to resist because she's trying to set us at odds. You never know who she'll pick on next."* This strategy is clearly unjust when it thwarts the recognition of individual merit and when it scapegoats certain employees. Jerome, a bank executive, elucidates similar management ploys: *"Every branch has their punching ball, their scapegoat, who's a little different behaviorwise, who's maybe new to banking, so they get blacklisted. It's unfair because they do the job they were hired for properly. It's more a matter of their personality, their attitude, that puts them in the doghouse. There'll be this uneasiness; these are the people who won't get a raise. It's really hard when the management harasses them in little ways, switching around their days off, stuff like that. A few years ago, with a manager who was really tyrannical, who made pretty many people cry, bouts of depression, some people broke down."*

The opposite of the scapegoat is, of course, the boss's pet. Indeed, favoritism and, specifically, "morganatic" affairs can prove every bit as unjust as malice aforethought. Helene spoke of a coworker who *"had a relationship that was, so to speak, intimate with a person she shouldn't have. So that ruined the atmosphere in the restaurant. Sure, she has plenty of advantages for the time being, so nobody says a word to her about it, nobody dares to. Some days, she leaves when she feels like it. She wants to stay home Wednesdays[4] to take care of her daughter, so that's what she does. That's not fair at all."* It is all the more unfair, as Helene explains, since the boss's lover's privileges increase the workload for the rest of the staff, who have to cover for her whenever she cares to take time off.

Instead of creating a harmonious atmosphere of camaraderie and mutual trust, in which each staff member's merit and responsibility are recognized and appreciated, the perversion of managerial power "spoils" staff relations, practicing—and thereby breeding—petty injustices and rampant hypocrisy. It morally depraves the workers who get caught up in its game, who learn to cheat and "save their own skin" by hook or by crook, to envy and "backbite" one another in order to maintain their own power and autonomy, in order to keep from being "cut loose." In some cases, to ward off moral degeneration, working groups resort to a form of absolute egalitarianism that categorically condemns any differential treatment—a regime that inevitably does injustice to individual merit and autonomy. So prevailing opinion then swings the other way, favoring merit and autonomy and thereby fomenting new injustices, which in turn call for the blanket remedy of abolishing all differences in treatment, and so on and so forth. Thus, the critique of power and its pernicious effects can be inexhaustible.

Emmanuelle, the head of an accounting firm, was sharply criticized by her staff for giving a special schedule to one employee, who had just adopted a child. Juliette recounts the antagonism she endured at the hands of fellow nurses for a love affair she had with a coworker on the medical staff. The pressure was so hard to bear that, in the face of the group's internal egalitarianism and its reverence for rank, the couple eventually had to break up. *"I had a relationship with one of the doctors, who wasn't much older than me. Word got round the ward a little, caused a lot of friction and jealousy among the nurses, who said I got promoted on the casting couch, when it wasn't that at all. Our relationship was outside the hospital, but that hurt me pretty badly. A lot of people turned away from me. People thought I was trying to get a higher position. We ended it because I was sick and tired of the rumors and the gossip, and so was he."*

For Caroline, manipulation and hypocrisy are in the very nature of power, which is about instrumentalizing individuals and relationships. Having attained the rank of high school principal, she could no longer bear the petty jealousies and tensions in the corridors of power, so she resigned: *"I dislike hypocrisy at work, and I realized that people in head positions are always trying to shoot each other down to make their own school look like the school where everything's great. They'll do anything to get new programs, and I don't like that. I realized that I'm not someone who enjoys having power, I don't like wasting energy on futile things. Example: If you change a teacher's room, she's bound to come complaining."* Caroline thus reminds us that power is a two-way relation. So it is that tyrants are often tyrannized, the coercive coerced, and the perverse perverted. As the only way to oppose power is to attain power, its attendant vices can infect its opponents.

The Power Vacuum

Despite all the reproaches heaped upon it, power is never criticized as such, for it is a necessity. In fact, weak, incompetent leadership, which ultimately puts the whole enterprise in jeopardy, is perceived as being especially unjust, as are the higher powers that fail to rein in petty tyrants. An execrable atmosphere prevails in the library where Henriette works because the head librarian *"can't hack it." "It's the department head's personality. Lots of stuff gets said behind people's backs. People get sidelined, no insults, but some loud spats. But the head librarian is afraid, he lets things get out of hand. There are no meetings, no communication between people, hence the bad vibe."* One schoolteacher we interviewed complained of the cowardice of the local schools inspector, who allegedly spent his time *"ducking criticism"* rather than doing his job, which included resolving minor differences at schools and arbitrating conflicts between parents and faculty. He systematically abided by seniority and routine procedures in order to avoid friction with both his superiors and the teachers' unions. Merit was never acknowledged, but neither were mistakes, and the teachers were at a loss as to exactly how much autonomy was accorded to them. Thus, weak leadership ushers in all manner of injustice. As Sennett demonstrated clearly (1982), although people distrust authority, they also expect it to reassure and protect them. Human nature dreads a power vacuum. Mailis is a nurse in the psychiatric ward: *"I was alone on the floor one night, and I was attacked by a patient. I reported the incident to the supervisor, but in the end all he did was move me to a different ward. I was never asked what I thought, whether I wanted sick leave—nothing at all. The patient, on the other hand, got left in the ward. So you move the nurse and not the patient. And the doctor doesn't even ask the nurse, 'Can you come see the patient with me in a session to talk it over?' To say that it was me who was acting within my rights as a nurse to knock on his door to give him his medication, and that the patient has no right to attack me."* Faced with conflict and trouble, the powers that be "ducked out of it."

Another reason why a power vacuum is unjust is that it poses a threat to a company's survival. Many employees feel they can only watch helplessly as their jobs fizzle away due to managerial incompetence. Nicole, manager of a sales agency, recounts: *"The last four months, I never saw my boss. He'd leave notes on my desk, and after a while I realized he wasn't even coming to the office anymore. We even had a visit from the CEO because our sales figures were too low. We couldn't pay our bills, the deliverymen were really dragging their feet, it was a mess."* Sophie, a maître d', thinks the mismanagement of the restaurant where she works is a waste: *"It's a nice place. In fact, I think it's a wonderful place. There's a lot we could do with it, but in the end, nothing ever gets done. They've been screwing it up for years: they're disorganized, the whole place is a mess, not financially, but in terms of service it's very, very disorganized. The longer it goes on, the less people feel like coming. It's not normal for the place to be going nowhere, the atmosphere is not exactly terrific, everybody gives each other a hard time, everybody's insincere."* Christine, an ex-chargée d'affaires, tells a more amazing tale: Her boss was such a "nice guy" that he ended up "sinking" his firm by taking staff out to lunch and paying them a half-salary extra—and all that on insufficient funds.

People have a very discerning perception of the issues involved in wielding power, the complexities of being a good leader, of constantly having to reconcile conflicting principles of justice. Good governance is a precision balancing act, as Lucie puts it, describing the tactics of her head nurse: *"We have a supervisor, a head nurse who oversees what we do, who calls us to order. She's fairly strict, but on the whole, if you don't screw up, if you're punctual and all that, things go smoothly with her. But it's true she doesn't try to establish friendly relations; we don't have a strong rapport, she tries to stay in her place and keep us in ours. We're well aware she's a quote-unquote superior."* In this case, team spirit is a factor: a tightly-knit crew working together, relying on one another, trusting in the group. Good governance alone can create a fairer world. Francis, who runs a small company, strives to maximize the merit and efficiency of his employees while taking their autonomy and needs into account. He is quite sensitive to the mood in the office—that of the team as a whole and that of each employee. *"Though I'm head of the company, I'm attentive to my employees' needs, because otherwise we'll run into problems in terms of the business. I can tell from their behavior—if an employee turns aggressive though he didn't used to be."*

Indeed, employees have to be trusted because, after all, they can easily find ways to harm a company and a boss that are treating them unfairly. Philippe, a truck driver, explains how teamsters who feel exploited by a tyrannical, temperamental boss "get even," even to the point of jeopardizing the company's survival. *"Certain drivers claim an extra hour of waiting every day. They do it every single day, and at the end of the month that adds up to one helluva lot of money. Personally, I don't feel like waiting an extra hour. The faster I can get the job done, the faster I make it home. The problem is that that affects the company: They do an hour every day, that makes 25 hours a month, and seeing as every hour after 200 pays time and a half, that's going to have an effect on the company, and if it's not doing well, that's going to affect me, and so on and so forth."* In a word, just about everyone has a little power of his own to use fairly or unfairly.

Recognition

"Due recognition is not just a courtesy we owe people. It is a vital human need" (Taylor 1995). But due recognition involves more than respecting differences of gender, race, and culture. Above all, it is a matter of recognizing the individual herself as the unique embodiment of a unique life story and social and cultural identity that are ceaselessly involved in her relations to others. It is important to define what we mean by "recognition," a buzzword now widely and indiscriminately used to refer to a variety of profoundly different phenomena. To wit, people complain of a lack of recognition when they feel underpaid. Those whose occupations are not sufficiently institutionalized, or who do not have enough say in decision making, say they are not getting the recognition they deserve. Nonrecognition is also a term of choice for insufficient prestige. In other words, (non)recognition has become a catch-all for most of the feelings of injustice that people express (Fraser 2005). The word is on its way to becoming the common denominator for a broad spectrum of claims, complaints, and social struggles, including such diverse issues as cultural or ethnic identity, gender inequality, exploitation, the fight for job security, entitlements and social safeguards, participatory rights, etc.

Honneth (2004) is probably right in defining recognition in terms of the formation of subjective identity and self-image, and rejecting Nancy Fraser's reduction of the concept to a mere consequence of social inequalities. Then again, recognition cannot be said to be "the normative core of a conception of social justice" (Honneth 2004) because no one such core exists. Recognition is not a principle of justice in and of itself because agents must also ask the question, Why is the absence of recognition unjust? And their answers to that question appeal to principles of justice that are more fundamental than recognition itself.

We will stay close to Honneth's basic intuition and define recognition as the formation of a positive relation to the self as it is both constructed and reinforced by others. From Hegel to Mead, theories of recognition remind us that identity is an ever-active and ever-imperiled social construct. Recognition is not an entity, but a process, and, as such, chiefly perceived in its denial rather than in its fulfillment. "It acquires a perceptible mass only in a negative form—specifically, only when subjects visibly suffer from a lack of it" (Honneth 2004). This negative or *intaglio* aspect of recognition results from its formation at the junction of two principles of justice. On the one hand, I desire recognition because I am equal to everyone else, hence the absence of recognition derives from contempt and inequality. On the other hand, however, this equality has the potential to negate the unique autonomy to which I also lay claim. Consequently, the demand for recognition is always ambivalent and carries two risks: that my equality will undermine my status as a unique individual, and that I will be confined within my uniqueness.

This definition of recognition as the tension between equality and autonomy is clearly corroborated by statistical analysis of our respondents' answers to the questionnaire. The more their criticisms focus on inequalities, the higher their index of perceived nonrecognition. And the greater their dissatisfaction about their lack of autonomy, the greater their frustration about the lack of recognition for their work too, which latter correlation is very prominent.

Dirty Work

For those who do "dirty work," the absence of recognition is a direct consequence of the different degrees of dignity allotted to different occupations. Those who do menial jobs come to be identified with them and confined to the lowly status society assigns to those tasks. Hence, the absence of recognition ensues from the symbolic order of inequalities and is its direct subjective expression. Maïté, a high school janitor, feels despised in an "ivory tower" that only values knowledge and its transmission. *"They're teachers, it's normal, they don't see us. They leave a mess, it's normal, that's what we're here for. When you want to hound a person, it's easy to do. Then you lose it, you fall apart, you don't know what to do, who you should talk to. I had a depression for the first time in my life. Our society is wrong to toy with people like that. It's a little like Hiroshima in my head, everything goes haywire."* Society doesn't see or hear the workers who do the dirtiest, the most menial and despised of tasks (even though no one denies the utility thereof) and ignores their experience and their skills. As Catherine, a nurse, told us: *"They tell us to submit ideas, but they also tell us to stay in our place, so it's not personally fulfilling at all. It's somewhere between 'say what you like' and 'do what I say.' … Then there's the moodiness of certain doctors, a lack of consideration for people. The doctors leave us to handle the human side, the people who are going to die. Sometimes, they can't even remember the patient's name. Doctors, they're top-notch technically, but it's the nurses who are there, it's the nurses who listen, it's the nurses who hold your hand. They need to have huge psychological strength. The doctors never put themselves on the line."* The lack of recognition goes beyond a low esteem for certain occupations: The work simply goes unseen. Lucette, who looks after the elderly, told us she liked her work, *"because we really do a lot for the elderly. But people think it's really degrading, that it's just cleaning up and nothing else. My employers don't realize the efforts I make and the work that's done, which they don't appreciate for what it's really worth."*

A worker's sense of being unappreciated, ill treated, even insulted, is often painfully acute in encounters with customers. In a society that places a high premium on social interaction, these interactions are inevitably fraught with the desire for recognition. According to their responses to our questionnaire, workers commonly feel disdained by customers, which constitutes a principal source of resentment, second only to that of being scorned by their superiors. Elodie, a cashier, describes her daily treatment from the checkout line: *"We say hello and we smile all day long, but after testing the waters you stop smiling. People look you up and down with disgust, they're thinking: She's young and already working the till. They're not necessarily aware that we're students. And if you showed them a picture of us after they've checked out, none of them wouldn't even recognize us because they don't even look at us.... The customers are very nasty, they think we're nobodies, whereas we have to be friendly all the time."* Even in small stores where the atmosphere is generally more cordial than in restaurants or supermarkets, and even where sales staff have a certain intimacy with customers, the feeling of being a nonentity sometimes prevails. Natacha, for instance, a saleswoman, cried after being insulted by a customer. But no matter how many anecdotes we cite, we shall never be able to convey the effect of the myriad affronts by all the "witches," "louts," and "assholes" who populate service-sector folklore.

The Decline of Symbolic Status

Members of some professions ascribed the sense of insufficient recognition to a symbolic fall from grace in the wake of the decline of the "sanctity" of the institutions where they work. That sense is particularly prevalent amongst teachers, almost all of whom woefully resent the criticism leveled at them by society. Their grievance may be somewhat exaggerated, however, for although teachers are convinced of incurring widespread public opprobrium, surveys show that the French continue to hold teachers in very high esteem.

Virtually all the teachers we met with told us they like their profession and enjoy teaching class and working with pupils. In most cases, however, they also believe parents and people in general do not appreciate their work, have little notion of what exactly they do or the responsibilities involved, and worse still, often think teachers are lazy. As Suzanne summed it up, *"We clearly aren't appreciated by the parents, some don't appreciate the hard work that can be involved, and the consensus is that we don't do a whole lot."* She added that this lack of appreciation is all the more unfair because parents often fail to rear their children properly and responsibly. They spoil their kids and, instead of backing up the teachers, they mistake schools for daycare centers.

Above and beyond these unappreciative parents, teachers maintain that schooling and education have been generally devalued in a society that is preoccupied with money and leisure and has turned its back on diligence and culture. The disregard for the profession is, they argue, due to the dwindling prestige of schools, which are no longer "sacred" institutions embodying the core values of the French nation, French culture, and the French republic. As a result, teachers may be liable to consider themselves "the new pariahs."

Their sense of injustice is exacerbated by the conviction that parents consider teachers a privileged and protected caste that *"is always on strike or on vacation,"* said Bruno. *"What people don't realize is that our work is not limited to time spent in the classroom. When people have a weekend off, that means they have a free weekend. It's not unusual for us to grade papers over the weekend. What's more, we are not paid for the meetings we attend. When people find themselves stuck with their kids for a week, they say it's tough going. What about us! We have them all day!"* Indeed, teachers complain less about the decline of their social status and working conditions than about the symbolic decline of their professional image: Once revered as epitomizing the grandeur of education, teaching is now seen as a province of privilege, and freely compared with other, more "profane," occupations. Indeed, such comparisons with professions hardly identifiable with the "sacred" principles of culture and the French republic are regarded as proof positive of nonrecognition. The implication that teaching is a job "like any other" is an intolerable affront to the "holy" role of the scholastic institution. However, let us be reminded that the widespread lament of nonrecognition in the teaching profession is not borne out by public opinion surveys. It could be construed instead as a corollary of the institutional myth of the decline of the great republic that had cast teachers as its underpaid but revered—and somewhat otherworldly—professional guardians (Dubet 2002).

Like teachers, doctors tend to associate a dearth of recognition with a decline in the prestige of institutions and professions. They feel their symbolic status is eroding when patients treat them as mere healthcare providers and threaten to sue them if the service is not satisfactory. Similar sentiments were aired by the group of small farmers we convened for this study, who bemoaned the public denigration of their profession. Their plight combines the themes of contempt for dirty work and the decline of symbolic status. The farmers say that at best, they are stereotyped as quaint rustics, at worst, as backward "hillbillies"—and that women deem them undesirable candidates for matrimony. They are, moreover, no longer esteemed for feeding the nation "by the sweat of their brow," but vilified as producers of "junk food" and as subsidized whiners, all too ready to stage violent demonstrations when it rains too much or too little.

Personal Injury

The full impact of nonrecognition is felt in attacks on a person's dignity, self-esteem, self-confidence, or on the foundations of his autonomy. Nonrecognition becomes a direct psychological attack when its victim is subjected to on-the-job "mobbing" or harassment and her status as a subject endangered or destroyed. This form of nonrecognition is not a diffuse process of tarnishing a subject's reputation, but a consequence of workplace relations that are intended to debase and destroy the subject.

"The unique voice of the individual" is thereby denied, denigrated, and stigmatized, and the resultant suffering is unique in each actual, individual case, because it affects the innermost identity of the victim. Many respondents to our survey told us they were subjected to hostility and mockery from their superiors and peers for displaying signs of their uniqueness, for resisting the ambient conformist culture by sporting piercings and tattoos, for cultivating a "look" of their own. Most of these nonconformists stated that they attach greater importance to these personal attributes than to their jobs or their serenity: *"They didn't pick me for the way I look. I've got a ponytail and I'm over 45—so what?"* It all boils down to a question of "character." But that is precisely the problem, because in the long term, the denial of recognition gradually undermines character, particularly if it affects the subject's perceptions of his most personal possession: his body.

Daniele has a pretty voice. When she called about a job as a receptionist, she was convinced she would be hired straightaway. *"There was no problem on the phone. They needed someone urgently. When I went in, you wouldn't believe the look the guy gave me. He didn't even try to understand, he just said that I wasn't right for the job, that I wasn't dressed properly. He was at a loss for words, and when he looked me up and down, I was very uneasy. Then he said something very hurtful: 'I don't think you will blend in with our customers.' That's when I knew he wanted to employ some cute chick, a little bimbo who'd look nice behind the counter at his campsite, and of course I felt humiliated.... One isn't just a body, there's a person inside, a person with a soul. Just because I'm fat doesn't mean I'm dumber than other people. Just because I'm a cashier doesn't mean I'm dumber than other people. I'm cultured, I take an interest in books, do my best to read. I'm not saying I went to a fancy college, but I do try to develop my mind."*

The denial of recognition can be crueler, or even more perverse, when employers instrumentalize individual stigma. A case in point is that of nightclub bouncers, usually of sub-Saharan or North African descent, who are instructed to refuse admission to "blacks" and "Arabs" and are deliberately used to keep their employers from being accused of racism. Our most upsetting interview in this regard was with Amadou, a 33-year-old African security guard at a sporting goods store, who sobbed in relating his ongoing ordeal. He is under orders to keep a close watch on the "riffraff" from the housing projects, including youths from his own neighborhood, who then generally seek revenge. On the other hand, he has to put up with occasional slurs like "dirty nigger" from white customers, and his boss actually blames him for such incidents when customers complain. Amadou is thus typecast as the black ghetto tough, reduced to his "race" and then subjected to racism. The bitterest twist to the story is that he can't complain to his employer because the latter is also black and refuses to admit that blacks may be victims of racism on the basis of the color of their skin, the proof being that he is black himself—and he's the boss!

For a woman's perspective, suffice it to quote Anne, a 22-year-old waitress, who feels at once denied recognition and "used" as a woman. *"I'm from an ordinary family, neither rich nor poor. My father's a grain farmer, and my mother's a secretary in the insurance business. I grew up in the country, in a very loving, untroubled family where boys and girls were raised more or less the same.... I went to college but I didn't like it because the professors weren't motivated and I need to be dealing with people who are motivated.... In my job I can really let loose. I like the contact with people, yeah, I don't like being alone. We're all totally relaxed, we've got a great rapport, we kid around the moment the work is done. The owners are young, they look out for us. They're really protective."* And yet all is not well: *"Sometimes, it's hard when there's an all-guy squad on duty. You've got to be able to take a joke, but it's a little crude, really macho. There are days you're not in the mood 'cause you're tired, 'cause you're fed up with it, you're sick of it. Very sexual gibes like 'you're flat-chested.' I don't think they really mean to be nasty, but they don't realize how hurtful that can be. Actually, that can really hurt. Because their mothers or girlfriends or kid sisters aren't around, they feel an irresistible urge to act up. They want to shock you. They don't use their heads. Sometimes you wonder if you can keep going with all that to put up with. And it's right then that the good vibe takes over with your shift and the owners and they let them know that will do."* In the course of the interview, Anne went on to point out that the "vibe" isn't really all that great because the women on the staff are confined to gender-bound roles. *"If one of the guys has a one-night stand with one of the girls, he'll tell the rest of the team all the details, and that's not very nice for her. Girls suffer more from that kind of thing because as a rule they're more liable to become attached, and I've seen some who quit, who changed professions because of that."* Anne had some more harsh words to say about repeated harassment from one of the bar's regular customers. At one point, she told her boss and even threatened to file a complaint: *"It's not a swingers club! That wore me out, I was fed up, so I left. You've got to be pretty tough to hang in there.... I'm pretty shocked by women who don't demand respect, who'll put up with any kind of talk or behavior, or even let themselves be pushed or even knocked around.... We're definitely treated a little like human cattle."*

Cecile, age 24, is a financial auditor for a private consultancy. A graduate of an elite university, she earns a decent living. But she, too, suffers from sexism on the job: *"They don't tell guys they lack maturity. We have to put up with comments about our legs, our breasts, our suits. They're 30, 35 years old and still can't keep themselves from trying to look up your damn skirt."* Once, when a colleague jocularly patted her backside, *"I threw my drink in his face. It was enough to ruin his clothes, but it wasn't as bad as the humiliation I'd suffered. The problem is, they tell me I'm too uptight. At times, I've been scared. The boss asked me to let a customer flirt with me so I could get some information, as though I were one of his chicks. I took that very badly. I've half a mind to take sick leave for depression, then he'd really have to foot the bill. Every Friday I feel like quitting. I'm beginning to have doubts about having a rewarding career as a woman."* The discrimination in these two socially contrasting but remarkably similar stories goes well beyond the question of the different status of men and women. The issue here is the ongoing personal harm caused by the denial of the self, the nonrecognition of the subject's dignity and individuality, and the reduction of identity to what others project onto the subject's body.

The Impossibility of Recognition

Like rules, which tend to fluctuate, and just authority, which is an unstable equilibrium, the demand for recognition is impossible to fully satisfy because it arises out of a sense of incompleteness and, more importantly, because no work organization or society can satisfy the claims for recognition of its every member (Dupuy 2004). If people are more important than principles, then justice will be depleted by the interplay of intentions and discrete interactions (Forsyth 1980). Furthermore, what is at stake in any given demand for recognition will be of vital importance to the subject but, in many cases, of trivial importance, if not ridiculous, to everyone else. Recognition issues are symbolic, hence by nature inexhaustible and incapable of fulfillment.

The crux of the matter is the psychological toll that work takes on any given worker, which is strictly personal and hard for others to appreciate, especially the worker's superiors. The psychological toll of an hour spent teaching a class, caring for a sick patient, or coping with impatient customers at a ticket office is felt only by the worker concerned, and it depends as much on the worker herself as on the nature of the work. Like fatigue, in Loriol's analysis (2003), it is a strictly personal experience, and it is difficult to imagine how it could be objectively measured in terms any more specific than pace, hours per day, or workload. Depending on the survey and the wording of the questions, the percentage of the population claiming work-related fatigue ranges from 23 percent to 78 percent. Where nonrecognition claims are based on subjective perceptions of work-related burdens and constraints, which is often the case where human relations in the workplace are involved, one would be hard put to conceive of an organizational system, labor code, or management style that could resolve every case fairly. Moreover, seeing as any effort to do so would involve the application of fragmented rules, it would inevitably give rise to feelings of injustice every bit as intense. Hence the prevalence of complaints about "whiners" on the staff who try to turn their alleged afflictions to good account. Fundamentally, the subject's conviction that his work is not recognized is based on the gap between the work he was hired to do and the work he actually does, but this gap is both functional and, indeed, desired by the subject himself to the extent that it generates a space in which to exercise his autonomy.

In many cases, moreover, nonrecognition claims hinge on details so trivial that, to anyone else, trying to exercise total control over such details would seem both unwarranted and undesirable. Recognition is akin to jealousy, and like jealousy it is often fixated on bagatelles: "They had coffee together," "He didn't even say hello," or even "My desk is too far from the window." Frustrations of this order could be overcome only by organizing work along perfectly egalitarian and mechanistic lines, which would, of course, inevitably breed new nonrecognition complaints to the effect that such rigorous rules fail to do justice to individual uniqueness.

Lastly—and this dimension will ring all too familiar to academics—recognition often involves symbolic objects and inexhaustible sources of conflict; and like envy, the desire for recognition is unbounded. After all, conflicts and disagreements over salary levels can be objectified, discussed, and negotiated; but when the bone of contention is the size of one's desk, or one's self-image as reflected in the opinions of others, depending on how much attention they pay, say, to their colleagues and their colleagues' publications, the wrangling over recognition can get caught up in an endless spiral. Claire, a university lecturer, gives a perfect description of the vertiginous quest for recognition. *"What I don't like about universities is they're full of people obsessed with power, though there is no real power here.... Nothing is clearly defined here. There's no real hierarchy. I don't have to answer to anyone, it's not a business, I don't have an account or a sales volume. So the problem is recognition: People here work because they're looking for recognition. And what does recognition mean at a university? Maybe it's something you can get from students. You can feel it, but it's never a sure thing, so you don't get any kudos for that. You do get kudos for your qualities as a researcher, but that's where things get a little fuzzy. You've got people here who are completely overawed by the international renown of whomever, Professor So-and-So. But if you look at the big picture, Professor So-and-So gets read by 15 eggheads. Is that international re-nown? As for me, I think the problem is that we don't get financial rec-ognition, which would sort out the situation. Now, don't get me wrong,*

I'm not in this for the money. But what is recognition? This is a milieu of strong-willed men, who were all top of their class, and they're very elitist. They think they're a lot smarter than the others, and they need recognition.... So they try to get power because they all have a hard time getting the recognition they need. They spend their lives seeking recognition." Claire knows whereof she speaks. She later told us she has no choice but to either "join the fray or back away." It may be ludicrous, but it's the only game possible in a world where workers have virtually no objective worth beyond the subjective conviction of their own worth. It goes without saying that in this realm of recognition, the obsession with personal autonomy is rivaled only by the fixation on equality within the ranks—added proof that recognition involves an ongoing compromise between autonomy and equality.

*   *   *

In the workplace, people talk as much, if not more, about issues of law, power, and recognition as about equality, merit, and autonomy. They can often discuss those issues more straightforwardly, for they are closer to personal experience. Moreover, those issues combine fundamental principles, articulating and engaging them in situations that are more practical than the "pure" underlying principles. Because these issues necessarily involve compromises, they are an inexhaustible source of critiques that are, above all, bound to be unstable.

It follows that the provisions of the labor code and collective agreements are perceived as rules, but also as resources that can be manipulated, as adjustable compromises between radical equality and local working constraints. On occasion, it may even appear more unfair to follow the rules to the letter than to ignore them. The critiques of power are even more ambivalent and diverse. Obviously, power is rejected when tyrannical and capricious, but it is also criticized when weak, remote, or, conversely, invasive. Finally, the demand for recognition is both urgent and inexhaustible, inasmuch as it is based on both a desire for autonomy and a need for equality.

The theoretical imperfection of the "secondary" principles of law, power, and recognition is largely responsible for their normative efficiency. In their attempt to unify the fatally disparate, they can never be stable. They are involved in the subtlest of interactions, in which they rely more heavily on categories borrowed from sociology than on fundamental principles of the philosophy of justice. However, though they are analytically secondary to equality, autonomy, and merit, they are clearly by no means minor or residual. Quite the contrary. But to understand them fully, we have to see how they are derived from more essential principles that are at a further remove from practical categories. Rules, power, and recognition are even more ambiguous than equality, merit, and autonomy, and they are interpreted in a wide variety of ways, some of which are mutually contradictory. This is why there is always a risk of misapprehension in using practical categories analytically. For they are too familiar to be ignored and yet too familiar not to be mistrusted.

Notes

1. It may be noted that management complaints about labor law are diametrically opposed to these views: Labor law protects workers from having to work, establishes privileges and castes, obstructs the realization of pure merit, and so forth. In a word, it is a tool in the hands of labor—just as labor views it as a tool of in the hands of management.

2. The 270 French labor courts (*conseils prud'hommaux*) adjudicated 176,065 actions in 2002, 90 percent of which were filed by employees (*Annuaire statistique de la justice,* 2004).

3. W. F. Trotter's translation. The original French reads as follows: *"La tyrannie consiste au désir de domination universelle et hors de son ordre."*—Translator's note.

4. French kindergartens and primary schools are closed all day on Wednesdays, secondary schools in the afternoon.—Translator's note

CHAPTER 5

Why Is the World So Unjust?

INDIVIDUALS BASE THEIR JUDGMENTS on all three principles of justice, despite the mutual opposition of those principles. Unlike most philosophers of justice, who strive to reduce the contradictions, individuals seem indifferent to achieving some ultimate coherency or establishing the parameters of an ideally rational, just world. After criticizing their working conditions in terms of equality, merit, and autonomy, which could be considered criticism *internal* to each principle, they elaborate *external* critiques, criticizing each principle of justice in terms of the others. To the extent that they espouse all three principles, many people successively adopt every possible position and proceed to work out all the critiques that ensue from each position. In our opinion, their critical strategy, which arises spontaneously, provides empirical proof of the profoundly contradictory nature of the fundamental principles of justice. It is a strictly sociological illustration of the "war of the gods."

Reasoning from the standpoint of equality, workers find that the reign of merit, identified with capitalism, exacerbates inequalities, and that of individual autonomy shatters the solidarity and moral cohesion that safeguard equality in democratic societies. But when they examine the world through the lens of merit, equality appears an immutable hierarchical order made up of unearned privileges that obstruct the free play of merit, while autonomy becomes a recipe for disorder and favoritism. Lastly, viewed through the prism of autonomy, equality becomes a form of lowest-common-denominator egalitarianism inimical to individual responsibility and creativity, and merit seems a cruel taskmaster, denying the individual's identity and ethical autonomy.

Each principle of justice structures a different ideological representation of society. Not all the individual's critiques are entirely original, for they draw heavily on the great critical tradition of social philosophy: the defense of community against capitalism, egoism, and anomie; the conjoint critique of tradition and moral disorder in the name of rational free-market competition; the critique of consumer society and instrumental rationality in the name of the subject's moral autonomy.[1] It is always fascinating to find social agents reasoning along the same lines as great authors they've never read, unless it works the other way around and it is the great authors that reason like people who are not trained theorists. All these critiques come from both the right and the left side of the political spectrum, so the end result is a sort of patchwork, but with a fairly stable internal pattern as individuals seem to adopt in succession virtually every moral posture available to them.

This process of developing external critiques has two main consequences. First, it locks the individual into a critical circle as she moves from one viewpoint to the next, and the image of a profoundly—and, in a way, necessarily—unjust world gradually comes into focus. Second, the more these normative viewpoints appear autonomous and mutually antagonistic, the darker, more pessimistic the image of the world becomes, even if the world itself is "not in such bad shape." This is how the modern perception of the social world comes to appear increasingly critical and pessimistic. At base, modern agents do not identify with society, for they adopt several conflicting points of view: The subject sees himself more as an outsider than as an insider, more as a skeptic than a believer (Dubet 1994).

Equality Versus Egoism and Anomie

At this juncture, it is certainly not by chance that we now take up Durkheim's concepts of egoism and anomie. In *The Division of Labor in Society* (1967), and later in *Suicide* (1967), Durkheim examined the threats to social solidarity posed by modernity, the division of labor, and capitalism (Allardt 1971; Durkheim 1967). He discerned two basic threats. The first is *egoism,* rampant individualism and the weakening of the latent social bond between individuals. The second is *anomie,* a breakdown in social controls and in the interiorization of social norms, without which individuals cease to control their drives, desires, and conduct by subjecting them to a common morality. Thus, insofar as the principle of equality rests on a latent conception of a just order and the cohesion of a group of equal individuals, it seems to be threatened by the ascendancy of merit, which leads to hypertrophic competition between egoisms, and by the realization of autonomy, which detaches individual ethics from common morality. In the one case, individuals think only of themselves; in the other, they have no moral standards anymore.

Egoism

Of our respondents, 60.2 percent feel that their workmates are increasingly "selfish." Merit accentuates egoism, undermining trust and human relations in the workplace. According to Martine, an office worker, *"We live in an individualistic society where everyone works for herself. Maybe your friend the next desk over has been working her butt off for 15 years without a raise or anything—so what, that's none of your business. It's everyone for herself."* "Brown nosing," cynicism, scams, and all-out war against all comers would become the rule in a world that encouraged purely self-seeking behavior. Thus, giving workers a merit-based raise or bonus is a strategy that foments egoistic competition. The remedy is to defend the equality of working conditions within each trade or profession, seniority, and the supremacy of qualifications, which protect the workplace from the arbitrary play of merit. Employees who have gone from a somewhat paternalistic, seniority-based system to the more "modern," merit-oriented style of management are rudely awakened to the rise of egoism. Karine, a supermarket cashier, describes how the mood at work has deteriorated since her supermarket was taken over and the new management moved in. *"It's a rat race, and everybody's trying to sabotage everybody else. We're more stressed out. As a result, we don't have a social committee anymore, we don't have a kitty for staff parties anymore. We used to do a Christmas party, we had an annual outing. All that's history now."* The merit contest has shattered the community. Unionists have long been blaming the decline in their influence on the individualization of merit, the selfishness of modern life, and the dearth of support from the community, especially the working-class community.

Subjects extrapolate from their experience to generalize about society as a whole. Many opine that the unadulterated capitalist ethos of money making and profitability is supplanting the old-fashioned corporate ethos of production and social integration within the company. Whereas industrial society had, over time, succeeded in more or less taming capitalism, it seems that nowadays the market and society are parting ways again as they did at the dawn of the industrial era. The new capitalist revolution is, so the argument goes, bound to destroy communities as it did in the days of the "Great Transformation" (Polanyi 1983). One young woman executive concurs: *"Even if the company's doing well, it has to do better, so you always have to cut quality to up profits. So I wonder, what are we here for? It should always be possible for people to make a decent living, I mean survive, but there are certain people raking it in and frankly, that's scary."* Though he has no reason to complain himself, Michel feels that *"inequalities are widening in an increasingly capitalistic world,"* and 67.4 percent of our respondents agree. They frequently adduce instances of companies closing down and laying off the workforce in spite of decent production and sales performance, and they decry the golden parachutes of CEOs who have succeeded in bankrupting their own businesses.

In France, opposition to international capitalism is often associated with hostility to the "American model," deemed the epitome of a society of merit-obsessed egomaniacs. *"Let's introduce ourselves American-style: What are you worth in dollars?"* Instinctively, we still tend to conceive of the community of equals as a national community, and to believe our close-knit French solidarity is menaced by an alien egoism. A full 63.3 percent of our respondents feel that France is losing out as a result of globalization. We should note that defining community in terms of class would hardly make any difference in the prevailing sentiment. Evelyne, a labor organizer, believes that the role of the unions is to overcome workers' egoism, but that immigrants sap working-class solidarity: *"We always find a good excuse for them. They know where to go for a handout; they know the laws better than we do, and us French taxpayers pick up the tab."*

Self-interest takes over in a "profit-driven society," lament 94.8 percent of our respondents. This is the familiar theme of "filthy lucre" and the corrupting influence of anonymous finance. In spite of the fact that most of us feel underpaid, we still have the impression the blind, anonymous flow of money is undermining the community and nurturing self-interest. Money is, moreover, a barrier between individuals. Unlike gifts, it promotes egoism by enabling individuals to disengage from the group. Specifically, it releases them from their debts to society, thereby severing the organic bonds between individuals, each of whom is always at once creditor and debtor (Mauss 1950). As Simmel demonstrated compellingly (1987), money is a universal medium enabling each of us to optimize our tastes and interests, provide for the future, sever our ties to the community, and buy our independence. However, though money makes us free, and that's the reason why we love it, it is also a vector of egoism, and that's the reason why we hate it.

The rejection is all the more adamant from the angle of equality, where "money mania" is perceived as both the symptom and the cause of the greatest inequalities and, above all, of the demise of solidarity when money becomes "cosmopolitan," globalized, faceless, and unprincipled. Thus, the critique of money is essentially moral in nature. In terms of equality, it dissolves the networks of interdependence and personal bonds that keep us needing others. Some of the craftsmen we interviewed virulently condemned the perverse role that money plays when commercial relations are reduced to a battle of self-interest, each party to the transaction seeking to "rip off" the other. Thus, equality still holds merit guilty for the crimes of capitalism, as if, without it, French society would be a harmonious community, whether of proletarians or virtuous and reasonable petty proprietors.

Anomie

Viewed from the angle of equality, the assertion of autonomy takes on the form of anomie, the deregulation of social control and morality. The ideal egalitarian society is threatened not only by egoism and capitalism, but also by individual immorality, which corrodes the moral cohesiveness of the community of equals. After all, while the advocates of merit may abide by the rules and keep their urges and desires in check because it is in their own best interest to do so, moral individualism enshrines the individual and his desires as the sole source of standards and norms. And one need only equate autonomy with narcissistic individualism to give it a very bad name.

Three-quarters (76.6 percent) of those surveyed agree that *"people are becoming less and less moral."* This sentiment is more widespread among right-leaning than left-leaning voters (Piketty 2003), but one needn't be an elderly conservative to feel the same way. Nicolas, a tree pruner, laments the collapse of communal solidarity he once knew in rural France. *"People don't stick together anymore. It's everyone for himself and to hell with you. I'm from the country, and when I get to Bordeaux, I don't see anybody, nobody looks at anybody else, everybody's rushing around. Somebody gets beat up, nobody looks. Things are really goin' down the tubes. Sure, I think it's the fault of the media. No doubt about it: You want to fight crime, throw out your TV set."* Many of our respondents think that by incessantly putting the horrors of the world on display, the media are setting a standard of tolerable inequalities in our society, as opposed to the patently unbearable ones elsewhere that we see on TV. The same people also feel that the media portray a world utterly devoid of moral rules and principles in the ongoing spectacle of perversions, insanity, murder, and mayhem. *"Just watching the tube, it's plain to see that everything's going down the drain,"* Nicolas added. One physician remarked, *"Well, you see all the crime, the consumption, that's enough of that! Things need to be put back in perspective."* Those who toil on "the social battlefront," healthcare providers, teachers, social workers, paint a devastating picture of their clients' moral destitution and abject anomie: Crumbling, deadbeat families and broken homes, the elderly abandoned by their grown-up children, aberrant childrearing methods, and child pornography concur to add moral degradation to material privation. Not only are people increasingly isolated, but in the very name of their freedom and autonomy they are becoming increasingly "clueless." Morally, "anything goes" in a society in which the only things keeping outrageous behavior in check are law enforcement and well-understood self-interest.

According to many of the workers we interviewed, employers and employees cheat and exploit each other, not only because they are selfish, but also because they are "amoral." In addition to being sly and utilitarian, people have been stripped of their moral values, which leads them to cheat shamelessly. Laura, an assembly-line worker, believes the work ethic is failing: *"We're not here to lounge around, we're here to work."* She condemns coworkers who "sabotage" the job as much as bosses who break promises. More generally, she believes things have gone wrong because the national framework that holds the system together is falling apart. She points the finger at immigrants collecting unemployment: *"You go work in a vineyard and you're bone tired for six days, you get sunburnt, and you sweat. Why in the world would anybody do that if he can live on unemployment?"* Those with no respect for the fundamental values of the community of workers—defined by extension, in this case, to comprise the French nation—are a moral menace. Not only are they foreigners, they are "free radicals" indifferent to the elementary moral constraints of solidarity that are necessary for equality, according to this working-class woman with far-rightist sympathies (Dubet 2004; Perrineau 1998; Wieviorka 1995).

Stigmatized as "rampant individualism," autonomy is also blamed for the erosion of professional ethics. Workers allegedly no longer take care of the equipment. According to older nurses, the younger ones go off duty without making sure the next-shift nurse has arrived to take their place.

Autonomy, equated with unprincipled individualism, constitutes a threat to the integrity of the community and the moral contract that are the foundations of elementary equality. From this standpoint, equality is undermined not only by free-market self-interest, but also by unbridled freedom, the distorted side of autonomy. If everyone has the right to build a life of her own, everyone will ride roughshod over everyone else. This argument is as old as the anathematization of money, for even though we all desire autonomy for ourselves, we are always ready to denounce it in others: Amorous choice becomes sexual promiscuity and the collapse of family values; self-care becomes narcissism; religious freedom oscillates between nihilism and communitarianism; and these prophecies of doom do not exempt manifestations of autonomy in the working world either. In short, autonomy brings decadence in train.

Merit Versus Privilege and Favoritism

Privilege

Naturally, belief in liberal equality and equal opportunity go hand in hand, for there is no justice in merit unless people can compete on an equal footing. As one company head told us, he would feel all the more assured of deserving his position if everyone else could have the same scholastic and career opportunities. One cannot take pride in merit if the deck is stacked in one's favor.

The other side of equality, however, that of the legitimate hierarchical order, seems profoundly unjust for two reasons. For one thing, this order appears to be an array of privileges that thwart and distort free competition and rightful merit. So egalitarians denounce the circumstantial inequalities of established safeguards, entitlements, and advantages. Second, the relationship between academic and professional merit is always strained, for it involves imposing one sphere of justice on another. It is arguably unfair for professional merit to be hemmed in by academic merit, which is earned by different means and which does not measure the same skills and attributes. For the champions of academic achievement, on the other hand, the problem is diametrically opposed: The mismatch between qualifications and positions is unjust—and smacks of "wheeling and dealing behind closed doors."

One of the most widely decried "privileges" is the lifelong tenure granted to French civil servants, regardless of their professional merit. A cushy government job simply sanctifies academic merit earned on the eve of entering the job market. In our survey, 23 percent of our respondents feel that the privileged status of civil servants is unfair. Another 9.7 percent would go a step further and abolish that status, while 27.8 percent think it discourages initiative. In all, "only" 18.1 percent of those surveyed find this status fair and feel it should be extended to the private sector, too. So about six people out of ten object to "excessive" job protection for "bureaucrats"—a sentiment that appeals to centrist and right-wing voters.

It is interesting to note that criticism of this privilege, particularly the lack of pressure to excel, is not uncommon among civil servants themselves. They are dissatisfied with the automatic career and salary advancement that is the rule in civil service, feeling that their merit goes unrewarded when they work harder and better than their colleagues. Sandra, a clerk in a government office, complains, *"Since it's difficult to fire a government employee, the boss takes advantage of the ones who actually work by giving them a bigger load."*

Of course, small business owners and contractors are all the more indignant about the privileges that go with civil service because they place an added burden on the taxpayer, and the absence of risk for government employees leads to an aggravation of risk for everyone else. Etienne runs a small gymnasium: *"I have this small business, and they never stop auditing me. They're always rummaging through all my stuff, trying to find a chink in the armor. But they know I have expenses, and my lifestyle's in clear view of everyone. Meanwhile, we pay taxes to maintain a bunch of lazy bureaucrats."* Etienne is exasperated with the teachers always going on strike, the rail workers clamoring for a 35-hour work week although they get to retire at 50 and travel for free with their families, national power utility employees getting free electricity, etc. *"When I was starting out, I worked 45 hours a week. The way things are going, pretty soon we'll have to bring them their paychecks at home. I know a few teachers, they stay home for depression every three weeks though they do 17 hours of work a week. C'mon, enough's enough."* William, a floorwalker, doesn't mince words: *"The thing that tends to get my goat is these continual strikes in certain trades, especially mass transit. They're not that badly off themselves, and yes, I feel it's wrong to paralyze the country…. They don't even know what perks they'll lose, and they're already on strike. A preemptive strike, they call it. That's blatant injustice for you. They're using their right to strike, fine by me, but that's over the top!"* Jane, an English teacher on a temporary contract, resents her tenured colleagues, who treat her with scorn and enjoy a number of advantages denied to her, including higher pay, even though some of them *"don't lift a finger."* The foregoing should suffice to give a sense of the prevalence and virulence of our respondents' criticism of civil service, which was practically a matter of course among those whose jobs hinge on their efficiency and merit. In their eyes, a large segment of the population is spared this ongoing ordeal.

Serge, who has a temporary job at a telephone company, is bitterly resentful of the permanent staff's protected status: *"All this business about rankings, the pseudo echelons…. The guys here don't rank any higher than the guys holing up in their offices, smoking cigarettes and drinking coffee all day long, waiting till 5 to knock off. They don't make more money, they don't have more skills, but it pisses me off a little, yeah, I have a hard time with that. They're always kvetching, and they're computer-game champs, it makes me steaming mad…. We're in a system that runs like a little Russian bureaucracy, with these petty czars terrorizing their department. That makes me a tad bitter. If I'm not happy, I can leave. If it bothers you, you just leave. There are plenty of much more serious injustices in life. What I say to myself, and to everybody else, is: You're free, go work the register in the supermarket."* Marc, a bank executive and unionist, admits that *"motivation gets dulled"* when private-sector employees see how government workers, defended by powerful unions, pile up the perks, whereas nobody pays any attention to the private-sector people anymore.

Although qualifications sanction a form of merit, many find their hegemony over the working world a sort of lifelong privilege based on an accomplishment that dates from late adolescence. Of those we surveyed, 64.5 percent think "it isn't right that academic qualifications should be a prerequisite for positions of responsibility." The most highly qualified are the least inclined to share that sentiment. Likewise, 84.4 percent of our respondents deem it unfair that "brainwork," jobs requiring the most qualifications, should be systematically better paid than manual labor. Qualifications are like money, it may be observed in passing: something everyone wants, especially for their children, while condemning the uses and abuses thereof by others in the professional world.

This brings us back to the denunciation of the qualified castes, of pay scales based more on scholastic achievement than "real-life" professional experience, or of the fact that collective agreements assign different pay to employees who are doing exactly the same work. Roger, a bank teller and union activist, bristles at the sight of young college graduates being handed executive positions that are eternally off limits to older, more experienced, and more competent staff: *"They walk into the bank and they're handed the job and a fatter paycheck than others who're doing the same job."* This puts Roger in a bit of a quandary, seeing as he also defends the collective agreement underpinning the system. Workers with no qualifications whatsoever in a society that is passing out more and more diplomas feel particularly vulnerable and trapped in menial, low-paid, subordinate positions in spite of any skills they may have had a chance to demonstrate. But *"without a high school diploma you got nothin'."* Worse still, in an age in which over 80 percent of high school students leave school with a diploma, not having one is not only a handicap, it's also a stigma, a telltale sign that one is way below average in terms of the aptitude, attainments, and "intelligence" that are expected of everyone.

In effect, the tension between these two proving grounds of merit, the classroom and the workplace, has never entirely abated. On the one hand, those who are "overqualified" for their jobs feel degraded and disdained by the working world. In an overeducated society, half the students who leave college after two years will end up blue-collar workers or lower-level white-collar staff (Duru-Bellat 2006). On the other hand, those who are "not sufficiently" qualified feel blocked and excluded when their posts are snatched up by the overqualified. Considering that this "educational inflation" and the instability of the employment market are unlikely to stabilize the correspondences between the two scales of merit, the two-way sense of injustice aroused by this mismatch is unlikely to subside. Many young PhDs, to wit, are reduced to doing odd jobs at university while waiting for a steady, prestigious appointment corresponding to their academic training. Sure of their academic merit, with a good dissertation and some publications under their belts, they think the tenured faculty they are working under monopolize all the privileges and comport themselves like a protected caste, while they—the subalterns—are becoming proletarianized intellectuals. What makes it seem all the more unfair to some is the conviction that they are more active and competent than the tenured set, who are locked into a routine and whose sole merit lies in having been born at the right time or in having "wangled" their way to their professorial posts. In this sense, the generation gap is also about merit: In the students' eyes, the older generation had less merit and more opportunities, so their positions look like privilege (Chauvel 1998). Arnaud, a young executive fresh out of a prestigious French university, makes the point clearly: *"When I see people like my dad, who did nearly the same studies I did, when I see what he did with it and where he is now, then it's plain to see you were better off starting work back in 1965. Now they tell you over and over again, 'You're not happy? The pay doesn't suit you? Check out the list. There are five guys behind you.'"*

Finally, there apparently exists a strange privilege, that of the poor who are overprotected by the social security system. A full 62.4 percent of the respondents to our questionnaire deem it unfair that recipients of unemployment compensation and welfare should draw benefits almost equivalent to the statutory minimum wage. Often without even realizing it, workers elaborate a critique of "inactivity traps" that form when the differential between unemployment benefits and anticipated pay (generally the minimum wage) is too slim to induce the jobless to take such unappealing jobs (Dubet/Vérétout 2001). The critique is not only practical and instrumental; it is, above all, moral, for merit goes by the board when those who don't work earn as much as those who do. In fact, they earn more since they don't have to pay the price of working. In order for the level of social protection to be equitable, it should not affect the intrinsic merit of work. The unemployed should not be earning as much, or almost as much, as the gainfully employed. *"That's where the idea of welfare is debatable,"* remarks Gilles from the National Employment Agency. *"That's the pernicious thing about state aid of any kind. Maybe work isn't a must for everyone in order to survive. Job seekers tell us that. You offer them a job at such-and-such a place and such-and-such pay, they say, 'Wait a sec, I'd rather stay on unemployment.' I really don't know what to think."* In other words, merit is only compatible with equality insofar as the latter safeguards the remuneration of merit.

This dilemma is particularly plain to the lowest-paid workers with the least job security, for they are socially close to welfare "beneficiaries." They are likely to know some in their family or building. After denouncing outrageous income disparities, Laure, a blue-collar worker and unionist, points out: *"People are encouraged not to work and then not to take an interest in anything. It's really outrageous, it's a flaw in society. It's as though society was saying: If you're on unemployment, we'll buy this for you, and the guy who goes to work's gonna be earning less than the guy on welfare. They give them everything, it's like people who have kids just to get benefits. Well then, if they let their kids turn into delinquents, their allowance ought to be cut."* Laure is not the only one to think this way. This line of reasoning is shared by almost all those who work hard and are particularly subject to the exigencies of merit. Jean-Baptiste, a department manager, speaks of his uncle as of a profiteer: *"What seems wrong to me is to see someone from my family who's better off than me without lifting a finger. I find that unfair because I think we're turning out welfare scroungers in France. I don't think it's right I should have to pay private health insurance and work my ass off; that I get up at three in the morning every day, while people better off than me don't pay taxes, they got medical coverage and don't do shit.... My uncle lives off it. He, like, begs them: He goes and sees his social worker, he moans and groans, he gets everything. He's got the same car as me, he's got his apartment, he's got it good."*

The Arbitrary Side of Autonomy

For merit to be fully realized, individuals need to start out on the same footing. But they must also be ensured of the neutrality and objectivity of the rules, procedures, and arbiters of merit. As in a sports contest, the entrants must be accorded the same starting conditions, the referees must be impartial, and the competition must play by the rules. Viewed from this angle, merit is a virtue.

But viewed through the prism of merit, the principle of autonomy is ambiguous. On the one hand, it goes without saying that individual freedom is indispensable to merit, and some theorists, like Nozick, make merit a consequence of freedom, which is held to be the foundation of any just society. On the other hand, however, to the extent that this autonomy is subjective, "irrational," mired in "special circumstances," it affects merit through the play of "connections" and "leverage" that people call favoritism. Merit then can no longer be objectively assessed, and the gulf between merit as intention and merit as performance appears to be unbridgeable.

In the workplace, suspicions of "foul play" are so strong and pervasive that many a worker, though attached to the merit principle, will end up rejecting or radically amending it. Measuring merit objectively seems impossible, and the methods currently used to assess it appear far more unfair than the hierarchical orders that are firmly ensconced in a global equality. Many teachers, in particular, come to the conclusion that, all things considered, automatic, seniority-based career advancement is a lesser evil than merit-based promotions, even if it means their merit will go unrecognized and they may be treated as "lazy" or "lousy" faculty members. It seems less risky to be judged by a grid of rules, a computer, or an inspector who comes around every seven years on average, than by the whims of the head of the school, peers, parents, or students. Robert, a tax office clerk, elucidates this reckoning: *"The shop runs on seniority. That has the advantage of being linear and systematic, and the disadvantage of disregarding motivation. All the systems are unfair, in fact, because if you set up a system to analyze performance, it'll be unfair if you don't pick the right criteria. The advantage of seniority is that it's a linear, objective system, quantifiable for everyone. I'd be in favor of a mixed system that takes both performance and seniority into account. There'd be something in it for everyone."*

In fact, mixed systems are the rule in most big organizations, but that does not allay suspicions about the ways in which individuals play on their autonomy to pervert pure meritocracy—which, in turn, reopens the never-ending case against favoritism. What makes this indictment all the more interminable is that favoritism promotes the less deserving and debases the others in its wake. *"The heads of the agency who had once been praised to the skies,"* recounts Marc, *"suddenly found themselves doing jobs that a 15-year-old kid could handle in two months. That's degrading."* Manuel, a warehouseman, feels that he has given a lot of himself but that his merit has gone unrecognized for one single reason: The new management team does not take to him. *"I'm planning to leave; I'm an ambitious guy. In terms of appreciation for my work, even if I didn't have the pay that went with it or the status, I didn't give a shit. I just wanted Mr. Martin to appreciate my work, that's all."* Manuel knew the 1,920 items in the warehouse by heart. After having played the merit card with so much conviction only to fall victim to the managers' whims, Manuel decided to withdraw into himself and protect himself. *"So you take notes, you fax and copy everything, you put together your personal file on the company, on the others. You work, but you cover your back. Everyone does their job, but no more than that."* When merit is suspect, the best thing to do is neutralize it, says Marc. The union shouldn't oppose highly "bizarre" promotions, but it should fight against penalties, even those that seem well-founded.

Because the autonomy and uniqueness of individuals are random and uncontrollable, the call for merit cannot be carried through to its logical conclusion. Merit claims arouse suspicion and foster self-imposed limits, even in those who believe deeply in merit. For example, although people resolutely deplore racial and sexual discrimination, most of those who broach these issues are opposed to any affirmative action program that would require official recognition of the individual's ethnic and social background, because it would affect the objectivity of merit assessment, even if it might comply with the principle of equality. And when confronted with individual autonomy, merit entails a perplexing spiral of conundrums, a set of deep-seated suspicions harbored by many a philosopher, starting with Rawls: Is merit defined by results or good intentions? Do we deserve our merit, our talents, our energy, and intelligence? And even if we are responsible for the way in which we make use of our talents, are we quite sure this use of them isn't just another effect of our socialization and our "genes"? In the final analysis, from the perspective of merit, autonomy presents both a threat to and a doubt about merit itself (Lucchesi 1995).

Autonomy Versus Egalitarianism and the Cruelty of Merit

Against Egalitarianism

The principle of autonomy affirms self-determination, the right to lead your life as you see fit and "be who you are." That freedom triggers a critique of equality in which equality is deemed a conformist constraint, a negation of the self in a society that is deemed oppressive. The obsession with equality engulfs the subject in a uniform society, manipulating his needs and, ultimately, annihilating his liberty. Without their knowing it, agents expressing views along these lines are carrying on a long-standing critical tradition beginning with Tocqueville's fears that the passion for equality would destroy freedom. This critique often comes from the right wing, but also from the leftward leaning who defend not so much equality as the individual's right to be master of her own life, to be protected against both the excesses of capitalism and the leveling effect of mass culture. This sort of criticism was vented by respondents bemoaning pell-mell the inanity of television, political propaganda, the manipulation of individual needs by consumer society, cultural mediocrity, and so forth. Denunciations of this sort clearly enable individuals to set themselves apart and thereby assert their own autonomy. Jean-Christophe, a dental surgeon, is appalled by *"reality TV where people learn how to dance in a day. I wish people would like things that aren't popular, I wish they'd dig deeper."* Others assert more crudely that the great injustice is the universal reign of *"stupidity,"* of public opinion, prejudice, aggressive conformism. *"Stupid assholes,"* workmates and bosses *"who think like the TV,"* racists and machos are among the sundry species in this widely despised bestiary. An individual who takes pride in cultivating particular tastes, or his own special style and look, considers his staffmates' call for equality an attempt to compel uniformity, to bring him into line. In perusing the transcriptions of the interviews, we sometimes had the impression our respondents were Chaplinesque protagonists: clearly not heroic figures taking on the pervasive pressures of society, but rather somewhat hapless types drifting through the working world, eternal outsiders, floating, labile, and yet somehow impervious to a surrounding environment that could destroy them by forcing them into the mold. The main thing is not to conform, not to "join in" or "sell out," to pass through society without stopping.

The critique of equality leveled by the principle of autonomy is at times far more virulent. Autonomy is built on responsibility, on the assertion that you pay your dues and owe nothing to others. There is something heroic about affirming that one is an autonomous subject, "lord and master" over oneself. A staunch autonomist reviles the various social policies designed to maintain an elementary equality because they induce their beneficiaries to be passive and to abdicate responsibility for themselves. At the very least, the code of autonomy isn't always conducive to compassionate indulgence.

Of the workers we surveyed, 51.1 percent think it "right that part of their income should be redistributed to the needy." Another 13.7 percent don't find it right at all, though 33.9 percent say "it depends." Specifically, it depends on how much the needy individual is to blame for his own misfortune. After all, it isn't right to help someone who has decided not to help himself or has "chosen" to be a victim. The principle of autonomy is not merciful towards the weakest in society, especially when they give themselves up to welfare and the vagaries of fate. Autonomists then blame the victims. Not only are state aid recipients cynical opportunists milking an "overly" generous system, they are morally responsible for their lot in life. In affirming that we are the cause of our fate, the norm of internality that governs autonomy implies that agents must fully assume the consequences of their acts and, from this point of view, it is difficult to conceive that "victims" are entirely what they claim to be.

Francis owns a firm with four employees. *"Those who feel like working ought to be able to work, people ought to stop bugging them, stop knocking them. In any case, the better off people are, the more they gripe. They think they've got everything coming to them. They're supposedly looking for work, but as soon as you give them a job to do, 'It's dirty, it's tiring, it's this and it's that.' Work is something you've got to earn: It's a salary, so it doesn't just fall into your lap, and you're not going to earn any money sitting in front of the tube. The school system hasn't kept up with business, and the ones you find on the job market have no desire to work. I see these youths who come in for an interview without an appointment, chewing gum, dressed in God only knows what, unshaven, looking a little dissolute: You've gotta wonder what kind of work they aim to do. I ask myself what could that guy do, he's gonna get blisters, he'll be afraid to work. Come on and show me what you really know how to do, you've gotta prove yourself."* This is a rather "populist" discourse, one would think. Is it really all that different, though, from that of social workers disparaging the benefits they procure for their clients? Or that of teachers reproaching irresponsible parents and pupils unwilling to exert themselves because television leads them to believe everything should come easily? Is it all that different from that of doctors talking about patients who seem to believe they've got everything coming to them and have consequently renounced all responsibility for themselves and abandoned all self-control, the ones who drink to excess, overeat, smoke too much, and expect the medical establishment to keep them in good health? *"There should be more control, more severity,"* says Jean-Christophe with regard to his patients. *"Many need to be helped. Others do nothing in order to be helped: They're parasites because no one ever explained to them that they could do something about their situation."*

Jean-Pierre, a hospital janitor and union representative, likewise verges on blaming the victims in the name of autonomy and professional dignity. *"My great strength's my work, ain't nothing about my work they can find fault with. My power's in my own hands, and I'll go talk to the organ-grinder before I'll talk to the monkey. I respect the chain of command. You need bosses, management all right, and that's a fact.... The CGT[2] is a union for the workers, defends the whole working class. Unfortunately, the bad thing is it also defends the bad apples, creatures who ain't defendable. Some folks are bone idle, if they can hide for three or four hours, they'll do it all right. Now that was in the private sector, they'd've been out of a job long ago—the kind of guy who, if you add it up, works 12 years outta 26."* Because the workingman's conscience depends on pride in one's work, it is not much more indulgent than the ethos of the small-time boss.

There again, the critique is not new, it is actually as old as the question of social welfare (Castel 1995). Though it appears self-evident that we must help the victims of the greatest injustices to remain in society, and that this obligation is all the more imperative in democratic societies, that does not answer the question of the victims' responsibility. The question is, moreover, all the more pertinent in democratic societies that put the highest premium on autonomy and personal responsibility. So how does one tell the "genuine" poor from the "phony" poor, the "real" victims from the "sham" victims, the "true" unemployed from the "welfare-scroungers"? The expansion of the social safety net does not eradicate the problem, for even if conservative administrations are always acting unfairly in cutting benefits, liberal administrations are not necessarily acting fairly in systematically augmenting them. The conservatives reduce everything to the principles of autonomy and responsibility and are tempted to leave social welfare to charity organizations, while the liberals are tempted to ignore the principle of autonomy in the name of egalitarian policies. Neither approach ever truly eases the tension between equality and autonomy, which is probably no more reducible than the tension between equality and merit.

The contradiction between autonomy and equality is not of a strictly ideological or political nature. It is also a practical problem for those tasked with allotting social benefits. A group of staff from the French National Unemployment Office, brought together for this study, debated the issue at length. How does one evaluate the share of responsibility and autonomy in the individual cases that come up? Jeanne: *"You ask yourself what you're getting mixed up in here. One time, you've got the rotten bosses who take advantage of others; another time, you've got the applicants who take advantage of others, who take us for a ride.… You've gotta wonder: What are we getting mixed up in here? I say to myself, I've spent the day getting things approved that aren't really legit, from time to time I get this feeling; sometimes you get sick of what you're covering up and what you could expose, report, or vice-versa.."* For Martin, *"Some people are more devious than others. You know perfectly well they're taking advantage, frankly. There are others who actually are out of a job, who are more vulnerable."* In order to overcome her qualms, Marion banks on the applicants' truthfulness: *"I can't work unless I focus on people's honesty, there's no other way. Otherwise I'd get paranoid, I'd change professions."* But that is a fairly rational wager after all, seeing as it is hardly possible to gauge a person's true intentions.

Against the Cruelty of Merit

Insofar as autonomy is based on the ideal of the subject's self-fulfillment, it cannot necessarily always be reconciled with merit, which is measured in terms of efficiency and performance. There is no proof that the most efficient subject is the most autonomous one. The Weberian theme of the "iron cage," a thoroughgoing critique of modern society's tendency to reduce subjects to their technical and instrumental utility, to cogs in the bureaucratic machine, is as old as the social sciences. It points to a specifically modern alienation associated with the dilution of subjective meaning in rationality. Citing Bauman (1988; 1991), Touraine (1992) posits an inevitable tug-of-war in modern society between economic and technical rationalism, on one side, and the subject's self-centered search for meaning, on the other. Whereas autonomy is on the subject's side, merit is on the side of instrumental rationality. This dichotomy manifests itself directly in human consciousness in two principal ways.

The first, mentioned above, is the internalization of unhappiness when individuals consider themselves responsible for their failures on the various scales of merit. Autonomy turns against itself. If I believe I am wholly free and responsible for my own actions, that deprives me of the consolation of blaming my failure on the community, on religious or social destiny (Sennett 2003). To quote Josette, who works in a daycare center, *"It's terrible to be labeled in your own self-esteem. It seems really unfair to your self-confidence."* The more a career demands commitment and motivation, the more the subject is affected by its objective correlative in terms of merit. He can only conclude that he himself is a failure. We encountered cases like this in teachers who, driven by a strong calling and commitment to their careers, gradually discovered that they were failing at their profession. Either they elaborated long and involved indictments of the students, parents, colleagues, and "the system" as the cause of their troubles, or (far more frequently) they began to blame themselves, sinking into a more or less latent depression. In either case, they have to live with the disappointment of always falling short of their own aspirations and demands on themselves. Others suspect that their strong motivation and professional integrity are being exploited; they are thereby being dispossessed of their autonomy, and they are "being had" by the pains they take to perform. Nurses have a *"super image,"* Valerie remarks, but their higher-ups exploit that image to their own ends: *"The people that hire us are aware of that image. They take advantage of it, because if you decide to work with people, you've got to have a pretty strong human side. So even if you don't have to stay, you wouldn't think of going if the patient's not doing very well. We'll do it without being told to, because afterwards, when we get home, we'll feel guilty the whole time, and they use guilt trips a lot.... They exploit our work ethic."* During their landmark strike in 1989, French nurses chanted *"Non bonne, ni nonne, ni conne,"* literally, "Not maid, nor nun, nor dumb."

In their quest for autonomy, to satisfy both themselves and their employers, individuals are continually contriving motivations for themselves, good reasons to pledge a subjective commitment to their work and to believe in it. However, their efforts gradually wear them out to the point of exhaustion, and the motivation is likely to snap if the work organization stops providing support and confirmation (Ehrenberg 1991; 1998). At that point, the desire for autonomy closes up like a trap, for in addition to being the artificial product of a management technique and the dominant free-market ideology, autonomy is also a deep-seated human need. After the employee has drawn upon her own personal resources to the "burn-out" point, she is then scrapped by the organization. As Cousin points out, the most surprising finding is that few subjects are indignant about the cruelty of this rule; many are convinced that it is inevitable for decline to set in around the age of 40 (Cousin, 2004). *"As long as they deliver, as long as they hold out, it's fine,"* says Serge, assistant manager in a department store. *"They give it all they've got, working crazy hours, no more private life. But when they're totally worn out and their results go down, it's a disaster. They either quit or we demote them. They're so physically exhausted they can't work up an interest in anything else. Those who don't manage to get past that point are in trouble, because they have no hope of making it, no hope at all."*

The second manifestation of the painful conflict between autonomy and merit is the feeling that everything is meaningless: The career to which one has committed oneself is not worthwhile because voluntary submission destroys one's autonomy. In this case, one's personal drive gradually comes to be perceived as an alienating liability rather than an asset in self-fulfillment. The subject is not only sacrificing his life to make a living, but he is also losing his soul in his work. Thierry, a computer programmer, could no longer bear his inane but highly paid job, so he switched. Many private-sector workers opt for public-sector employment, even if the salaries are lower. They prefer more interesting work and a more congenial, more "fulfilling" private life. Didier was doubtless heeding a "calling" when be became a doctor, but he finds the "commercial" relationship with his patients, the competition with his colleagues, and the exacting control exercised by the national health insurance administration unbearable. As a result, he feels as though he has been betrayed by his vocation. Christian, another doctor, launched into a far more radical critique: *"I've always loved doing it, it's what I've always wanted to do. I like everything about this profession, everything. What I dislike is collecting the fee for the procedure. The longer I practice, the more it riles me. There's a business side to practicing that is undeniable and absolutely must be eliminated. You have to please the customers or they'll take their custom elsewhere. But there are times I don't feel like pleasing the customers."* And yet René was quite successful: *"I made plenty of money, I sure did. Then, after 15 years, my wife split and took the cash. I make €120,000 a year, working like a bureaucrat from 8 to 6. That's too much, I'm perfectly aware of that; it's pointless, doesn't make you any happier. There you go! Our society is morally decadent,"* pronounces this doctor, son of a blue-collar anarchist. René is sometimes as bitter and despairing as Dr. Destouches alias Louis-Ferdinand Céline.[3]

Jean-Baptiste is the exceptionally dynamic floorwalker who finds "good stress" stimulating. However, he admits that, owing to the exigencies of money and profitability, the only criteria of merit, an autonomous commitment to work, wrecks your private life. *"If you succeed, that's a good thing; if you get over it, then at that point it's perfect. If you're unlucky, and you fail, as is often the case in this job, you've lost four or five years."* Jean-Pierre says his work is exciting, but it's *"a dog's life."* As a matter of fact, he is separated from his wife, who couldn't stand his being so consumed by his job.

This type of experience bears out the critique of capitalism as a system based on the manipulation and control of freedom and autonomy. Subjects seeking self-fulfillment and gratification in their careers are frustrated by the exigencies of the market and a work organization that appropriates their desire for autonomy to the point of voiding their lives of any meaning. Many workers seem to be fairly conscious of this mechanism. The young executives and floorwalkers in our focus groups described this form of exploitation dispassionately. They explain that they play the game nonetheless, convinced that it's their only avenue to autonomy, aside from quitting. This is a graphic illustration of Weber's contention that the ethic of self-fulfillment at work can be compared to an athletic compulsion. As in sports, the contestants encounter blows, injuries, defeats, and doping, but they also have a shot at glory—albeit fleeting—and they revel in the "adrenalin surge" of competition.

"Everything's Getting Worse"

"In reality," there is no evidence that the world is getting worse. It would be easy, if somewhat lengthy, to show that, although certain social indicators are on the decline, others are on the rise. It would also be possible, if not as easy, to show that many of these indicators simultaneously point to both favorable and adverse trends. Furthermore, we must beware of the human penchant for idealizing the past. The French tend to look back fondly on *les Trente Glorieuses,* their 30-year postwar economic boom, as a golden age, ignoring the fact that it was marred by "Fordist" working conditions, inadequate social safeguards, limited educational opportunities, poor-quality urban housing, low wages, poverty among farmers and the elderly, repressive moral values, subjugation of women, the war in Algeria, etc., etc. They recall only economic growth, full employment, a budding consumer society, and upward mobility. Devoured by change, modern societies seem forever tempted by nostalgia for a series of "good old days." But let us put these reflections aside in view of the massive fact with which we are confronted in the interviews: For the agents, everything's getting worse.

Of our respondents, 67.4 percent think inequalities have widened. A full 68.4 percent agree that our society is increasingly unjust, and 79.8 percent believe the privileged and underprivileged are becoming more and more privileged and underprivileged, respectively. And, as noted above, 94.8 percent of those surveyed believe that money reigns supreme, and 63.5 percent that France is being harmed by globalization. Nevertheless, this overwhelming pessimism applies far more to society as a whole than to the individuals themselves, who take a more moderate view of their own career situation. When they were asked, "Are you optimistic about your career future?," 39.8 percent said yes, 18.9 percent said no, and 40.7 percent were undecided. Uncertainty is therefore more prevalent than pessimism. Some 41.7 percent say their lives are better than those of their parents, 28.1 percent say they're worse, and 28.8 percent see no significant difference. All things considered, though people are not resoundingly optimistic about their own fortunes, they are radically pessimistic about social trends. How do we account for this dissonance?

Unhappiness

To begin with, we should note that individuals have every reason to be pessimistic and unhappy. Linda, age 34, daughter of Portuguese immigrants, works as a nurse's aide in a retirement home. As a girl, she played nurse to her infirm parents: *"I can't blame them for it, it wasn't their fault."* Then, at 19, she became a single mother. *"When you get pregnant, the social workers say, 'You've got to keep the baby, you'll be helped.' It's not true, it's unfair."* Shunned by her family, Linda raised her child without any welfare benefits. Once, she applied to a social services agency to pay the gas bill and was told, *"All you have to do is put aside €15 a month.' I slammed the door and never set foot in there again."* So much for birthright equality.

Work provides no relief, of course; everything comes to a head. Linda deplores her boss's arbitrariness: *"He has no consideration for the personnel." "The bosses were people like one day you're up, next day you're down. It's so hard. For example, when they made mistakes, they'd basically put the blame on us.... We were treated like total nobodies."* Once, the manager insulted Linda for failing an examination. *"He invaded my personal life. He invaded everything to tear me apart. I was angry, I wanted to fight back, but I didn't know my rights."* In short, a textbook case of power and recognition.

"The retirement home isn't getting anywhere, we need more hands to take care of the people. It's a question of money. Our dear bosses are raking it in; they save on personnel because we're also very poorly paid for the amount of work we do. We don't count the hours. I say we're doing volunteer work, for the amount of work we do. In the private sector, you work overtime that isn't paid. We have to attend meetings, which is during our time off. At Christmas, New Year's, you have to do a good deed, so you have to go in and it isn't paid. Sunday's paid like every other day." In short, a textbook case of merit and exploitation. And due to the fact that scheduling is arbitrary and unpredictable, Linda can hardly structure her private life, or even her career: *"People appreciate me a lot because I take a lot of interest in my work, but the boss is always nit-picking."* So much for her feeling of autonomy.

It is hardly surprising that Linda should take a gloomy view of society: *"The people who are out on the street, it's a disgrace. The people who are underpaid, their work isn't appreciated right. We're moving too fast, we should take a step back. People are selfish—we can't relate anymore. It's everyone for himself, holing up at home. It's distressing, we're all shutting ourselves up when we ought to be sticking together. We should all be the same, even if we have more money or we got a better education. We should help each other out a little, there's too much difference between social backgrounds.... It always comes back to the same thing. If you're still taking home less than a thousand euros a month after six years on the job, you'd rather stay on unemployment for three years and get the same salary. I understand those people, but that's not a solution. We hide poverty, we'd like to hide it."* And seeing as everything's getting worse, things were better before. *"Before, people were good to others: They didn't try to find out your social background, they didn't look at what was around you, they looked at the human being. That's what's been lost. And yet that's what's most beautiful about us. Every person's got something precious, it may be from what you learned in school, from anything."* Linda's nostalgia doesn't seem to have anything to do with her age, she's only 34. Rather, it is a way to believe that a better world is not impossible, since there was one "before." Linda isn't benefiting from any of the principles of justice. Her unhappiness at work and at home, all her criticisms and complaints, mutually reinforce to produce a dismal, hopeless view of the world.

Frustrations

Linda's "absolute" unhappiness may be juxtaposed with the "relative" unhappiness of everyone else, a reminder that pessimism derives partly from relative frustration and comparisons (Davies 1962; Gurr 1970). Suffice it to cite two out of a host of cases in point. Charlotte, a 26-year-old ticket agent at French Rail, is overcome with indignation fueled by frustration. College educated, she feels her job is beneath her. She is constantly comparing herself to those below her, who are uncomfortably close, and those above her, who are maddeningly far. *"We ticket agents have no clout. When there's a strike, we count for nothing—just a notch above the cleaning ladies. Our bosses are all men, so there's subjugation involved: They've got a way of acting with us, talking to us, giving us orders, saying: 'Do it like this, do it like that.' I'm shocked when people who're loaded come up to the window and look down on me: 'You're nobody, you're just a civil servant.' Every day, I mean every day. They see me sitting behind the window, but I don't know what they're imagining: that I didn't go to college, that I'm a nobody, that I don't have a life? I'm a very proud person, and that really gets me. See, I'm making just over welfare, I earn minimum wage. I'm a nobody and I have no say, nobody listens to me. How should I put it: You don't have money, you come last, you get the short end of the stick every which way. You've got to drive a crappy car, you can't afford anything else. You're last in line because the name of the game is bucks. I've got job security, that's all I've got. If I was alone, I wouldn't be able to go on vacation—I could, but I wouldn't get far."* Charlotte and her partner have just bought a house: *"Some people tell me I'm lucky! I don't know what's so lucky about it."*

Nordine, a housepainter, feels a victim to every injustice when he compares himself to temp agency workers and the long-term unemployed: *"The happiest ones these days are most likely the temps. They're always changing jobs; they go to a company and then get unemployment. They get paid while they're unemployed. They've got their time off and then, since we're very short on labor, they make a lot.... There's no justice in France. Plus, it's all arbitrary, it's money that talks. How come they love getting unemployment? Because they moonlight, that pays a lot more, and they're sitting pretty at home. Ain't that paradise? Plus they've got all the other benefits, they get free driving lessons, job training.... Some'll even say they've got it coming to 'em, but c'mon, that's goin' a little too far."*

These two portrayals were selected from the bottom of the wage scale, but we could add dozens of others from the middle or even the top of the social ladder, for, inasmuch as everyone draws comparisons, everyone has grounds for bemoaning the injustice of their lot. However, this interpretation is not entirely satisfactory because it fails to explain the basic dissonance between the sense that everything is in decline and the fact that most people by and large consider their lives decent and fair. In fact, as we saw in the chapter on equality, most of the working people who compare their situation to that of the homeless in France, or to the "world poverty" and "remote misery" reported by the media tend to come to the conclusion "I'm OK myself." Apparently, the comparison mechanism works both ways: It can aggravate frustrations, but it can also mitigate them, depending on the comparative criteria applied. So we need to find a complementary explanation for the dissonance between this purportedly crumbling world around us and our sense that our own lives are not so bad.[4]

Critical Spirals

Our hypothesis is that the pessimistic, even alarmist, prevailing view of society as a whole, notwithstanding our feeling that our own lives aren't so bad, is due to the heterogeneity and mutual antagonism of the structural principles of justice. Inasmuch as subjects simultaneously apply several criteria of justice, the odds are that one of them will not be satisfied, for it is difficult to imagine being content in terms of equality, merit, and autonomy at one and the same time. Even more clearly, the adoption of any single principle of justice will inevitably breed criticism of the others and their adverse effects on the favored principle. And since subjects espouse all three principles, they are caught up in a critical spiral that gradually detaches them from their own situation. The critical spirals they articulate are neither incoherent nor irrational; in many cases they are actually near-complete executions of the syntax of the principles of justice. The spirals follow their own trajectories, but are encountered in individuals of every stripe. In other words, the world appears to be unjust simply because the gods are at war, and they cannot all emerge victorious. Oftentimes it was as an interview was drawing to a close that our interviewees would reduce the equation to the conclusion that, as far as they were concerned, things weren't so bad. This critical mechanism, or normative spiral, then detaches from the individual's personal experience to create a widening gap between self-awareness and world-awareness. As Simmel suggested (1988), the distance between the categories used to interpret the world and to interpret the self estranges modern man from his own experience. This reasoning with regard to the feelings of justice bears a certain resemblance to Beck's analysis of the "risk society" (2001): The fact that everyone's safety is increasing mechanically contributes to the fear of risk. The variety and strength of the principles of justice thus breeds a sensitivity to injustice that is relatively detached from personal experience because it is caught up in its own critical dynamic.

The result is a dynamic of perpetual circulation between contradictory principles of justice. In their desire for equality, merit, and autonomy at one and the same time, moreover, subjects do not always perceive the contradictions. The same individual will, by turns, espouse free-market, egalitarian, moralistic, individualistic, and solidarity-based views. This dynamic will tend to accelerate criticism inasmuch as each viewpoint on justice almost automatically calls for apologies and new critiques from other angles, and so on and so forth in an endless spiral.

* * *

Criticism is structured by elementary rules, by basic mechanisms that inject logic and rationality into the normative activity of social agents. These mechanisms trigger all the other possible critical mechanisms, generating an endless spiral of criticism as the subject shifts from one viewpoint to another, continually changing her perspective on justice. The criticism and feelings of justice are comparable to language, which is also structured by basic rules that make it possible to write all possible texts, just as the rules of musical harmony open up all the creative possibilities of musical composition. Individual critical activity, or creativity, appears to be all the more open-ended because the fulfillment of one principle of justice betrays the other two, so it is highly unlikely that critical consciousness can ever be fully stabilized. If we agree that modern society is characterized by the ever-increasing autarchy of the principles of justice because we are increasingly "democratic," or attached to equality, "capitalistic," or attached to merit, and "individualistic," or attached to autonomy, modern subjectivity is becoming more and more critical. Our view of the social realm is becoming increasingly pessimistic because society can never fulfill all the principles it has set for itself. At some point, however, both subjects and sociologists must stop the vertiginous whirl of the critical spiral: At least locally, the critical score must stabilize. Ultimately, the representation of the world and self-awareness separate. More precisely, feelings of injustice take root in immediate experience and detach themselves from the images of society that are swept up in the dynamic of critical processes.

Notes

1.   Virtually all the great names in the social sciences could be mustered here: from the counterrevolutionaries to Marx and Durkheim for their critiques of the deleterious effects of capitalism and individualism on the community; from Smith to Hayek for their critiques of egalitarian and moralist fictions; from Simmel to the Frankfurt School via Weber for their critiques of the reification of culture and the loss of meaning. For these eminent theorists as for social agents, these critiques are all intertwined.

2.   Federation of French labor unions (affiliated with the French Communist party)

3.   That is, the great, acerbic, and highly controversial twentieth-century French novelist.—Translator's note

4.   For our present purposes, we are leaving aside the convenient but difficult-to-verify hypothesis that public opinion is "manipulated" by the media. In all likelihood, the media (especially television) convey conflicting representations. One is soothing: Rich people are just like us, money can't buy happiness, France is blessed with the best of everything, people are wonderful, etc. The other is disturbing: The world is a horrible, dangerous, violent place engulfed in crisis; poverty is rampant; the future of the planet is in jeopardy, etc. Television doubtless manipulates opinion—but every which way.

CHAPTER 6

The Social Distribution of Feelings of Injustice

JUDGMENTS OF JUSTICE are the product of an axiological rationality: The agents examine the "pure" principles and combine them to elaborate their moral reasoning. However, these judgments are affected by the social and cultural conditions in which workers are placed. Although the "priority of the just" governs many moral judgments, they are also decisively influenced by living and working conditions, interests, groups, and cultural identities. To analyze how norms of justice are parsed by social conditions, we need a method that can identify and measure statistical correlations between the agents' evaluations and the various aspects of their social situation. This chapter, in an effort to understand how judgments of justice are distributed in the social realm, is based on the findings of a questionnaire survey.[1]

Apparently, French society is no longer experienced as being ruled by class; to a considerable degree, feelings of justice fail to fit the ideological pattern of the class-conflict model (Dubet/Martuccelli 1998). This state of affairs has two consequences. The first is an extension of the field of inequalities perceived as unjust. For example, although inequalities based on age or gender have always existed, their visibility increases when the social realm is no longer described as a "simple" hierarchy between social groups defined by their position in the system of production (Fitoussi/Rosanvallon 1996). The second consequence involves the mechanisms controlling judgments of justice, which become pragmatic rather than political or ideological: The agents judge their personal situation rather than that of their social group, applying the principle most apt to give meaning to their individual experience. As a result, the unique individual context becomes the overriding determinant of assessments of justice, pushing ideological allegiances and class consciousness into the background.

The Distribution of Injustices and Social Status

A class-based breakdown of injustices shows a connection between positions in the social structure and moral tenets, and several classic empirical studies describe the tendency of the upper classes to valorize merit and autonomy and that of the working class to valorize the principle of equality (Selznick 1969; Kellerhals/Coenen-Huther/Modak 1988). The "ruling class" believes in the justice of the social order. They are conservatives, and their allegiance to merit leads them to impute the workers' woes to a character flaw rather than to the social system (Lerner 1986; Bègue 1998). Inversely, the working class is more sensitive to the injustice of society as a whole (Hamilton/Rytina 1980). They are egalitarians, blaming their tribulations on an unjust social system. Our findings, however, do not fully corroborate this breakdown.

A Loose Connection Between Justice
Principles and Social Stratification

Although conceptions of justice do vary with social group, the variation is slight and not systematic. While certain disparities persist at the two ends of the social spectrum, there is a genuine consensus on a certain number of issues. Broadly speaking, class differences are less about preferences for such and such a principle than about the objects to which, and the ways in which, the principles are applied.

Elements of differentiation. The higher one climbs on the social ladder, the more legitimate inequalities in income seem to be. In our survey 40.8 percent of managerial and senior staff, as against 16.3 percent of blue-collar workers and the sample mean of 24.8 percent, find the salary gap between cashiers and sales managers justified. An executive's propensity to approve of a salary gap in his own favor attests to his allegiance to a model of personal success that prizes dynamism and the ability to make the most of one's opportunities. Talent-based inequalities seem legitimate as long as the fundamental equality of the players is respected and the chances are the same for everyone. On the other hand, executives are more critical of the effect of social inequalities on scholastic achievement, but they feel that if everyone can compete freely on the talent market, the wealth accruing to the winners becomes less of an outrage. This is why the income levels to which individuals take offense rise as a function of social standing: Blue-collar workers consider "indecent" a monthly salary of 6,000 or more, executives and company heads 10,000 or more.

Finally, the "class struggle" obtains in the truly significant opposition between company heads and the rest of the gainfully employed population: Of company heads, 58.3 percent find the pay disparities within their company fair, as against only 14.2 percent of blue-collar workers. Likewise, only company heads are more likely than average to approve of renewing a temporary employment contract several times before granting an employee a permanent job. The self-employed[2] are the most in favor of giving precedence, in offering continuing education courses, to the most deserving employees or the ones who contribute the most to their companies, rather than to those who simply request a course. Thus, the self-employed, and company heads in particular, appear to be the most strongly attached to the principle of merit.

Elements of consensus. However, merit is not valued only by the ruling class, or equality only by the working class. On each of these principles, there are distinct elements of consensus between the various social groups as well. For example, there is fairly widespread agreement on the "functional" legitimacy of just inequalities and on the lower limit of morally acceptable inequalities. The distribution of the responses to our question on the earnings disparity between doctors and cashiers reveals a consensus on functional inequalities. Because a doctor fulfills a recognized social function useful to everyone, it is generally agreed that she is serving the common weal, so this inequality is grounded in civic values. A sales executive, on the other hand, is always suspected of contributing little to society (see Table 6.1).

Moreover, all occupations agree on the minimum acceptable monthly compensation (around 1,000). They refer to the same conception of "primary goods." A basic wage is one that enables a person to live decently, regardless of any calculation of merit or difficulty. So agreement on the legitimacy of certain inequalities, social integration, and a living wage may be said to provide a shared foundation for the conception of inequalities.

Opposition between the "top" and "bottom" of the social scale fails to explain certain differences in arbitrating between equality and merit. All socioeconomic classes find it legitimate for workers in certain occupations to retire early: Across the board, between 70 percent and 80 percent of our respondents share this opinion. Answers to the question "Do you find it right that academic qualifications should be a prerequisite for positions of responsibility?" actually turned out to be a sort of textbook case of statistical independence between two variables (see Table 6.2).

All of the foregoing questions weigh merit against equality, and in each case, the workers' socioprofessional differences fail to explain their differences of opinion.

Table 6.1 Judgments of Wage Differentials

Survey Question: A doctor earns four times as much as a cashier. In your opinion, this gap is:

Occupation	Not Answered	Too Small	Fair	Too Large
Farmer	0.0	2.8	62.5	34.7
Craftsman/Shopkeeper	0.0	6.9	72.4	20.7
Company Head	4.2	0.0	66.7	29.2
Executive, Brainworker	2.5	8.9	61.1	27.4
Intermediate Profession	2.0	4.0	61.4	32.7
White-Collar Worker	0.7	4.1	66.7	28.5
Blue-Collar Worker	1.5	4.2	54.4	39.9
Whole Sample	1.7	4.6	61.6	32.1

Survey Question: A sales executive earns four times as much as a cashier. In your opinion, this gap is:

Occupation	Not Answered	Too Small	Fair	Too Large
Farmer	0.0	0.0	23.6	76.4
Craftsman/Shopkeeper	0.0	6.9	48.3	44.8
Company Head	4.2	0.0	54.2	41.6
Executive, Brainworker	3.2	1.9	40.8	54.1
Intermediate Profession	3.0	0.0	17.8	79.2
White-Collar Worker	0.7	1.0	24.4	73.9
Blue-Collar Worker	0.9	0.6	16.3	82.2
Whole Sample	1.7	1.0	24.8	72.5

Attachment to the principle of autonomy is not confined to a particular socioprofessional group, though it is true that the upper echelons of society are more likely to prioritize the attainment of personal fulfillment through their work (see Table 6.3).

Yet this observation in no way detracts from the legitimacy accorded to the principle of autonomy: It simply attests to a form of personal investment in one's work that largely depends on how much fulfillment it can provide, as we shall see below. On the other hand, the *right* to regard one's work in terms of one's personal interests and aspirations is universally acknowledged (see Table 6.4).

So the idea that continuing education courses should be offered to those who want them rather than to those who deserve them or who contribute most to the company is endorsed across the board. What is more, the order of the responses is virtually the reverse of that of the responses to the previous question about what is the most important aspect of work. After intermediate professions, white-collar workers prove the most strongly attached to the principle of autonomy. In their eyes,

**Table 6.2 Attitudes Toward Academic Achievement
as Justifying Positions of Responsibility**

Survey Question: Do you find it right that academic qualifications should be a prerequisite for positions of responsibility?

	N/A	No	Yes
Farmer	2.8	69.4	27.8
Craftsman/Shopkeeper	6.9	65.5	27.6
Company Head	0.0	58.3	41.7
Executive, Brainworker	1.9	61.2	36.9
Intermediate Profession	0.0	68.3	31.7
White-Collar Worker	1.0	66.7	32.3
Blue-Collar Worker	0.3	63.4	36.3
Whole Sample	1.4	64.7	33.9

Table 6.3 Importance of Aspects of Employment for Personal Satisfaction

Survey Question: What is most important to you about your job?

	Making Money	Being Part of Society and Having a Normal Life	Finding Personal Fulfillment at Work
Farmer	33.3	12.5	54.2
Craftsman/Shopkeeper	37.9	10.3	51.8
Company Head	41.7	0.0	58.3
Executive, Brainworker	19.1	17.8	63.1
Intermediate Profession	21.8	13.9	64.3
White-Collar Worker	34.6	26.6	38.8
Blue-Collar Worker	53.8	22.7	23.5
Whole Sample	36.9	21.2	41.9

neither individual merit nor productive contribution suffices to justify entitlement to take continued education courses, which should correspond to the personal aspirations of those who apply for them.

Shared principles in different contexts. The remaining elements of differentiation do not concern the degree of allegiance to the various principles of justice. Merit and equality are valued by all occupational groups, but in different contexts and in respect of different objects that involve different "spheres" of justice (Hochschild 1981; Toernblom/Foa 1983; Walzer 1997). Blue-collar workers advocate equality when it offers them status-based guarantees. This group, followed by the intermediate professions, is the

**Table 6.4 Attitudes on Who Should Be Offered
Continuing Education Opportunities**

*Survey Question: In your opinion, which employees should be given preference
in offering continuing education courses?*

	Those Who Request It	Those Who Deserve It	Those Who Contribute Most to the Company	Other
Farmer	59.7	18.1	12.5	4.2
Craftsman/Shopkeeper	41.4	27.6	17.2	0.0
Company Head	50.0	25.0	20.8	4.2
Executive, Brainworker	66.9	13.4	5.1	12.7
Intermediate Profession	76.2	11.9	4.0	6.9
White-Collar Worker	74.9	13.2	6.2	4.3
Blue-Collar Worker	61.0	23.0	11.5	3.9
Whole Sample	67.4	16.9	8.3	5.5

The responses do not total 100 percent because some respondents did not answer the
question.

most inclined to find seniority-based compensation fairer than compensation based on on-the-job merit and performance. On the other hand, they
endorse merit more strongly with regard to redistribution: Whereas only
13.7 percent of the respondents find it unfair for part of their salary to be
redistributed to persons in need, 20.5 percent of the blue-collar workers
object to redistribution. A full 62.4 percent of the total sample find it unfair that certain welfare recipients draw benefits nearly equivalent to the
minimum wage; 64.7 percent of blue-collar workers and 61.2 percent of
white-collar workers agree. Blue-collar workers adhere to the work ethic
that calls for observance of the rules of merit, and it is in the name of this
ethic that they stigmatize "the undeserving poor" and "welfare queens."
But they display a sense of solidarity, too, in favoring the protection of
the most vulnerable and the safeguards for aging employees.

At the upper end of the social hierarchy, this picture is reversed:
Equality is applied less frequently to status-based benefits and more frequently to justifying redistribution. In the survey 76.4 percent of executives and 91.7 percent of company heads find seniority-based pay unjust,
as against 71.5 percent of our aggregate sample. Inversely, only 5.1 percent
of executives find it illegitimate that part of their salary should be redistributed to the needy, and neither executives nor company heads stand
out from the rest in finding it more or less unjust that cumulative welfare
benefits should amount to almost the minimum wage. Hence, it would
be simplistic to reduce upper-class representations of justice to a social
Darwinist meritocracy in which only the most talented or dynamic deserve

to be rewarded. Executives, like blue-collar workers, hold composite conceptions of a just world, for they are divided between "morality and money," between equality and merit. They combine a solidarity-oriented conception of redistribution with an individualist endorsement of success (Lamont 1995).

Injustices Experienced in Different Contexts

If social background and status fail to explain individual preferences for one or another of the principles of justice, they are even less apt to account for the way workers judge their own experience. Agents interpret their situation using *the whole set* of principles that are at their disposal. All socioeconomic groups consider themselves victims of injustices in terms of equality, merit, and autonomy. They all have their own respective reasons for frustration based on these three principles, and these reasons have to do with the issues and problems besetting their respective occupational realms (see Table 6.5).

Differences at the extremities. Clear-cut differences between socioeconomic groups are only apparent at the furthermost poles of social stratification. In between the two, the incidence of subjective injustice proves surprisingly homogeneous, as attested by the overall indices of injustice of the various socioeconomic groups.[3]

The disparities here between socioeconomic groups are slight. Only company heads show a markedly lower index than the others. Blue-collar workers, for their part, cite the greatest number of reasons for feeling ill used. But this working-class specificity is relatively inconsequential

Table 6.5 Concentration of Feelings of Injustice

Survey Question: In your opinion, which employees should be given preference in offering continuing education courses?

	Overall Index of Injustice
Farmer	5.69
Craftsman/Shopkeeper	4.41
Company Head	**2.58**
Executive, Brainworker	**4.25**
Intermediate Profession	5.26
White-Collar Worker	5.02
Blue-Collar Worker	**6.15**
Whole Sample	5.23

Bold type designates statistically significant deviations.

because it is not homogeneous and tends to refer to situations of cumulative social hardships.

When asked, "In today's society, do you think you are: relatively privileged, relatively mistreated, or living under normal conditions as a result of your work?," barely 8.1 percent of the workers answered that they were mistreated. This low percentage shows that, in the minds of our respondents, being mistreated applies only to an extreme violation of fundamental equality, the state of being a social outcast. Blue-collar workers tend to consider themselves mistreated more frequently than others, but this propensity remains slim, concerning only 14 percent of the group. "All other things being equal," the two most significant variables of perceived mistreatment are finding one's work demeaning and being subjected to poor working conditions. Aside from the arduousness of the labor itself, then, loss of pride in working-class identity appears to be a key factor here. The sum of these two factors brings to 36.4 the percentage of employees with inferior qualifications who feel mistreated. So there does seem to be a typically working-class brand of perceived injustice associated with the humiliation of inferior status and the arduousness of working conditions.

On the other hand, the tendency to harbor this sentiment increases significantly as social disadvantages add up. The cumulative effect is a truly profound feeling of injustice. Segmenting the sample, we find a working-class population who find their jobs demeaning, feel discriminated against at work due to their cultural background, and are able to land only insecure temp agency jobs. Seventy-one percent of this subgroup feel mistreated. Manual labor in and of itself does not account for this feeling, but the sense of injustice "explodes" among manual laborers when adversities are compounded.

Equality. Frustration related to the principle of equality cuts across the entire sample of socioeconomic groups whenever they are confronted with another "caste's" contempt. The feeling of being despised is not confined to the condescending attitude of the affluent towards the working class: Between 25 and 35 percent of all workers in every socioprofessional group said they were victims of contempt, and only company heads were by and large spared (12.5 percent) (see Table 6.6).

Contempt is not simply an effect of the social structure. It is endemic to a wide variety of workplace situations and occupational sectors. As Table 6.6 shows, certain sources of contempt cut across the board. One's superiors are the chief source of subjective contempt for all the groups, including those in management. Only those who have no direct superiors, the self-employed and company heads, are truly spared this experience. No one is entirely safe from friction with their higher-ups. Conflictual relations are inevitably an opportunity for reasserting differences in rank

Table 6.6 Conceptions of Others' Demeaning Attitudes

	N/A	Coworkers	Superiors	Customers	Service Users	Friends and Family	The Media	Society
Farmer	66.7	1.4	0.0	2.8	2.8	0.0	23.6	26.4
Craftsman/Shopkeeper	75.9	3.4	0.0	17.2	6.9	3.4	6.9	3.4
Company Head	87.5	4.2	8.3	4.2	0.0	0.0	0.0	0.0
Executive, Brainworker	73.2	6.4	12.1	5.7	4.5	0.6	6.4	6.4
Intermediate Profession	71.3	6.9	13.9	8.9	8.9	0.0	3.0	3.0
White-Collar Worker	6.8	9.1	18.2	14.6	5.5	2.2	2.6	6.7
Blue-Collar Worker	66.2	7.9	22.4	9.1	2.7	3.0	1.5	8.8
Whole Sample	68.0	7.4	16.2	10.2	4.6	1.8	4.2	7.9

The responses can add up to more than 100 percent because each respondent was allowed to choose more than one response.

and reactivating the "pecking order" that simultaneously unites and divides the various categories of employees. The risk of being subjected to coworkers' contempt is even more widespread, except among farmers and craftspersons/shopkeepers, who often work alone—as though the absence of coworkers were the only protection against peer contempt!

Other forms of contempt are more specific to certain groups and occupational sectors. Customer/user contempt afflicts those who deal directly with the public on a daily basis: teachers, social workers, nurses, employees in retail and services, etc. Generalized contempt, imputed to the media and society, is not reserved for those who possess the least "symbolic capital." Naturally, it affects people whose work has historically been viewed as degrading, like farmers and manual laborers, who have watched the dignity and pride associated with their class erode within recent memory. But it is also felt by those subjected to the symbolic decline of their institutions, the ongoing competition with the "hot" culture of show business and the media, and the fading of the sacred aura surrounding a social function long identified with the universal values of the public weal, the state, the nation, culture, progress, and reason.

Merit. The arithmetic of unacknowledged merit is common to all occupational groups because there is no single standard for measuring effort and because all occupations require some degree of personal investment (see Table 6.7).

In Table 6.7, the percentages of those who deemed the question inapplicable to their case give us an occupational breakdown of pay satisfaction. This brings to light another contrast between blue-collar workers and company heads, the former citing the greatest number of reasons for feeling underpaid, and the latter being the most satisfied in terms of every comparison proposed. Outside of this opposition, only 10 percent to 20 percent of the respondents in the remaining socioprofessional groups feel fully satisfied. In view of their working conditions and occupational hazards, blue-collars feel their merit is ignored; white-collar staff fall within the average range of satisfaction, except as regards occupational hazards. Those in intermediate professions feel their salaries are not a fair reflection of their qualifications and responsibilities, while executives are most likely to give responses close to the sample mean, except that fewer of them complain about their salaries. Shopkeepers also hover about the mean, save for comparisons based on seniority and the opposite sex. Lastly, farmers fall in with laborers' complaints about working conditions and occupational hazards.

The standard of merit, the nature of the effort for which recompense is expected, varies from one occupational sphere to another, depending on their respective exigencies and constraints (Godechot/Gurgand 2000). This is why merit can never be a "value" confined to a single social group, even though its formalization may vary from one group to another. As

Table 6.7 Reasons for Feeling Underpaid

	N/A	Compared to Coworkers	Compared to Working Conditions	Compared to Occupational Hazards	Compared to Academic Qualifications	Compared to Responsibilities	Compared to Coworkers with the Same Duties	Compared to Coworkers with More Seniority	Compared to Coworkers of the Opposite Sex	Compared to Superiors	Compared to Personal Investment in One's Work
Farmer	8.3	70.8	72.2	50.0	19.4	54.2	23.6	15.3	11.1	9.7	72.2
Craftsman/Shopkeeper	20.7	51.7	48.3	37.9	17.2	37.9	27.6	6.9	3.4	3.4	55.2
Company Head	58.3	29.2	20.8	20.8	12.5	20.8	16.7	12.5	4.2	8.3	29.2
Executive, Brainworker	19.1	42.0	26.8	28.0	37.6	54.1	28.0	22.3	12.7	36.9	59.2
Intermediate Profession	12.9	57.4	41.6	43.6	51.5	63.4	32.7	22.8	9.9	44.6	56.4
White-Collar Worker	12.9	54.8	42.3	26.6	37.6	43.8	34.7	21.5	13.4	46.2	50.2
Blue-Collar Worker	7.3	58.9	64.4	50.5	29.6	38.1	38.7	28.4	16.6	55.0	49.8
Whole Sample	13.0	54.9	48.2	36.9	34.3	45.2	33.5	22.8	13.3	43.1	53.1

Each respondent was allowed to choose more than one response.

a result, it is easier to understand why the social perimeter of feelings of exploitation is so elastic. Subjective exploitation, a radical form of the feeling of unacknowledged merit, is always based on a perceived imbalance between contribution and compensation. In the absence of a universal standard for measuring effort, people in any occupation can feel exploited. Furthermore, this feeling refers as much to an "objective economic infrastructure" as to the strictly subjective forms of fatigue. Once again, although all the socioprofessional groups develop the feeling of being exploited, albeit to varying degrees, the factors that arouse or aggravate that feeling are specific to each of them.

For example, blue-collar workers feel exploited because their work is hard and physically exhausting and the hours are long, and because working-class tradition tends to interpret this suffering in terms of exploitation. A full 46.5 percent say they are exploited, but the proportion rises to 60 percent when they compare their wages to their working conditions, 72 percent where working conditions are deplorable, 74.5 percent where the work is dirty, and to 67.5 percent if they are unionized. And yet symbolic dimensions also figure prominently: The fact of feeling despised or experiencing tension with superiors or moral harassment amplifies the laborer's propensity to feel exploited.

Executives, for their part, are more inclined to feel exploited if they feel that they are poorly paid, that bonuses are not fairly distributed, or that they are disparaged in the media. For members of the intermediate professions, finding one's work tiring and stressful exacerbates feelings of exploitation. And among white-collar staff, a long workday or work week, scheduling privileges accorded to certain coworkers, and feeling looked down upon by coworkers significantly magnify the impression they have of being exploited.

Autonomy. Though not all occupational groups attach the same importance to self-fulfillment in and through their work, all of them have an ambivalent relationship to autonomy, which they regard at once as an accomplishment and as an obstacle to that accomplishment. The desire to assert one's subjectivity at work cuts across all social classes, whose sources of fulfillment vary according to the nature of their occupational activities (see Table 6.8).

To wit, nonsalaried workers prize the autonomy and inherent values of their profession. Farmers like their work because the results thereof are "concrete" and "tangible," because the work is varied, and because they are autonomous (47.2 percent say farming allows "scope for initiative"). But they are the most liable to suffer from fatigue and isolation. Small-scale self-employed workers give fairly similar responses. But they also derive satisfaction from customer relations (69 percent), while exhibiting an above-average tendency to find their work tiring.

Table 6.8 Reasons for Liking and Disliking One's Job

Sources of Job Satisfaction	Varied	Scope for Initiative	Useful	Human Relations	Constructive Pressure	Tangible Results	Pleasant Atmosphere	Responsibility
Farmer	68.1	47.2	34.7	25.0	1.4	51.4	15.3	37.5
Craftsman/Shopkeeper	34.5	34.5	13.8	69.0	0.0	41.4	20.7	55.2
Company Head	41.7	41.7	12.5	54.2	8.3	29.2	29.2	83.3
Executive, Brainworker	49.0	54.1	33.8	65.6	4.5	16.6	13.4	48.4
Intermediate Professions	57.4	47.5	37.6	75.2	5.9	10.9	16.8	37.6
White-Collar Worker	42.8	30.6	24.2	64.6	4.8	15.8	35.4	33.0
Blue-Collar Worker	40.5	25.4	25.7	32.0	5.1	35.6	39.3	23.3
Whole Sample	45.6	35.3	27.1	53.4	4.7	24.4	29.9	34.5

Each respondent was allowed to choose more than one response.

Table 6.8 Reasons for Liking and Disliking One's Job (continued)

Sources of Job Dissatisfaction	Monotonous	Insufficient Scope for Initiative	Fatiguing	Dirty	Lack of Human Relations	Unpleasant Atmosphere	No Responsibility	Causes Anxiety
Farmer	2.8	1.4	76.4	26.4	12.5	4.2	1.4	31.9
Craftsman/Shopkeeper	17.2	0.0	69.0	10.3	0.0	0.0	0.0	27.6
Company Head	8.3	0.0	37.5	4.2	4.2	0.0	4.2	29.2
Executive, Brainworker	9.6	3.8	42.0	3.2	3.8	10.8	3.8	34.4
Intermediate Professions	8.9	8.9	49.5	5.0	1.0	11.9	7.9	42.6
White-Collar Worker	28.0	14.4	41.1	9.6	5.3	16.3	14.6	19.4
Blue-Collar Worker	34.7	16.0	62.8	38.1	4.8	12.4	16.0	11.2
Whole Sample	23.3	11.3	51.2	17.7	4.9	12.4	11.4	22.2

Each respondent was allowed to choose more than one response.

Executives and company heads find in their responsibilities a vital source of professional accomplishment, but also a source of stress and anxiety. Managerial staff, increasingly assigned to advisory rather than executive posts, also bemoan the mounting competition among their peers (only 13.4 percent of them checked "pleasant atmosphere" among the reasons for liking their jobs).

The intermediate professions are torn between being "happy" about their work on account of the variety of activities involved, the scope for initiative, and quality of human relations, on the one hand, and being "unhappy" about the "anxiety" caused by those same relations. White-collar staff derive satisfaction from the workplace atmosphere and human relations but suffer from the lack of initiative and autonomy. Blue-collar workers often find their jobs dirty, monotonous, and fatiguing but also "sociable" and rich in tangible results: The survey shows that 35.6 percent of them say "you can see the results," as against 24.4 percent of our respondents all told. *On the whole, workers are both happy and unhappy about their jobs, though the various occupational groups do not base their arithmetic of happiness on the same aspects of work.*

A "Pragmatic" Approach to the Principles of Justice

The "theories of justice" adopted by workers are only loosely connected to their social position, while their perceptions of injustice basically seem to be linked to the nature of their work and the context of their workplace experience. Hence, our data suggest that feelings of justice are essentially based on a matrix of *pragmatic* considerations: Workers adopt principles of justice, not only because they are generally valid, but also because they serve to give a certain *meaning* to their work experience. More precisely, they take a moral point of view, not only because such a perspective is capable of passing the "test of general validity"—of obtaining the assent of an indefinitely large number of people (Taylor 1998)—but because it yields the most congenial explanation of their situation. Their spontaneous theories of justice depend more on their experience of work than on their social status or ideological allegiances. In other words, individuals draw up moral maps of the social realm based on their own experience. They develop a sense of justice arising out of a more subjective necessity, that of putting a positive construction on their personal identity (Joas 1999).

The Local Context of Perceived Injustice

What are the best predictors of the different perceptions of injustice? In a class-based society, perceptions of injustice would be directly linked to the "gaping" inequalities inherent in social stratification. Job status would correlate closely enough with ideological orientations to structure assessments of justice. Left-wing ideologies would offer the most vulnerable members of society a framework of egalitarian inspiration within which to denounce their sufferings as the result of class domination. The ruling classes, for their part, would develop a liberal political rationale, an ideological expression, as it were, of their belief in a just world that holds everyone responsible for her own misfortune and prohibits her from blaming it on the social system.

But our findings markedly diverge from that scenario. The variables of status and ideological positioning appear, *ceteris paribus,* largely inoperative, whilst the various characteristics of work prove, in contrast, highly explicative.

Equality. To wit, this factor serves to explain perceptions of injustice based on the principle of equality, which proceed from local, contextual injustices rather than global inequalities inherent in social stratification. All things being equal, once again, it turns out that occupation, pay, age, and gender have no more influence on the probability of declaring oneself ill treated than left/right-wing political orientation, belief in God, or union membership. The same goes for feeling oneself an object of contempt, which, *ceteris paribus,* does not seem to be connected either to status or to political allegiances, but to damaged human relations: Specifically, friction or outright conflict with one's superiors or customers or being a victim of or witness to moral harassment or racist persecution significantly augments the probability of perceived contempt. We found that the nonrecognition and arduousness of work explain *in and of themselves* the feeling of injustice based on the principle of equality, regardless of status or allegiance to a more or less egalitarian ideology.

Merit. Agents view merit, likewise, within the localized framework of their relations to coworkers and employers. Merit is not experienced collectively, much less as a consequence of a class-based representation of society. Dissatisfaction with one's pay is only marginally connected to status-related or ideological variables. Controlling for gender, age, socioprofessional group, and academic qualifications, the feeling of being underpaid for one's work depends on the level of pay itself and the onerousness of the work in question. First, the effect of pay levels is uniform: Virtually all socioprofessional groups tend to consider themselves underpaid if they earn between 871 and 1,250 a month. Beyond 2,500, the tendency to consider oneself underpaid drops off steeply in every social class. Here, unrecognized merit is a personal assessment, disconnected from any belief in a shared class destiny. The yardstick of income ambitions is unrelated to the social group to which one belongs, for pay is gauged in terms of "absolute" value. Controlling for status-related characteristics, for example, the fact of being subjected to deplorable working conditions and feeling degraded by one's work significantly increases the probability of declaring oneself underpaid.

Finally, the feeling of inequity intensifies when employers fail to play by the rules. A "no" answer to the question "Does your employer always comply with the labor code?" shows a very close correlation with feeling underpaid, whatever the respondent's social status, the onerousness of his work, or his political orientation. Unfair wages are not "class wages," but wages that fall short of what the worker deems the heavy price of having to bear conditions of employment that flout the rules of labor law.

The feeling of being exploited scarcely bears any relation to political orientation or ideology. While an extreme left-wing stance is very slightly significant, being unionized or believing in God is of no consequence; nor is socioprofessional group, level of education, or earnings, age, or sex. Contextual elements, on the other hand, figure prominently: Workers who complain of deplorable working conditions, degrading work, friction with their superiors, and their employer's flouting the labor code are manifestly more inclined to feel exploited.

Autonomy. The sense of being subjected to encroachments on one's autonomy is by and large unrelated to a representation of society in which those on top, holding the bulk of the power, enjoy a de facto autonomy permitting greater subjective involvement in their work, while those at the bottom, who are heavily dependent, enjoy only the side benefits of work: sociable staff relations, family life, leisure-time pursuits, and the like.

This image is not inaccurate, but incomplete. One of the questions we put to our respondents was whether their work corresponded to what they felt like doing. The responses are a telltale index of self-fulfillment because they measure the degree of subjective appropriation of one's work. Unsurprisingly, our analysis of these responses shows that a sense of accomplishment is more easily acquired by executives and company heads than blue-collar workers or lower-level white-collar employees. Although employment that corresponds to one's education is highly significant in this regard, political orientation is of no consequence. On the other hand, a certain number of contextual factors have a non-negligible effect. The probability that workers will say they "chose" their work steadily declines with worsening working conditions and increases to the extent that they are allowed to set their working hours themselves. The same goes for recognition of one's work. Feeling appreciated heightens the propensity to feel that the work satisfies one's desires, whereas those who complain of racist or sexist remarks in the workplace are less likely to report satisfaction. Despite pronounced differences between professions, these various contributory factors have an across-the-board impact and exert an independent influence on a worker's capacity to experience his work as a subjective accomplishment. Thus, the socioprofessional pyramid cannot be reduced to an opposition between a subjectivizing apex and an alienated base.

An examination of the factors of stress and fatigue leads to identical conclusions. Here again, status variables are only slightly significant, as is avowed political orientation. While stress tends to be more of a middle-class phenomenon and fatigue a working-class affliction, the same processes are involved in their production. Work intensity; lack of recognition; and substandard workplace relations with peers, superiors, or customers prove to be influential factors in either case. There is a correlation between hearing racist remarks at work and feeling fatigued, while a perceived loss of prestige or harassment at work heightens the propensity to feel "stressed." Fatigue is more pronounced among those who don't set their own working hours, while stress is exacerbated by friction with one's superiors.

In the final analysis, feelings of injustice stem more from a personal *situation* than from a collective *condition*. To be sure, the work situations to which these judgments apply are not randomly distributed in the social sphere, which is the reason why the distribution of subjective injustice is not independent of social stratification. The link between stratification and perceived injustice is *strong,* but *indirect*; workers apply their assessments of justice not to social inequalities as such, but to their work experience itself.

Conceptions of Social Justice and Workplace Experience

While it is easy to understand that feelings of justice at work are closely connected to workplace experiences, one might imagine that more general conceptions of social justice depend on broader contexts, both on positions in the social structure and on ideological and political frameworks. Were this the case, class positions and political opinions might figure more prominently. However, experiences in the workplace have an independent impact that in many cases goes beyond that of status or ideological allegiances. Assessments of justice are also, and above all, normative productions designed to give meaning to a situation experienced.

Equality of opportunity. The sense of equality varies by social category solely when applied to equality of opportunity prior to the realization of merit. Other things being equal, the higher a worker's income, the more likely he or she is to condone as legitimate the pay gap between a sales executive and a cashier. Likewise, a right-of-center political stance augments the probability of sharing this acceptance. And yet, certain factors of the workplace experience *itself* have an independent effect, irrespective of earnings, status, and political orientation. Those who consider themselves underpaid, discriminated against, and looked down upon are more apt to opine that the remuneration of talent is a pipedream. It is this experience of inequity that gives rise to calls for egalitarian treatment backed up by status-based guarantees, the only remedy for what are perceived as arbitrary mechanisms of distribution. Conversely, as high-earners are more inclined to believe they themselves are the "cause" of their success, they are more favorable to the free play of aptitudes.

Nuanced combinations of equality and merit. Working-class circles value equality when it comes to career advancement, and merit when it comes to income redistribution. This opposition is progressively reversed the higher one climbs on the social ladder. One of the most telltale questions we asked was whether seniority-based pay is fairer than merit-based pay. Other things being equal, neither social status nor political orientation directly affects the response. The tendency to valorize merit increases, however, with the degree of commitment to one's work; that is, with the number of hours regularly spent working. The more they feel underpaid or exploited, the more respondents will valorize merit. Views on redistribution exhibit the same patterns. Political leanings are more significant here: A left-wing standpoint increases one's propensity to find it fair that beneficiaries of state aid should draw benefits nearly equivalent to the minimum wage, or that part of one's pay should be redistributed to the needy. But experienced injustices have an independent effect. Feeling exploited raises the probability of being opposed to the principle of redistribution, as does feeling underpaid. In neither case are the status variables (occupation, qualifications, pay bracket) significant. In short, the propensity to feel society should be organized in a way that takes merit more clearly into account is linked to personal experience of unrecognized merit. That experience gives meaning to the injustices and privations endured.

This result is counterintuitive. While we would instinctively expect those who feel exploited to be more egalitarian and more disposed to denounce exploitation, it turns out on the contrary that being unfairly treated, and being aware of it, is not enough to prioritize equality. Also necessary is an ideology linking experienced injustice to a collective condition and to the social system. These last two prerequisites do not seem to be met nowadays; instead, the experience of merit-related injustice tends to induce workers to call for a "new deal" that would provide for their individual self-preservation (Della Fave 1974).

However, nobody fully believes that merit alone is capable of guaranteeing social justice, if only because it does not safeguard the most vulnerable members of society and because the "chances" of having talent are not the same for everyone. Workers are, then, ambivalent. Members of working-class categories hold egalitarian views on work because their lack of autonomy in the organization of workplace operations leads them to feel they have less control over their career paths. They are more inclined to privilege job-promotion rules based on such stable and predictable status criteria as seniority (Selznick 1969). On the other hand, given their proximity to marginalized groups, they develop strategies of distinction that lead them to stigmatize beneficiaries of state aid (Élias 1997). Hence their meritocratic sensibility with regard to the redistribution of wealth. Conversely, the upper classes have greater power at their disposal and "believe" more readily that their fate hinges on their own actions. Consequently, they are more willing to rely on merit alone, while the symbolic distance they maintain from marginalized groups enables them to be magnanimous about matters of redistribution.

Situational autonomy. It is doubtless in the realm of autonomy that agents show the most pronounced tendency to take a pragmatic standpoint on the rules of justice. This is evidenced, once again, by responses to the question "What is most important to you about your work?" Our respondents had three answers to choose from: "making money," "being part of society and leading a normal life," or "self-fulfillment at work." The third choice, of course, reflects a strong attachment to the principle of autonomy, and we have already seen how the upper classes are set apart by a marked preference for that response. Here again, assuming "all other things are equal" enables us to substantially relativize the effects of status and political sympathies, which have no influence on the responses. The propensity to valorize personal self-fulfillment at work depends on several factors. The first has to do with organizational autonomy: Ample scope for initiative and the freedom to set one's own working hours are both highly significant. Further, it depends on the recognition accorded to the employee: Doing a rewarding job doubles the likelihood of choosing the response "self-fulfillment at work." This interplay of factors shows that the attachment to the principle of autonomy does not hinge on status or ideology, but on the effective possibility of subjectively identifying with one's work. Here, workers adopt the moral perspective most conducive to conferring a positive meaning on their experience: The more self-fulfillment they get out of their jobs, the more apt they are to prioritize self-fulfillment. Those whose work is less creative and autonomous are more apt to prioritize other aspects of work, since a stronger attachment to autonomy would be demeaning to themselves.

Priorities based on criteria unrelated to status. Status-related variables do not explain the variance when it comes to evaluating the role of age or qualifications in the distribution of earnings or responsibility. In neither case does a worker's position in the social hierarchy impact her preference for equality or merit. *Ceteris paribus,* we find that only the respondents' ages allow us to predict their responses to the question, "Is it fair that young employees should be paid less than older employees?" The youngest are most liable to disapprove of this inequality. Likewise, educational level is more closely related than status or political orientation to affirming that academic qualifications should be a prerequisite for positions of responsibility.

All these outcomes lead to the same conclusion: The inequalities built into the social structure do not in and of themselves dictate workers' perceptions and conceptions of justice. Workers examine their own personal situations first, and based on those observations they construct normative images of a just society that will give their experience a positive signification. As to the attitudes most clearly associated with certain social groups, they can be explained not by a shared representation of the social structure, but by the similarity of the personal situations in which the individual group members' judgments arise.

Perceived Injustices and "Off-the-Job" Inequalities

What are the roles of qualifications, gender, ethnic origin, and job insecurity in the formation of perceptions of injustice? At first glance, these inequalities cut across all the various socioprofessional groups, for one can be a man or a woman, an immigrant or a "nonethnic" French national, more or less qualified, with a more or less steady job, at the "top" or at the "bottom" of the social pyramid. In point of fact, these distinctions run diagonally or "on a slant," for there are clearly more immigrants, high school dropouts, and temporary employees at the bottom than at the top of the social pyramid, just as there are more women in low-tier jobs than in the top or middle echelons of management. But these diverse variables can be isolated by methods of statistical analysis, and the resulting figures show they substantially influence perceptions of injustice.

The Lost Nobility of the College Graduate

The "inflation" of diplomas and degrees, partly an outgrowth of increased mass access to education, has not been accompanied by parallel growth in the number of qualified jobs. Ever since the mid-1970s, each wave of newcomers to the job market has been more qualified than the preceding generation, but the number of management-level jobs has stagnated. University degrees have been "depreciating" as a result: They no longer guarantee attainment of the social standing to which the baby boomers could realistically aspire (Boudon 1973). And since the mid-1970s, first-time job seekers have been faced with a less congenial employment market with less scope for upward mobility on the strength of their academic credentials (Chauvel 1998; Goldthorpe/Mills 2004). For many, this situation is all the harder to accept in light of the fact that French society continues to bear the stamp of a republican meritocracy in which qualifications-based upward mobility used to be a realistic prospect as well as a norm of relations between the generations. The generations entering the job market after what is known in France as the "golden decade" (1965–1975) have had to reconcile this legacy with a changed economy (see Table 6.9).

The higher one's academic qualifications, the more likely one is to feel underpaid in terms of those qualifications. Qualifications largely dictate aspirations, and the unqualified make a virtue of necessity by accepting lower wages and less prestigious social positions. For the others, a university degree works like a "title of nobility." The holder feels entitled to a sort of social upgrade (Bourdieu 1989). But this "entitlement" is crumbling: Nearly half of those with university degrees are dissatisfied with their pay. The odds of considering oneself well paid in terms of one's qualifications rise with social standing and salary bracket, but fall with the level of academic qualifications. For instance, only 12 percent of those who earn more than 3,500 per month feel underpaid in terms of their qualifications. Another 23.5 percent of those with three or more years of higher education under their belts feel the same way. In other words, university degrees give rise to salary and status aspirations that structurally exceed the real prospects in present-day France.

Naturally, having a job for which one feels overqualified radicalizes this tendency. Those with degrees for 3 or more years of higher education are 1.7 times as likely as vocational school graduates to feel underpaid in terms of their qualifications when they feel their job actually *corresponds* to their qualifications, and 2.7 times as likely when they don't. Under these circumstances, the phenomenon of educational inflation *cum* overqualification creates a prodigious breeding ground for relative frustration. A steadily growing cohort of college graduates are now doomed to see their

Table 6.9 Views on How Well Earnings Reflect Qualifications

Survey Question: Do you think your earnings correspond to your qualifications?

	No Response	*No*	*Yes*
No Qualifications	3.7	11.1	85.2
CAP/BEP* Vocational Training	1.9	26.2	71.8
High School Diploma	0.0	29.0	71.0
Two Years of Higher Education	0.0	53.1	46.9
Three or More Years of Higher Education	0.0	55.4	44.6
Whole Sample	1.3	34.3	64.4

*Certificat d'Aptitude Professionnel (Vocational Aptitude Certificate), Brevet d'Etudes Professionnelles (Vocational Studies Certificate): lowest-level vocational qualifications in France.

professional hopes dashed when they enter the job market. And the structural mechanism that produces this perceived injustice is built into French society, unlike any of the other injustices we've described thus far.

Though overqualification alone has no effect on subjective mistreatment, its influence increases when grievances pile up. Only 4 percent of those in intermediate professions feel ill treated, but the figure comes to 14.3 percent when the work doesn't match their qualifications. Overqualification is, moreover, the sole status variable with an independent impact on subjective contempt. It also seems to significantly reinforce subjective exploitation: The overqualified believe their employers are getting a good deal—and giving them a raw one. Finally, the encroachment on the overqualified employee's subjective autonomy takes the form of thwarted ambition. Regardless of position and other status-related characteristics, the very fact of being overqualified for a job increases the probability of a worker's feeling his job does not satisfy his desires or suit his tastes.

Contrary to what one might think, this devaluation of academic credentials is an incentive to adopt the "free-market" vision of a society in which individual career paths are driven by merit. *Ceteris paribus*, most overqualified workers find it fairer to base salaries on merit than on seniority, and unfair to pay young employees less. This tendency to accord greater legitimacy to on-the-job merit actually leads them to espouse views that run counter to their own interests, for they are more inclined to object when positions of responsibility are reserved for academic achievers. Here again, those whose merit goes unrecognized all the more roundly condemn any status-based prerogatives that undercut the pure recognition of talent. The overqualified are every bit as pragmatic as other workers when it comes to mustering representations of the world that justify their career paths. By championing merit, they view their difficulties from a vantage point that casts them as victims whose academic merit is undervalued.

Job Insecurity and Subjective Discrimination

For over 20 years now, the French unemployment rate has hovered between 8 percent and 10 percent. That same period has seen a marked increase in unsteady jobs, part-time work, fixed-term contracts, temp work, and the like. And yet, job insecurity in and of itself does not spoil the worker's attitude toward her work, which depends on other factors such as having a recognized profession or trade, and skills that guarantee relative autonomy in the exercise thereof. A sharp distinction should therefore be drawn between the worker's attitude towards his work and towards employment: It is not the quality of the work that is a core complaint of those with unsteady jobs, it is the precarious nature of their employment as such (Paugam 2000).

Employees without job security are not significantly more likely to feel exploited than the rest of the workforce. Of our respondents, 33.6 percent feel exploited at work: That breaks down into 31 percent for those who have never been on unemployment versus 42.3 percent for those who have been on unemployment at least once in their working lives. But this difference is not statistically significant and actually disappears if we control for various factors of status: pay, working conditions, and so on. The same goes for terms of employment. Employees on short-term contracts are no more apt to feel exploited that those with permanent jobs. Temp agency workers are the most inclined to feel exploited, but that difference is not statistically significant either. Nor does the fact of working full-time or part-time—by choice or not—have a significant impact on subjective exploitation. Thus, job insecurity in and of itself does not lead workers to feel their merit is going unrecognized. It is entirely as though merit were an issue *inside* the workaday world, whereas the problems plaguing those without job security have to do with *entering* that working world. Consequently, they view their situation in terms of *discrimination.*

Workers who've been out of work for over a year at least once are singularly prone to feeling discriminated against: A full 26.8 percent of them state they've been victims of discriminatory hiring practices, as against an average 11 percent for all our respondents. There is a significant link between past experience of long-term unemployment and the sense of being a victim of discriminatory hiring. In our survey, 25.5 percent of temp workers and 17 percent of insecure jobholders say they were victims of discriminatory hiring, as against under 10 percent of steady jobholders. It is not only a matter of racial discrimination: Some workers also point to discrimination against scholastic underachievers and physical differences, such as handicaps, obesity, and the like. Here again, we find the distinction between views on employment and attitude towards work: Job insecurity really only affects the former. Generally speaking, job insecurity leads to a sense of feeling ill treated by society. This tendency is not confined to blue-collar workers, 71.4 percent of whom feel mistreated when job insecurity is compounded by a drop in status, poor working conditions, and a sense of being discriminated against. Executives and members of intermediate professions working on a part-time basis also show a significantly above-average propensity to consider themselves ill treated. Thus, job insecurity engenders a frustration that falls within the register of fundamental equality, and that experience is not confined to the working class.

An "Irreducible" Gender Divide?

Women seem to attach greater importance to interpersonal relationships at work than men do. Is this difference an effect of gender, arising out of the conditions of female socialization and internalized social stereotypes that dictate specifically female attitudes? Or should it be attributed to the specific economic spheres in which women work, their position in the hierarchy, and the types of employment in which women predominate (Maruani 2000)?

According to our findings, more women than men prioritize personal self-realization through and in their work. If we control this divergence for differences in the working conditions of women, the pattern still holds: We see that 1.4 times as many women as men chose this response. Women are more attached to the principle of autonomy: Consequently, they are more prone to complain of stress. Even if we control for status variables and different contextual factors of stress, women are still 1.5 times more likely than men to say they are suffering from stress.

Nonetheless, the gender divide is not quite as clear-cut in terms of professional accomplishment. Asked "What do you like about your job?" 25.4 percent of our female respondents picked "human relations at work," as opposed to 16.4 percent of the men. This effect remained significant when we controlled for every other difference—*except* place of work: It turns out that working in direct contact with the public, rather than in an office or factory, traveling or in the field, significantly augments the probability of prioritizing human relations at work and, above all, defies the gender divide. It might be argued that the latter effect is but the consequence of the higher concentration of women in such "relational" professions. Working in contact with the public blurs the gender line because anyone who chooses this line of work presumably finds human relations rewarding. So in this case men adopt what Carol Gilligan (1986) terms a "feminine ethic." Men doing "women's work" take on "female" attitudes.

Women, who tend to have lower-paid and less-secure jobs than men, are more likely to feel they are victims of discrimination. The results showed that 4.1 and 4.5 percent of our female respondents said they were subject to sexual discrimination in the hiring process and at work, respectively. These percentages may seem small, but they overlap with the statistically significant differentials between men and women. Furthermore, 16 percent think they are poorly paid compared to their male counterparts. Above all, they are more affected by their family situation and the difficulty of reconciling private and professional life. Other things being equal, the probability of a woman's feeling work has a harmful effect on her personal life depends on her family situation, which is not the case for a man. A woman living in a couple with children is twice as likely as a single woman to think her work has a negative impact on her personal life, whereas the same categories of men show no such variance. Likewise, the probability of job-related health problems depends on family situation for women, but not for men.

Thus, gender has three distinct effects that converge in women's experience. First, the gender divide is linked to the conditions of socialization and social models internalized by each sex. Second, this divide is related to the predominance of women working in "human relations" sectors, but in fact it has more to do with the nature of the work than with gender, for men in the same working contexts attach similar importance to human relationships. Finally, women experience a distinctive subjective discrimination and difficulty: To the extent they feel more responsible for family life than men, work poses a greater threat to the stability of their personal lives. Thus, culture, work, and the social division of labor between the sexes combine to produce a distinct gender divide.

Racial Discrimination

Racism at work or in gaining access to work leads the victims thereof to feel degraded, despised, and ill treated (Bataille 1998). While 8 percent of all our respondents find their work degrading, the figure comes to 34.2 percent for those who feel discriminated against at work on the basis of their ethnic origins, and 14 percent for those who feel, on the same basis, subject to discriminatory hiring practices. These two forms of discrimination lead 76.3 percent and 47 percent of the respective victims to feel looked down upon, as against 32.2 percent for the global set of responses to our questionnaire. And these correlations obtain even in cases of identical status and working conditions, where immigrants have the same jobs as workers "of pure French extraction."

Perceived racism has an independent effect on perceived ill treatment in present-day society. To verify this correlation, we set up a "racialization score" by adding the responses to our questions about feeling despised on account of one's ethnic origins, being the victim of racist harassment, working in an environment in which racial slurs are commonplace, and, finally, feeling the victim of discriminatory hiring or discrimination at work on the basis of one's ethnic origins. Given similar socioprofessional situations and working conditions, the probability of feeling mistreated rose by a factor of 1.3 for each additional point in the "racialization score." We found that 12 percent of those subjected to racist harassment, 18 percent of those who feel despised for their ethnic origins, and 26.3 percent of those discriminated against at work on the basis of their ethnic origins feel they are ill treated at the hands of society, as opposed to only 8 percent on average for our sample as a whole.

Generally speaking, subjective racism at work compounds subjective injustice in most of its dimensions. Though it does not significantly affect feeling underpaid, it does appear to play a part in feeling exploited, particularly among members of the intermediate professions and blue-collar workers, who are more apt to feel exploited if they feel they are victims of racially driven harassment. Controlling for status and working conditions, the airing of racist remarks in the workplace doubles the probability of subjective work-related fatigue.

Thus, women, the academically overqualified, victims of racism/racialization, and workers without job security develop feelings of injustice directly related to their social situation. Regardless of their working conditions, workers without job security say they're the victims of discrimination. The overqualified resent the disregard for their formal training. Women say that, "as women," they are not treated equally. Lastly, the racialized say they suffer from racism. Above and beyond class stratification and working conditions, these social injustices overdetermine feelings of injustice in the workplace.

Subjective Injustice Spans the Political Spectrum

Agents do not conceive of society as an integral system that can be changed by identifying the dominant groups and attempting to influence their actions. The prevalence and virulence, in France, of a condemnation of the neoliberal ethos is symptomatic. Social evils are not imputed to a dominant agent, but to an anonymous, impersonal system that people identify more with its ideological rationality than with who controls it. This trend markedly affects assessments of justice: Because it is harder to blame a class adversary for their sufferings, workers blame their immediate environment. Our subjects invariably attribute injustices not to capitalism and its champions, but to their "sadistic little slave drivers," unscrupulous employers, or their peers. And when the perceived injustice is blamed on society itself, the culprits are aspects of our society that lie outside the traditional scope of class conflict: racism, inequalities between the sexes and generations, job insecurity, and so on and so forth. Under these conditions, workers are unable to map their sufferings onto an organized representation of social conflict in which the ruling elites are held responsible for the injustices sustained. So it is more in moral than political terms that agents interpret their experience of injustice.

The Realm of Political Representations

Politics and morality appear to be the two principal dimensions that inform our respondents' representations of the social domain. That is confirmed by our factorial analysis of the correlations between their responses to questions about political life and society (see Figure 6.1, next page).

One axis corresponds to political orientation, the other to a positive or negative moral assessment of the trend of latter-day individualism. The horizontal axis maps respondents to points on the political spectrum, contrasting those who seize upon traditionally right-wing issues (e.g.,

Figure 6.1 Representations of Society

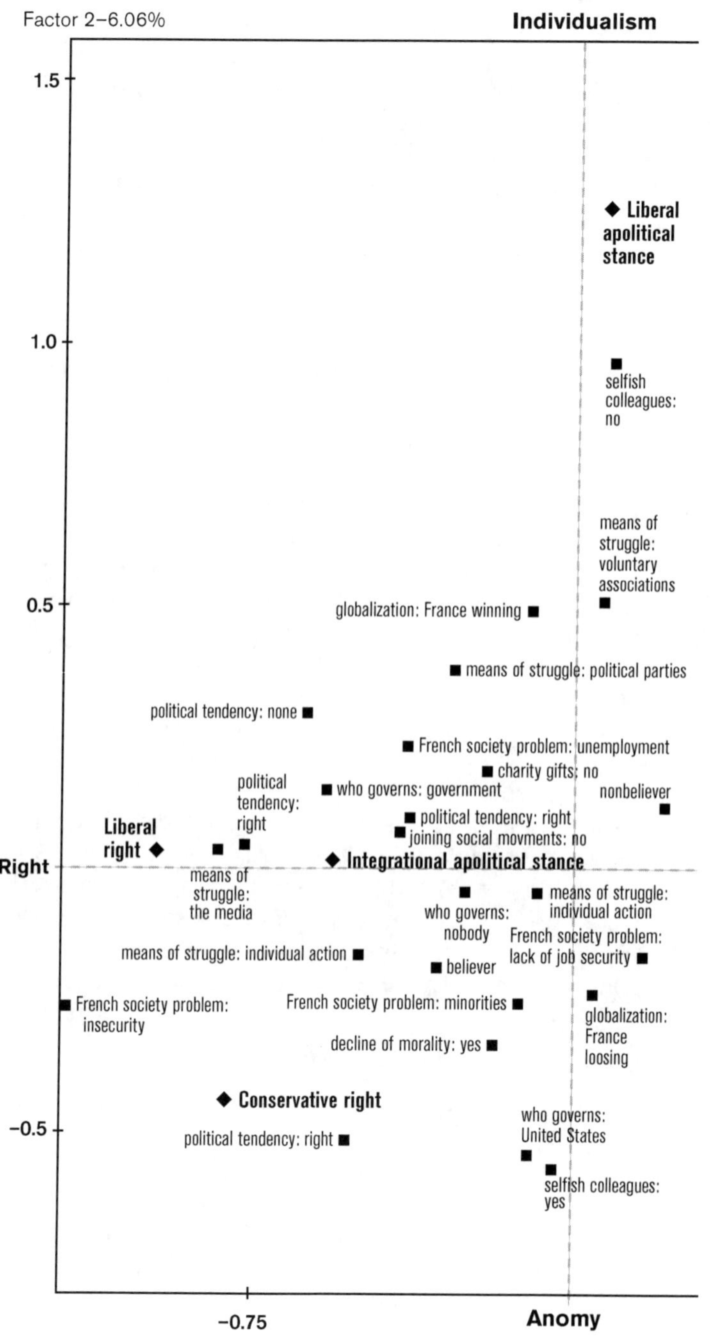

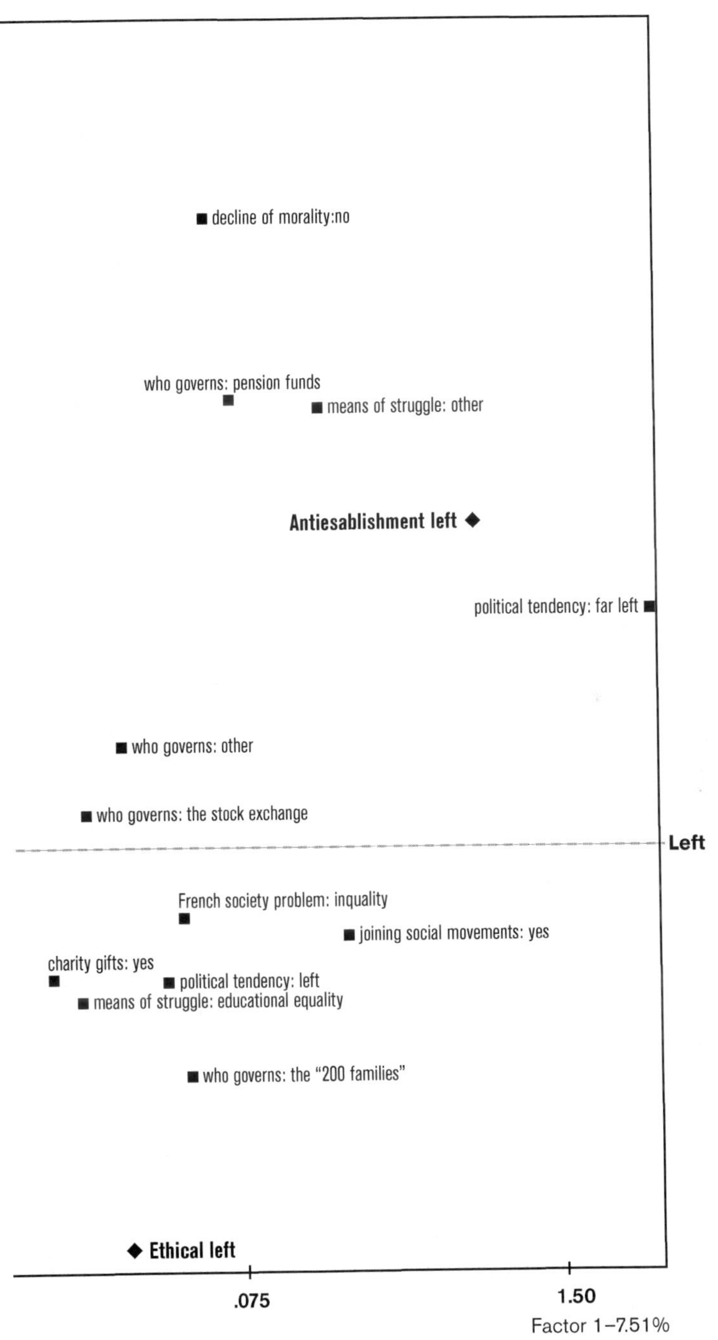
decline of morality:no
who governs: pension funds
means of struggle: other
Antiesablishment left
political tendency: far left
who governs: other
who governs: the stock exchange
Left
French society problem: inquality
joining social movements: yes
charity gifts: yes
political tendency: left
means of struggle: educational equality
who governs: the "200 families"
Ethical left
.075
1.50
Factor 1–7.51%

crime) and believe the government controls society and the economy, with those who take up left-leaning causes (e.g., the struggle against inequality and job insecurity) and believe society and the economy are controlled by a small, self-enclosed elite or by the stock market. The vertical axis differentiates workers according to their responses to questions like "Do you think your fellow workers are becoming more and more selfish and individualistic?" or "Do you think people are becoming less and less moral and it is hard to trust people?" but also "Do you think France is gaining or losing from economic globalization?" In other words, the horizontal scale maps current social issues along political lines, in terms of the mechanisms of economic and social regulation. The vertical scale maps these problems along moral lines: It refers to the development of moral pluralism and global culture, a trend increasingly linked to individualism and nonconformism. It distinguishes between those who take a positive view of these trends and those who are anxious about the loss of values, the decline of social solidarity, and the spread of anomie, and who regard outside influences as a menace to our national identity and to the integrity of French society based on its national values.

Using an automatic classification algorithm, we can distinguish between six main types of attitudes (shown in boldface on the above chart). These attitudes correspond to specific combinations of the two pairs of dichotomies. Each political sensibility, for example, is split in half according to whether it is associated with disapproval of the loss of values.

A *liberal* and a *conservative* view of current-day society coexist on the right side of the political spectrum. The former may be characterized essentially by contrast with the latter. Though its adherents are politically right of center, they do not discourse on the subject of moral decline. They reject most of the forms of collective action listed in our questionnaire. And they show an above-average inclination to believe that the government controls the economy and that the media is the best means of bringing pressure to bear on decision makers. The *conservative* sensibility, in contrast, involves an above-average tendency to bemoan that coworkers are more selfish and people less morally principled than they used to be. Of these, 23 percent consider crime one of the crucial problems in France today, as against 5 percent of our total sample. Furthermore, a greater number of them state that they are religious.

The same dichotomy obtains among left-of-center respondents. One *moral* stance on the left side of the political spectrum mixes a marked fear of the ascendancy of the market and the outside world over French society and political life with an eschewal of individualism, seen as the triumph of selfishness and anomie. Those who take this stance are more likely than the average respondent to opine that the stock market, the United States, or the "200 richest families" run the economy. They also criticize more than others the amorality and selfishness of their coworkers. The contrasting left-wing sensibility of *protest*, with fewer advocates, appears to focus exclusively on strictly political and economic issues and practices: France is losing out as a result of globalization, the pension funds run the economy, salvation lies in social protest movements, and so forth.

More surprising is that the same polarity cuts across the group of those with no avowed political orientation. *Liberal* apoliticism is characterized by a high frequency of "no" answers to questions about the selfishness and individualism of people in general and of coworkers in particular (74 and 83 percent, respectively, versus 22 and 36 percent for our global set of respondents). Workers in this category are more apt to think France is gaining from globalization, but also that the stock market runs the economy. The other form of apoliticism might be called *integrationist*, for its exponents exhibit a more pronounced inclination to deem unemployment one of the principal problems facing French society. They are also more liable to believe the government controls the economy and that the unions are the best means of struggle. Finally, 94 percent of them feel the population is becoming increasingly amoral, as against 76.5 percent of our global sample.

A More Moral than Political Interpretation of Experienced Injustice

Workers resort to an essentially moral vocabulary to situate their suffering within the larger framework of society and the workings thereof.

Equality on the left and merit on the right. Our data corroborate many other surveys. A right-wing political stance is associated with a more pronounced belief in the value of merit, which supposedly explains and justifies existing social inequalities. A left-wing political stance is linked to a preference for equality and a tendency to separate the value of the individual from his or her social status (Bréchon 2000). This divergence influences perceptions of inequalities: We see 46.2 percent of avowedly right-of-center respondents find the wage gap between a sales executive and a cashier excessive, as against 80 percent of left-leaning respondents. It also impacts views on income redistribution: There, 84.9 percent of right-wing workers, as opposed to 55.2 percent of left-wing workers, find it wrong that welfare recipients are entitled to benefits nearly equivalent to the minimum wage. These tendencies all confirm that, other things being equal, ideological orientations have an independent effect on conceptions of the just society.

Injustice viewed through the prism of morality. Conversely, political orientation has no effect on feelings of injustice about personal experiences at work. This result confirms the disconnect between political interpretations of the social realm and individual experiences of injustice. Assuming the left/right divide is the political expression of a central social conflict, we are forced to conclude that the subjective experience of injustice is not an inherent part of this conflict. However, subjective experience does tie into a moral assessment of the social realm. Rather than ascribing social evils to a perverse system, agents blame them on the perversion of people in general, on the character and "mindsets" of their peers and superiors at work, on the social frameworks within which their feelings of injustice develop. There is, for instance, no significant correlation between feeling despised or discriminated against at work and one's avowed political orientation. On the other hand, those who feel despised or discriminated against are significantly more likely to bemoan the general spread of amorality in society and the selfishness and individualism of their peers. So subjective exploitation appears to bear virtually no relation to political orientation, but it does coincide with a tendency to feel that society in general and coworkers in particular are growing increasingly selfish and individualistic.

In the final analysis, sweeping judgments on society that distinguish left-wing from right-wing political orientations don't seem to have any connection to subjective injustice in the workplace. Instead, that sense of injustice is related to moral representations of the world in terms of anomie and selfishness and to optimism/pessimism about changes in society. That helps explain why the left/right divide and the contours of the political realm itself seem to be blurring, why so many voters wander and waver, and why partisan politics does not seem to directly "represent" the various groups of workers.

* * *

The syntax of the feelings of justice gives rise to complex configurations for two main reasons. The first obviously has to do with the plurality of the principles of justice itself, which multiplies the perspectives and criteria of judgment. The second has to do with the complexity of the social fabric, owing to which inequalities are not neatly meted out to homogeneous subsets of the population. While company heads and the worst-treated manual laborers seem worlds apart, everyone in between is enmeshed in far more heterogeneous working situations that vary with each particular context. Superimposed upon these working contexts, moreover, are inequalities of a different nature, involving discrimination, inequalities between the sexes, mismatches between education and employment, etc. Thus, subjective injustice is not subsiding with the fading of the image—doubtless a reconstruction—of a class-based society: Instead, it is simply spreading out in atomized, individualized form.

Everyone in our survey believes equality is desirable, the merit principle just, and autonomy an essential value. But these principles of justice do not neatly divide up the various representations of society; they do not align with social divisions based on political affinities. Rather, workers have a "pragmatic" relationship to the principles of justice, which they apply according to their needs rather than according to consistency with a certain world view or collective interest. Indeed, workers come up with made-to-measure moral configurations to endow their experience with a meaning that will render it at once controllable and desirable. Ultimately, this relationship to the principles of justice bears a certain resemblance to the way in which new believers make use of religious dogmas, which they carve up into discrete components and then reassemble into a customized spirituality to meet their personal existential needs (Hervieu-Léger 1999). Thus severed from political and social dividing lines, injustices break up into myriad injustices experienced in the constricted circles of collective work relations. Workers may suffer at the hands of their peers and superiors, from racism or job insecurity, but they won't impute this suffering to a clearly identifiable social adversary.

Notes

1. This survey, conducted throughout the Aquitaine region of France in late 2004, involved a sample of 1,144 gainfully employed persons above the age of 18.

2. Craftspersons, liberal professions, shopkeepers, etc.

3. This "index of injustice" is the total number of responses from each individual attesting to a feeling of injustice.

CHAPTER 7

Injustice and Action

THE CONNECTION BETWEEN PERCEIVED INJUSTICE and action is not as direct as one would be tempted to think. Although most people vehemently denounce injustices and illegitimate inequalities, collective action often seems to pale in the face of the wrongs a subject has experienced, and the anger and indignation he takes away from the experience. It is not enough to be appalled by injustice to take action; what's more, it seems that those who do mobilize are not necessarily more sensitive to injustice than those who don't. The first to act are those who can, and their motives are often only very indirectly linked to injustices experienced at work. In our questionnaire survey, the "injustice score" we computed for nonunionized employees is only slightly lower than the score for unionized staff, and just barely below the figure for those who go on strike.[1] Why do we find this disconnect between perceived injustice and action?

Many theories and analyses of collective action seek an answer to this conundrum. On the assumption that there is nothing natural about collective action, seeing as frustration and discontent prove insufficient spurs to action, they investigate the various factors that do conduce to action: the forces of community cohesion and social division, the openness of the political system, individual levels of absolute and relative frustration, the capabilities of organizers of collective action, the interplay of the various inducements to action, the employers' response to workers' demands, etc. The literature on labor movements has examined all these factors one by one.

Without meaning to supersede any of the various theories of collective action, to which our material scarcely has any answers to offer, we'd like to investigate the nature of the connections between perceived injustice and action more closely. Although it seems obvious that collective action arises out of a sense of injustice, that sense can also serve to thwart action. The gap between perceived injustice and action may be explained, in large measure, by the dynamics of perceptions of justice. We shall elaborate five arguments to that effect:

1. It is a truism that many people feel their situation is just because they benefit from just inequalities.
2. The definition of injustice always depends on the conviction that injustices partake of a world order; agents may hypothesize, "upstream" of the social realm, a just world that reduces social injustices to manifestations of chance, destiny, or "human nature."
3. The principles of merit and autonomy necessarily give rise to doubts about the victims' grievances: They can always be suspected of being responsible for their own lot.
4. Individuals by and large think they themselves are not entirely innocent. They may feel they are aiding and abetting the world's injustices in any of a thousand different ways. Deep down inside, they don't always feel they have the moral right to complain, even when it is a matter of denouncing injustice.
5. The very makeup of collective action is almost always out of phase with feelings of injustice, either because it is deeply entrenched in work collectives and of a very defensive nature, or on the contrary because, in our day, the search for a social adversary who can be accused of causing injustice *with intent to harm* leads us far afield from the initial experience of injustice at work. When the cause of injustice seems to be "the system" itself rather than identifiable social agents, it may seem ludicrous to "take arms against a sea of troubles."

Just Inequalities

It's important to remember that, though the critique of injustice is grounded in the principles of justice, so are those inequalities that we deem just. Consequently, each principle may induce every one of us to believe that our lot is fair, and that the inequalities we benefit from are fair because they partake of the order of things in a hierarchical system, or because we deserve our place in the system, or because we are responsible for what happens to us. That doesn't preclude criticism of society as a whole, but a person hardly has reason to take action as long as her lot seems fair and inequalities far removed. Witness the aforecited policeman Alain, who finds the bureaucratic rationale of the police force perfectly fair and that those who complain have no good cause for doing so, unless it be ignorance of the rules or smoldering deep-seated frustration. Or Sylvain, a high school teacher, who finds that inequalities resulting from competitive examinations are part and parcel of a perfect meritocracy and that everyone is in his rightful place as long as nothing upsets that hierarchy. Finally, let us recall the company heads who think that they owe everything to their own merit and freedom, and that they are no more "privileged" than doctors who have passed difficult exams to do a job that is useful to everyone. Even if all of them denounce injustices, they target only the ones that are remote from themselves and that, in consequence, hardly compel them to take action as long as nothing destabilizes their own positions, which seem perfectly legitimate to them. In a word, as each principle of justice establishes a just order, many avail themselves thereof to meet their own purposes.

Sometimes, even workers in apparently less favorable situations are liable to harbor this notion of a just lot in a fairly just world. Magali is a cashier, the daughter of a blue-collar worker; after leaving school with mediocre marks, she married a storekeeper and scarcely sees any reason to complain. *"I haven't got any problems with injustice apart from the pay and the hours, but we work it out. We're not well paid, but that figures, seeing as how we didn't go to college."* She adds that family life is her main priority and that at any rate *"there's no way for us to change things."* Magali has doubtless internalized the domination to which she is subjected, but she's not entirely taken in: She compares her life to those of her circle and, all things considered (amenable boss, shopkeeper husband, life in the country, the kids), if she does have some reasons to complain, she doesn't have many to fight.

All that goes to show that individuals often combine a formidable capacity to criticize inequalities and injustices with a far more moderate and conciliatory view of their own lot. On the one hand, they seem to have a relatively stable image of what is an acceptable position in contrast to outrageous inequalities. On the other, they must break out of the spiral of criticism by putting their lives in perspective compared to those of others both very near and very far. The responses to our questionnaire indicate that, even though racism, sexism, and harassment are widely condemned, when they happen to materialize in the workplace, the sources of these injustices are often considered to be woven into the very fabric and structure of society and are therefore "out of reach." And unless we believe in a universally altruistic disposition, it is hard to imagine people taking action against injustices that do not personally affect them, or more precisely that affect them subjectively without manifestly impairing their working and living conditions, their dignity and aspirations. One can be indignant without taking action or without seeing what kind of action to take.

If everyone is free and responsible for his own life, then "everyone has what he deserves and deserves what he has." People like Henri, a maintenance man, refuse to see themselves as victims: *"Apart from the wages, I'm the one who lays down the working conditions, and seeing as I'm on the go all day long, I shouldn't go blaming anyone but myself. If I'm like that it's nobody's fault. You got no one but yourself to blame. If you look beneath you, you figure you haven't got it so bad; if you look above you, you really got it bad. But it's also the upshot of my life. I'm like that because I didn't know better or I didn't go to college, I didn't have enough ambition. There's always a reason for being what you are. Don't be fooled: The guy who sits on his ass and won't budge, if he's in that fix it's 'cause he made a choice. You are what you are."* It will always be remarked that Henri's ambition, or rather the lack thereof, is itself socially determined, so he is deluding himself. But that will hardly get us anywhere, for the fact that Henri appropriates this determinism as a subjective liberty goes to the very core of the principle of autonomy. For that is what autonomy is: a relation to the self perceived as being under the regime of freedom. To deny Henri the share of autonomy he claims would be to accord him only a negative freedom, the freedom he would have gained by knowing the social forces that determine his action, the freedom he could only acquire by reading the sociologists who, to produce their analyses, proclaim that they are akin to subjects, thereby substituting a different fallacy for the worker's delusion of free will. The dignity of workers demands an amplification of the principle of autonomy, a stubborn refusal to see oneself as a victim, a sort of elementary pride that proclaims. Though the world is unjust, my own lot in life in not inevitably so (Lamont 2002).

Destiny and Sin

Diametrically opposed to these calls for freedom and responsibility is an implicit belief in a moral conception of the world that renders human injustice a sort of inevitability. Individuals form representations of world justice within moral frameworks that are more or less directly derived from religious views of the nature of things and of man. If destiny reigns supreme, in the form of either chance or necessity, the struggle against social injustices may seem to be in vain, because it can never alter the eternal recurrence of the order of things. If the root of injustice lies in human spitefulness, social injustices seem inevitable consequences of a perverse nature, in which case it would be wise to temper any urge to revolt. In the shadow of this fundamental justice or injustice, the condemnation of *social*—i.e., *contingent*—injustices appears either a delusion or a ruse of the *demi-habiles,* the "half-clever" people, of whom Pascal (2000) spoke.

One Big Lottery

One way of accepting one's lot and coming to terms with an unjust world is to concede that chance and inevitability play a part in the assignment of the individual's place in society and individual destiny. How can we fight the combined forces of chance and necessity that control our lives? This *Weltanschauung* is less common among those who believe in the designs of the gods than those who believe in the play of birth and genes. *"I could have been born a hood, I was lucky to be well-born,"* muses Michel, a doctor. *"That's the first inequality and there's nothing I can do about it. Take Down's syndrome, health, intelligence: You've got people who can take the* bac[2] *20 times and they'll never pass it, and you've got kids who pass at 14. Now who's fault is that?"*

At base, so the argument goes, merit is not what we think: What we call merit and autonomy is the fact of having been born in the right place, at the right time, with the right potential. Marc, a teacher in adult education, shouts it out loud: *"Life's terrific! I'm a grandfather, got a house, the weather's fine, I'm in good health, I play golf, I love the mountains, I sing in a choir, I know how to make foie gras. Life's worth living! I've had more luck than merit."* So if the world's one big lottery, why fight it?

And then there is the random nature of encounters, emotions, personalities, observes Thibault, a technician: *"We're going to talk about injustices, we can put it that way. That's often the way it is in life: You've got to come at the right time, that's a fact. You're not going to make the world over again. I bring you three people, there'll be one you really dig right off the bat, one you could take or leave, and one who rubs you the wrong way. And then the day you have an important choice to make, you'll tell the guy you like best. The minute you're born there's inequalities. There's looks, for starters: Some people look good, others not so good. Then, when it comes to smarts, there's lots of guys don't need to study much, and others who have to study hard.… It's normal to cash in on connections. It's unfair, but if you've got them, you might as well use them."* If the individual's place in society is assigned by chance, it goes without saying that some will be out of luck, and there is no point in interfering with this lottery, which is, ultimately, neither just nor unjust. But those who are aware of what they owe to birth and chance also explain that they can't fully relish their pride in their merit and their freedom. That, in turn, keeps them from placing too much blame on the victims, seeing as the latter are not wholly responsible for their lot in life either. Though strictly deterministic conceptions of action and society generally underscore the radical injustice of the social realm, they may also induce us to substitute wisdom and compassion for action and revolt. When subjects turn out to be "Spinozists," whether or not they know it, their only choice is between tempered fatalism and an indignation that may be but a purely personal way of "saving their souls."[3]

Human Nature

Those surveyed in the course of this study seem to lean less toward fatalistic beliefs, secularized or not, than towards a faith in an anthropology of evil, postulating that man is naturally wicked. In this sense, the belief in "original sin" has survived the decline of religious convictions by metamorphosing within other types of discourse. If injustices do not trigger action, it is because they lie buried in the very nature of human beings. As Michel puts it: *"Nothing will put a stop to jealousy, hatred, spitefulness, stupidity."* What surfaces here is a latent conviction that the principles of justice are incessantly being violated because men are evil. Denunciations of "stupidity," "sadism," and "jealousy" occur in most of the interviews, and a full 31.5 percent of the respondents to our questionnaire think these vices are human and justice is impossible. Katarina, a waitress, sums it up thus: *"At any rate, injustice has always existed and always will; it's part of human nature. As soon as you give someone a little power, they get the impression they're king of the world—they've got power over others and they'll make the most of it."*

This sense of "sinfulness," this radical pessimism about human nature, likewise permeates the thinking of Elodie, a cleaning lady at a hospital: *"I used to do the cleaning in a ward where you'd see people dying pretty often. And you see people dying all alone, though some have loads of friends and family around them, others are all alone. A poor grandpa who'll be happy to see you—just you, the cleaning lady— because they don't have time to talk to anyone. The elderly, they don't get enough respect. It's true that not every family can keep them, but then again a visit a week wouldn't kill anyone either. But I saw some laid up for two months, nobody came to see them—that's disgusting. You hear some of them saying, 'I'm a burden to my family, they're sick of me.' You say it ain't so, but you know full well that when it comes down to it, for the family it is a burden.... You see some coffins being lugged out all loaded with flowers, all rolling in dough, and others without a thing. I've seen people refuse to pay anything at all 'cause they'd let one of our terminal patients smoke, that's what gave him pleasure. Everyone's at loggerheads, nobody wants to take care of them anymore."* Samy, a social worker, thinks injustice is in the nature of things, for the psychoanalytical axioms taken for granted in his profession involve a notion of innate sinfulness: *"There are inequalities between brothers and sisters, and there's nothing you can do about it because man is not in-fallible, we reproduce what we see, I mean I wouldn't want to play the armchair psychologist but....*" With the "id," the death urge, and envy, the underlying anthropology of psychoanalysis is hardly more optimistic than the creed of original sin (Dejours 1998).

Fabrice, a hotel maintenance man, believes injustice is, above all, a moral battle of evil versus good, hate versus love: *"Man is his own worst enemy, we're becoming crazier and crazier."* And the logical answer to hatred is not action, but love: *"I've got someone who loves me, whom I love. You've got to love your work, you've got to love people, you've got to love your family—love with a capital 'L.'"* The fight against injustice is less a social struggle than a matter of personal virtue and love. Not everything about social injustice is social: The boss's malice and coworkers' jealousy are not mere outgrowths of capitalism.

Audrey, a manager, describes various "irrational" injustices: racism, contempt, the ill-treatment reserved for temporary staff, everything that serves no other purpose than to give the tormentors pleasure. The problem she broaches is that of malice: the fact that people go far beyond the "rational" pressure and threats that may be "necessary" for the company and the system to run smoothly, even if it is a system of exploitation. This desperate outlook leads to utter skepticism, and Audrey rages against the unions that *"play dirty"* by systematically thwarting the employer, manifesting the same will to dominate, committing the same acts of social violence as those they are combating. Indeed, iniquity and moral corruption are not confined to the upper echelons and do not halt at the social divides. Nor are there any compelling reasons to believe that those who fight injustice are more just than the others. Jacques-Henri, also a manager but a union member as well, brings up this moral corruption: *"At this teeny-tiny level of the union, at this microscopic, even mediocre, level, you find the same ambition, the same desires, as in the political scene—the struggle for power."* One might well ask, however, whether this image of generalized immorality is not also a roundabout way of justifying one's own cynicism; if the world is a jungle, then we won't be taken in and might as well put ourselves resolutely on the side of the predators. After all, the idea of original sin implies that there are ulterior motives even in the act of denouncing injustice, for there are some personal benefits to be reaped from indignation, notably that of "cleansing one's conscience."

Although the mistrust of labor unions and political parties is generally attributed to political factors, to their image of being corrupt, impotent, or indifferent to people's aspirations, it might also be due to a moral detachment deriving from the very representation of the origins of injustice. The "Eastern" belief in fate and the Judeo-Christian beliefs that are readily transformable into a modern, "scientific" belief in determin-ism, chance, or an anthropology of evil pose formidable obstacles to the transformation of feelings of injustice into collective action. To put it in strictly normative and moral terms, there is a "way out" of the duty to fight injustice that consists in viewing injustice as a moral problem of good against evil, a problem of virtue and beliefs about the underlying causes of the nature of things. Is this a consolation, an opiate of the masses, or a form of worldly wisdom? It is difficult to decide. But those who think there is a moral basis for perceived injustices are neither the least critical nor the least generous; they simply believe inequalities are not, at core, strictly social. Many, in short, reject an optimistic anthropology that postulates that man is good and the causes of injustice lie outside the individual; they are, in their way of thinking, closer to Pascal and Hobbes than to Rousseau and Marx.

Are the Victims Really Innocent?

From the point of view of merit and autonomy, not every situation that might appear unjust turns out to be truly so. More precisely, we cannot help wondering whether putative victims of injustice really are victims, whether injustice strikes by chance, and whether misfortune does not befall those who deserve it. Needless to say, this suspicion does not proceed from some vague view of things in terms of reincarnation in which misfortune strikes to punish obscure wrongs committed by one's ancestors or in a previous life, but from doubts about the intentionality of the victims of injustice. Do they make good use of their autonomy and freedom, and, if not, why take action on behalf of those who do not fully deserve it?

The Victims Are Also Guilty

Messianic revolutionary movements were based on the assumption that the victims of evil and injustice were ipso facto wholly innocent, virtuous, impervious to the moral taint of injustice. A victim of racism was not in turn a racist in his own right, a subjugated woman was gentle and kind, a proletarian was simple and giving, and so on and so forth. Therein lay a deep-seated faith in the immanent justice of the world and an essential political fiction, for one could only venture to destroy an unjust world if one believed the good would then take the place of the wicked (Cohn 1983; Lanternari 1979). Those who inveigh against injustice still adhere more or less implicitly to this eschatological fantasy, but oftentimes, once they come into closer contact with "real-life" victims, they are dismayed to discover that victimhood does not expunge all taint of moral corruption; those aggrieved by the wicked are not necessarily good. As we move down the chain of abstraction from principles towards individuals, a collective injustice does not automatically translate into individual injustice. Fabienne, a social worker who describes herself as "leftist to the core" and antiracist, cites a case in point: *"I know this body shop, an excellent firm. The owner's black, from Martinique. His apprentice is Moroccan, so at first I figure it's going to work out fine. Goes to show how dumb we are! Two days later, the apprentice calls me up and says, 'You see, he's racist. He talks down to me, disrespects me.' I go see the bodyworker, 'Farid, nothing interests him. He sits in his corner, no curiosity, doesn't ask any questions. I ask him to do something, he sighs and says, 'In a minute!' Farid's like all his kind: He's not into working, they're slackers, they're violent, they're noisy.... Farid's like Calimero, who ends every story with 'It's unfair, it's so unfair!'"* Though a priori every black person is supposed to be nonracist because a victim of racism himself, not so this employer. Then again, does Farid really want to work? Who's the victim, who's the perpetrator? Fabienne doesn't know what to think any more, for this little incident has blurred the lines on her mental map of justice.

It happens, too, that victims will "take advantage" of their victimhood, using it as a smokescreen from behind which to torment others. Arnaud, a teacher, recalls how a black teacher took a schools inspector to court for racism: *"You're so afraid of being confronted with this problem of racism that you can't tell anymore what's okay and what's not, because you systematically run the risk of being labeled a racist, and that becomes a real ordeal. The moment you say a thing to a person of color, you're liable to be called a racist. And then there's racism towards whites, of course; people of color can be awfully racist."* One would like to identify with victims of injustice, but they have to prove themselves worthy of it by refraining from behaving as badly as their victimizers. Though everyone admits women are generally treated unfairly, that doesn't mean some of them don't take advantage of their "weaker-sex" image to tyrannize others. The condemnations of contempt and abuse of power cited in the preceding chapters should suffice to satisfy us that many women bemoan both "feminine jealousy" and the reign of terror under tyrannical female superiors. If human nature is bad, there is no reason why victims should be an exception; if good, there is no reason why it should not be corrupted by injustice.

Generally speaking, when one refuses to be victimized, to be trod upon, when one fights back, one can denounce social injustices while refusing to indulge victims who seem by and large to acquiesce, whether out of helplessness or cowardice. Luc, a crane operator, who describes his employer as an unscrupulous exploiter, adds that his workmates do nothing about it: They sell out for tiny favors, which basically makes them as immoral and dishonorable as their boss. Acquiescing in the injustice to which they are subjected, they become as unjust as their masters, since they could always resist in order to preserve their dignity and autonomy.

The inmates, so to speak, end up collaborating with the guards, selling out for a modicum of security and a few advantages, or because they want to avoid conflict. The principle of autonomy often falls within the scope of an analysis of "voluntary servitude" (La Boétie) in which the dominated end up taking pleasure in their domination, so one can never wholly identify with them. Sometimes, in fact, the absence of sympathy for the victims turns into outright antipathy. Louis, a blue-collar worker, denounces the exploitation of manual laborers. But he feels no solidarity with his coworkers, victims like himself, because they just don't deserve it. Of one such unworthy he says, *"He's heavy, crude, vulgar. People like that, sometimes you just don't feel like seeing them. It even gets so bad you even wonder if there was a genocide and he got stuck in it, that'd be a good thing. He's really something else. You're not allowed to physically eliminate someone, it's prohibited by law, so you have to put up with them. You bottle it up and wait for the day to go by."*

From the standpoint of autonomy, everyone, in theory, has the power to resist, to refuse to let himself be entirely dominated. Moreover, one is never a victim "by chance." Jerome, a bank teller, describes the game of tyrants and scapegoats as a perverse relationship in which the victim, while remaining a victim, actively contributes to her own misfortune: *"The girl's very paranoid, so that causes friction, things blow up in a flash. And the fact is people trip her up a little unfairly because she does a pretty good job. But what with her personality, you don't really feel like helping her out. It's tough: She considers herself persecuted and the arguments go on forever. When she's working she puts up a rear-view mirror: We ask her, 'Why've you got a rear-view mirror?' 'I can't stand seeing someone moving behind my back.' Naturally, the way she reacts leads to decisions that aren't necessarily fair. We tried to talk to her several times, but she shuts up like a clam. After all, you can't force people. We advised her to see a psychiatrist, to take sick leave if necessary—it's no problem, we've got good coverage. 'No, no, I'm perfectly fine. You're a bunch of bastards.'"* One could hold forth ad infinitum on this anecdote: Is the woman insane? Has she been driven insane? Is the group content in being united and protected from the boss's whims by a scapegoat? Or does everyone derive some pleasure from feeling normal or making someone else suffer? All these questions will occur to the parties to such a "situation," and we know that fellow staff members are considered a prodigious source of injustice at work.

This stern view of victims could be deemed an ideological effect whereby the most dominated members of society adopt the norms of internality, of a "neoliberal" ideology that compel them to blame the victims. Though reasonable, this explanation is not sufficient, for the neoliberal credo rests on autonomy, a principle of justice we also know to be opposed to domination. It is in the name of our autonomy that we denounce the abuse of power. Even if we inveigh against the "alienating" effects of autonomy, we cannot utterly discard a principle we deem vital for ourselves. Beyond mere belief, this principle is also a *necessary fiction* for those who actually work "on the injustice front." Everyone has had his chance at some point, so the argument goes, and those who have not seen fit to seize it hardly have any right to complain. Indeed, social workers often say part of the population is "unemployable," incapable of extricating themselves from the quicksand of dependency in which they have submerged themselves. What can one say to the long-term unemployed to get them to break out of their predicament—that they are not entirely victims and should take themselves in hand? Nearly all the schoolteachers in present-day France concur in criticizing schools as factories for the reproduction of inequalities. Most of them know that birth and cultural and social "handicaps" play a decisive part in their pupils' careers. And yet, like social workers, they cannot resign themselves to the fatalism of these determinisms and regard the victims of social inequalities and injustices purely as innocent victims. They are condemned to a "duty of hope," to postulate that everyone is capable of pulling through, of succeeding if only just a little bit. For without this hypothesis, without this "fiction," in which everyone has a modicum of autonomy and merit at his disposal, the teachers' work would be wholly devoid of meaning. They have to believe that every underprivileged person can elude his or her fate, every pupil can succeed. Otherwise, they would have to give up their vocation, reduce social work to a blend of caretaking and aid work for the poor, reduce education to a mechanical reproduction of inequalities in which teachers would be, at best, impartial referees of a contest played out in advance. What would we think of a social worker who said to a client, "In your situation and in your predicament, there's nothing you can do but wait"? What would we think of a teacher who said to her pupils, "Considering your birth, your neighborhood, and your parents' status and background, it makes no sense to study because you'll never make it through school"?

Even if the belief in individual freedom is a fiction, even if it is cruel to impose a norm of internality that makes people blame themselves for their own misfortune, there is scarcely any alternative, and renouncing the fiction would be even worse. So it is that every poor person is told that she can escape poverty if she really wants to, and every pupil that he can succeed if he really wants to. But "where there's a will there's a way" means anyone who fails can always be suspected of not really wanting to succeed. If we hold that merit and autonomy are fundamental principles of justice, our compassion for the victims cannot be unadulterated. It is easy to see why they are always suspected of too obligingly succumbing to their fate. We can still denounce inequalities and injustices, of course, but the denunciation subsides as it comes closer to the victims and to the use they have made of their autonomy. Ultimately, there is no reason why a social worker, unsettled by the situations she comes up against on a daily basis, should not suspect that plenty of the poor are "taking advantage" of the system. Nor is there any reason why a schoolteacher, even if he is caustically critical of scholastic inequalities, should abstain from scolding and penalizing underprivileged children for not working hard enough to seize their opportunities. Even the most combative unionists may well feel that certain employees are simply not defendable. And as it is difficult to walk that narrow, precipitous line, there is always a risk of lurching from compassion to hatred for the victims.

The Shadow of the Underclass

As we have seen, joblessness is perceived as the most scandalous form of inequality; a majority of people reject racism, and, in our interviews, many respondents describe "the projects" as neighborhoods plagued by every form of social injustice, privation, and human misery. However, their condemnations of injustice do not necessarily imply that they see the victims thereof as being innocent and likable. On the contrary, these people seem threatening and dangerous. Because they live below the threshold of tolerable inequalities, this underclass also represents an inner barrier separating society from a "barbaric" netherworld not truly deserving of compassion. The "dangerous classes" (Chevalier 1978) are perceived as guilty victims. The youths are seen as juvenile delinquents and "riffraff," and the immigrants are blamed for failing to assimilate and harboring militant Islamic fundamentalists, drug dealers, welfare cheaters, etc. The urban riots that break out periodically in French housing projects (as in the fall of 2005, for example) give this underclass a particularly "dangerous" image (Dubet 1987; Kokoreff 2003).

Time and again in the interviews we heard about how immigrants cut in front of native-bred French people in line, who don't dare protest for fear of being labeled racists. Not only are these immigrants treated as the equals of French citizens, but what is even worse, they take advantage of their victimhood to rip off honest taxpayers. On closer inspection, it is argued, the victims of injustice are not as blameless as is generally believed. Boris, a young white-collar employee who rails against his exploitation at work and his deplorable working conditions, is even more incensed when he compares himself to his next-door neighbor: *"It's not necessarily the most destitute who are the most disadvantaged. What drives me crazy is one of my neighbors who doesn't do a thing all day, but with her three kids she gets €1,200 a month and she pays €75 a month for a house. I figure more power to her, but on the other hand there are people who are all alone and working their asses off for nothing. But there's nothing for them, whereas her, just because she's a single mom, blah-blah-blah, blah-blah-blah!"* When people complain about those living "high off the hog" on welfare, they usually mean immigrants in the housing projects. The underclass is resented for not "staying in their place," for taking advantage of their entitlements, for sinking into an aggressive form of dependency of the sort that keeps others from intervening when they cut the line, and that is seen as a threat to equality in a national community that has become too open and too generous.

The underclass is also denied good-victim status because they still possess a quality the rest of us have lost: solidarity. Instead of suffering from the anomie and selfishness criticized by many of our respondents, the "dangerous classes" have clung to their families and "clans," networks that provide the support of which we feel deprived. The lonelier we are, the more they seem to stick together, because they're different and remote, and the more threatening their solidarity seems, giving them a collective strength we lack. As Robert Merton pointed out, the virtues of the "in group" become the vices of the "out group." When the underclass lacks both cultural values and solidarity, it is a threat to us; when it does have them and shows it, that, too, is a threat. When these people are out of work, they are taking advantage of our generosity; when they have jobs, they are degrading our working conditions.

The stereotype of the juvenile delinquent from the projects provides the handiest justification for a radical redefinition of the victim as culprit. This youth is striving to acquire the most conspicuous signs of equality offered by our consumer society, without obeying any of its rules, submitting neither to work and merit, nor to virtue and self-control. More damning yet, the juvenile delinquent is clever enough to cry victimhood, whereas the true victims are the poorest and most deprived. *"It's always some poor guy who gets mugged,"* Boris says. *"It doesn't usually happen to somebody who's superrich. Lots of times, it's just a working stiff, and I say goddamn it, the guy sweats all his life for a little nest egg, and then they steal it from him."* It doesn't matter whether the thief is slightly poorer and more deprived than his victim: The robbery breaks the continuity of the critique of social inequalities (Lagrange 2003; Robert 1999). Insidiously, the dangerous classes have found a way to exploit society's compassion: *"The more trouble they make, the more attention they get,"* whereas the "real" jobless and "real" victims of exploitation, those who toil and suffer, go unheard, unseen. Indeed, the wretched make a livelihood of their wretchedness, turning compassion into a dangerous and naive sentiment. Perrine, an esthetician, reports, *"I support Les Restos du Cœur,[4] and I donate to the charity. But if I volunteered to serve, I'd blow my stack because when I see these people standing around on the sidewalk waiting for the truck to be unloaded, I'd yell at them, 'C'mon, can't you give us a hand? Can't you help us do you a favor?'"*

"We're All Part of the System"

To take action, you have to believe the victims are really innocent, and you also have to be convinced that you yourself are not guilty of or party to the injustices you condemn. This is another instance in which social agents reduce the scale by questioning themselves rather than asking about others. Is a person really capable of protest when he feels trapped in the machinery of injustice by all the little moral compromises of day-to-day life? In other words, the individual suspects himself of being guilty, and the doubt aroused by these guilt feelings seems to make him prefer producing justice in his immediate surroundings to changing the world.

The Injustices We Create

Because agents endorse several principles of justice and attempt to arbitrate between them, they have the feeling they are never entirely fair, for in adopting one principle, they are quite likely to betray the others. This latent tension and guilt are especially acute among those whose work involves providing services to others. For example, the primary school teacher faces a daily dilemma as he strives to treat all the pupils as equals, while rewarding the most outstanding for their merit, and enabling each student to develop her personality and creativity. Teachers quite naturally despair of achieving all these goals, and the profession is haunted by latent guilt. Likewise, employees at the French state employment agency, which distributes benefits to the unemployed, have a vague feeling they are aiding and abetting certain injustices. Regardless of their ideals, they know they are caught between employers offering unfair wages and excessively harsh working conditions, and the jobless who are taking unfair advantage of the welfare system. They are also aware that their practices are not always entirely fair. According to Jeanne, *"Some of my colleagues routinely strike people from the rolls."* Marion adds, *"Waiting in line for two hours, that's outrageous, and I'll say so myself: It's outrageous. We're all extremely uncomfortable. We see the people waiting, and when we finally interview them, it's awful. Just horrible. For them it's a grueling wait, but it's intolerable for us, too. I really mean it."* Yet peer pressure, force of habit, and the workload conspire to stifle initiative, and the civil servants end up getting used to their clients' ordeal, even if it is an ordeal for them, too.

Guilt seems inherent to certain occupations, even if their organic ideology of those occupations primarily consists in denying individual responsibility and blaming anything that goes wrong on "the system." For example, nearly all our workers began by criticizing employers and politicians and ended up describing the scandalous practices of certain workmates, which nevertheless go unreported. Generally, after having asserted that the government and the system are to blame for educational injustice, teachers turn to the inadmissible practices of some of their colleagues, adding that they do nothing about that. Nurses' aides and nurses make the same allegations, and collective action for the sake of group interests is never entirely devoid of latent guilt. *"I've worked with some nurses who didn't always have good working conditions, but tried to do their best,"* Dominique told us. *"But you always have some who don't give a damn and don't work, who aren't conscientious. You don't just treat a broken leg, you treat the whole person.... It can turn ugly when there's a cultural clash. Naturally, the gypsies turn up in groups of 10 or 20, but that's part of their culture, so it's important. When it comes to Arabs, you hear the nurses making remarks like, 'Damn them, here they come again. See that? She's bringing him his couscous!'"*

But the "caring professions" are not the only ones plagued by guilt. In some occupations, creating injustice is part and parcel of the job itself, as fledgling MBAs discover when first confronted with the harsh laws of the market. Benjamin works in a bank: *"Usually, when a company is struggling, the first to demand payment are the creditors—in other words, the banks with the bank accounts. Every morning, I'm facing the screen, knowing that I have a choice of bouncing the checks or not, knowing if I refuse to pay, I'll definitely be dropping them in the shit, whether they deserve it or not. That's the question I ask myself, and I don't care if it's cold in the office or if I'm going to sit there till eight, when that's the priority. If I put 'No,' what happens then? Have I taken everything into account? Anyway, I don't know, there's a thousand reasons why a business can fail, but that's the question I'm asking myself all the time.... It's too easy to say I'm going to close my eyes and just treat everyone the same, here I go.... The people might be bastards, they might be crooks, they might be folks who made the effort to come around and then you've got to decide because it's enough to make you blow your brains out! You can't shoulder all the misery in the world. We're not saviors.... I've seen people come to the bank with their whole family, it's like emotional blackmail. Well, that sort of thing, even if you're right to turn them down, you've just got to grit your teeth and bear it. When you've got someone crying on the phone and you hang up, you can say, 'OK, I did it.' It's too easy to say it's the capitalist system. There's six billion of us keeping it running and I'm going to see no evil, hear no evil, and ask myself no questions. We're supporting injustice, no doubt about it.... I'm a big boy, I can tell myself things are worse elsewhere, I've got to make up my own mind."*

Edouard, another young manager, recounts how he had to do the dirty work as the "repo man" for a car dealership. *"I took the keys away from some customers. I saw people cry, I got called names: 'I'll kill you if you take my car!' The first thing they need in life is a car to get to work, so that's a helluva bad break. You have these people on the phone, you tell them to come and turn in the keys, and that's the worst of all. They bring back the keys, they leave on foot. Me, I've got my car parked downstairs."* Unless these young managers change to another line of work, these guilt-ridden experiences will probably arouse caution rather than rebellion. Neither foolish enough to believe in the virtues of capitalism nor entirely innocent, they are caught in a cross-fire zone, in which they will probably choose compromise and moderation over radical revolt.

And yet, despite their latent feelings of guilt, individuals who engage in such a radical denunciation of wrongs, even those that are very "close to home," never portray themselves as heroes who are out fighting injustice. Apparently, they bear silent witness to injustice without intervening, because taking action would be too costly, make too many waves, or lay them open to ridicule, because once they got started there would be no end to their indignation, etc. They look on as coworkers are sidelined, passed over by flagrant favoritism, even publicly humiliated, without saying or doing a thing, even though they'd have faced no risk in protesting. All these instances of petty cowardice make us, in spite of ourselves, party to the injustices we denounce so vehemently.

Moral Hedging

Many of our interviewees condemned the injustice of "string pulling," but 60 percent of the respondents to our questionnaire consider it an acceptable means of helping out a friend or relative. Individuals concede that there are venial sins, acts that are unjust in principle, but perfectly understandable and excusable in practice, for, in an unjust world, compromising one's principles is the only way to adapt. Let us take an example from outside the working world (Caillet 2001; Dubet 2000). When high school and college students were asked about cheating on exams, they replied that although it is a moral failing and an injustice, it is basically excusable as long as it remains within certain limits. For example, cheating can be tolerated when it keeps the weakest students from dropping out, when it is done as a favor to a friend, or—if neither of those conditions is met—at least it involves taking a risk. On the other hand, cheating is condemned whenever it gives an added advantage to students who are already the highest achievers, or when, especially on an entrance exam, it will automatically disqualify those who do not cheat. Basically, cheating is tolerated insofar as it contributes to student equality and group solidarity.

Attitudes are similar in the working world, where most individuals denounce major injustices in the name of universal principles, while indulging in the minor injustices, the little compromises, that serve their survival or advancement. Delphine, a nurse's aide and shop steward, admits that she draws some advantages from her union activities: time off from work for union activities, first choice of the freebies and discounts offered by the company's shop committee, and protection from superiors who won't risk a clash with the union, to name a few. Ultimately, she does not judge any of this especially unjust, because these little perks don't harm anyone.

Naturally, there is some chance that her coworkers would decry these "perks" as outrageous privileges. Similarly, individuals will criticize favoritism while admitting that, fortunately, they themselves happen to have a good rapport with the boss. Gilles, an agricultural laborer, is a case in point. He stays late after work to finish unloading the truck: *"There's but one sucker, and I'm it."* But he acknowledges that his sacrifice is not entirely selfless because, in exchange, the boss grants him a slightly more flexible schedule and lets him use company equipment. Teachers, another example, are often sticklers for bureaucratic order, and yet the ones with the most seniority feel they have earned the right to negotiate their own classroom schedules and teaching assignments. Their colleagues are not incensed enough about it to protest, hoping perhaps that someday they, too, will enjoy the very same privileges.

Despite stringent egalitarianism and pure merit, workplace relations have to weave in a thousand little arrangements that are expedient to both the organization and the individual. From this perspective, no work organization could withstand an excess of virtue, seeing as the areas of autonomy that workers have to stake out are arguably relative privileges as well. As trivial as they usually are, however, these privileges are bound to create injustices that seem less trivial to others. Those without such privileges might consider Delphine a member of the union "caste"; Gilles, the farmhand, "the boss's pet"; and the teacher dictating her own schedule a privileged "dignitary."

But all these special dispensations, this rule bending and connivance at petty injustices may not prove to be a zero-sum game. While most agents participate to a greater or lesser extent, the gains of some are not necessarily equal to the losses of the others. Power, recognition, and special dispensations are not finite entities, and every work organization can create and distribute as much or as little thereof as it sees fit. In doing so, the organization opens up an abyss between the principles of justice and daily interactions at work. Viewed through the prism of the principles, these practices effectively stymie any inclination toward collective action, should one be tempted to believe that the feeling of injustice should immediately give rise to collective protest. Everyone knows or senses that these practical compromises are infringements of the principles of justice.

Local Justice

One of the ways agents cope with their vague sense of guilt about moral compromises is by establishing limited zones of justice within their immediate sphere of action. If it appears pointless to fight for sweeping change and to dream of a perfectly just world, it seems wiser and more reasonable to create a livable, just world around oneself. If it is impossible to change the world—*"it's not within our power, at our low level"*—if human nature is bad, and only one's friends and family matter, then, as Sandra, a secretary, says, *"The unions and political parties are putting us on."* So Sandra tries *"to be nice"* to her coworkers, and volunteers for an NGO because *"they're actually doing something."* Instead of tilting at windmills, it's better to do something tangible and immediate. Christine, a secondary-school teacher, has had her fill of mass protests and high dudgeon, especially seeing as the most radical critics of educational injustice among the faculty are also the most elitist teachers in practice, favoring the best students and ignoring the weakest: *"I'm an outlaw because the whole faculty decided that students would get a zero on their record for every homework assignment that isn't handed in. It's unfair to the students because some of them have serious problems to contend with at home."* Sometimes, an act of decency may seem miniscule when it merely involves being polite and respectful in an extremely brutal working environment. *"It's a drop in the bucket,"* says Max, a 22-year-old surveyor. *"The workers have to put up with the foreman bawling them out all the time—do this, don't do that—for no reason, sometimes. He makes them slave away but cheats on their pay. He puts them to work on rainy days and reports it as 'normal weather.' The workers don't get paid for all the hours they put in: It's all gravy for the owners. I say good morning, I'm pleasant, I kid around. It's very important to say good morning, to call the guys by name. 'At least this guy says hello, he's not a stuck-up kid.' Well, that's something, at least."* These miniscule acts of decency may carry more weight when performed by supervisors who believe a blend of moral duty and intelligent management will make their personnel feel fairly treated. Serge, a department head, explains how he tries to combine several principles of justice: *"That everyone gets roughly the same job to do, but everyone's got their 'secret garden,' I'd call it, where they can do their thing without answering to anyone. I try to pay attention to things like vacation time because I think it's a source of friction, so I try to make sure it's not always the same guys who get first dibs."*

Many have a sense of inhabiting a relatively safe haven from the world's injustices, a refuge to be preserved at all cost. Occasionally, the relationship to the world is reversed, and the workplace, which calls for trust and solidarity, seems much fairer than the rest of society. A shared team vision eclipses the pettiness of the dog-eat-dog world. *"We trust each other,"* says Veronique, a pediatric nurse. *"We always sub for each other when necessary, and we're on a first-name basis. There's hardly any sense of a pecking order. There's mutual trust, we're happy to be together, we kid around, we're tight. And you know tragic experiences create a bond, too. A team that's been through a tragedy will hold a meeting to talk about what happened, how we feel about it. We're on a first-name basis with the doctors. If they make mistakes we're allowed to object, we can talk certain things over, we can give our opinion. At lunchtime we eat with them. It's not a compartmentalized hierarchy."* The staff are willing to acquiesce in a few injustices in order to preserve this sanctuary of peace and fairness: *"Many of us do our best to avoid conflict, we even laugh at the scapegoats behind their backs."* Laughter and banter ultimately disarm the "go-getting" staff members who are always complaining. Indeed, a sense of humor is also a must in dealing with patients, who may display anxiety, hostility, or strange behavior.

This individual resolve to be fair could be dismissed as paling into insignificance in the glare of appalling wrongs. The workers portrayed above are assuredly not heroes, committed activists, or makers and shakers of history. Nevertheless, they are capable of saying no to the injustices that affect them directly, without blaming them on others or the system. It must be remembered that, in the worst situations, under the harshest and most abusive regimes, it is precisely these unassuming individuals who have demonstrated time and again that the long road to justice is paved with quiet acts of kindness, unique, individual forms of resistance, as much as by the heroic exploits of larger-than-life figures espousing great causes. In history, as in Milgram's experiments as analyzed by Moore (1978), it is the "everyday people" who refuse to submit to authority. They are the ones who may be able to avoid becoming what Browning (1994) termed "ordinary men."

We Have No Right to Complain

Veronique's account raises a question that is often ignored because agents do not explicitly address it: Is the working world invariably more unjust than other spheres of activity, such as the home, school, or daily life? Veronique refuses to join in the incessant grumbling of her fellow staff in the emergency room who, in her opinion, parade their difficulties in order to gain more entitlements. She herself is daily confronted with the greatest injustice of all: childhood diseases and death. *"Personally, I don't have the feeling of being wronged in life. I don't like these people who feel persecuted. Sometimes you have to examine your conscience to see whether you have something to do with it or not, right? When I leave the hospital, it's back to our own world. But I think something we learn there stays with us. We keep things in perspective, and that keeps you from feeling persecuted because there are plenty of rotten things that happen to you on the side. Plus, we live pretty well. We get a decent salary. Last summer, when the heat was hellish, there were people who had to work in that heat, and that's enough to make me say we have no right to complain."* Michel, the doctor, also refuses to complain, because he has worked in other countries. Elsewhere in the world, children are starving, he points out, whereas France spends a great deal on health care for the elderly, which is a telltale sign of a *"a rich, extremely privileged country."* Sylvie, an engineer, also equates grumbling with self-indulgence: *"We are privileged, we are rich. We could help others with what we throw away. I am part of the selfish core of society."*

The condemnation of injustices, including those to which the subject herself falls victim, does not necessarily give her a moral right to complain. Everything depends on the selected basis of comparison: Many of our interviewees point out that, as members of the middle class in a rich country, they are among the world's most fortunate. And yet, they are not satisfied with these expanded terms of reference. Those who appeal to arguments of justice will also be inclined to question their share of responsibility for, or acquiescence in, the wrongs they condemn and, in consequence, the moral legitimacy of any collective action that is not necessarily endorsed by the wretched of the earth. One is even more hard put to justify a condemnation that omits to specify what one owes to the sufferings of others. Reading the interviews we collected, we may have the sense that the polyarchy of justice principles quickens people's critical faculties. At the same time, however, it creates a gulf between injustice and action, a fundamental self-doubt. After all, when people are obliged to juggle various principles of justice, they also become more skeptical, more self-critical, and more morally circumspect.

The Gulf Between Justice and Collective Action

It would, of course, be a gross, even absurd, exaggeration to claim that the obstacles to collective action are purely moral, deriving more or less directly from immanent representations of justice and human nature or from the moral consequences of the principles of justice themselves. In fact, there are far more practical, and simple, reasons why collective action falls so far short of workers' grievances, even where their demands seem wholly justified and an "impartial observer" could not but share their indignation.

Act Up or Shut Up

Collective action is costly. In addition to the economic cost of a strike or quitting one's job, there is a far more widespread, and probably heavier, price to pay in social terms. Michael's story graphically points up most of the obstacles to collective action. A 22-year-old nurse's aide, Michael witnessed elder abuse in the retirement home where he worked. Why did he choose to say nothing and simply leave? *"Their conduct was so shocking, it even got violent. I never went as far as reporting it to the higher-ups because of the fallout: I mean you've got to be careful what you do because the person who acted violent, his job's on the line. In a way, you might say that'd be fair. He starts getting violent again, maybe he shouldn't be staying on there. But, you know, a retirement home ... the people—how should I say it—the people who had the most experience were definitely sick of it, see, the job had left its mark on them, and the way they acted was sometimes worse. We'd find patients with horrible bruises on their thighs. Everyone's pretty well aware who does what in the team. I said, 'No, no, I won't put up with that. You say you're sorry and never, ever do that again in front of me.' But I never went and told my superiors and the director, 'So-and-so's an abuser.' I couldn't bring myself to do it.... Sometimes the families report it, to scare us, see, but they never go all the way. They figure, 'It's my own fault, I never should've stuck my mother in a home, this'd never have happened, so I've got no right to take it any farther. These people there are taking care of my folks, and if they don't do it anymore, who will? If the home gets shut down, who's going to take care of them?'"* Michael adds, significantly, that his fellow workers, and fellow villagers, would never have forgiven him for risking the closure of the home by reporting the elder abuse, and that he didn't feel up to taking on the union. So he opted to leave.

Michael's self-justifications set out a nearly complete catalogue of the obstacles facing those who wish to take action against injustice. Michael felt too small; he was loathe to break ranks; he feared the adverse consequences of reporting the incidents (possible closure of the home); and he sensed he would get no support, either from the community or from his natural allies, the patients' children, seeing as they themselves felt guilty for "abandoning" their parents. Furthermore, Michael can "relate" somewhat to his abusive coworkers, "worn out" by their work. These are all daunting deterrents to the types of action foregrounded by theories of mobilization.

After all, Michael could not act alone, and the uppermost impediment he faced was the feeling of betraying his fellow staff and villagers and the fear of ostracism. Catherine, a school psychologist with much sturdier safeguards than Michael had, tells of all the trouble she had after reporting a home help for child abuse. *"Don't make waves,"* said her superiors; *"We don't report people,"* said the union; *"You're causing chaos,"* said her colleagues. Mother's helper kept her job, Catherine changed hers. Social capital, while essential to collective action, also inhibits the condemnation of injustices that don't affect the group as a whole. Protesting an injustice is always a bit of a betrayal of one's immediate circle.

It goes without saying that tacit or explicit threats also prevent workers from taking action. "Love it or leave it" was one of the formulae of resignation, and one of the widespread threats, we heard frequently in the course of this study. The fact that the harshest and most iniquitous working conditions tend to erode solidarity bolsters the efficacy of the threat. Julien, a warehouseman, sometimes sounds like one of the first labor movement firebrands, hell-bent on rousing the masses from their passive stupor. Julien tried to start up a movement in his company, but *"people won't take a stand because they're afraid."* Nothing changed because Julien's coworkers feared they'd lose the little they had. What's more, according to Delphine, a cook at a hospital, whose staff can strike without fear of losing their jobs, cupidity can be another obstacle to action. *"If you ask me, it's the money and that's sick. If you talk to them about paychecks, it's yes; if you don't talk to them about paychecks, it's no."*

Many of the employees we interviewed said labor unions are reluctant to take on injustices because they cannot undertake anything that might weaken group cohesion. Note that our study showed that only 18.2 percent of workers trust labor unions to struggle against injustice. We can conclude that a certain gap exists between collective action and feelings of justice because, by definition, any collective action must concern injustices that impact the broadest possible collectivity, and it must mobilize fairly uniform principles of justice. On the other hand, this presupposes that the labor collective is not itself a generator of, or permeated with, injustice, and that the movement can espouse a cause outside the collective. Insofar as collective action is facilitated by rank-and-file unity around a cause and against an adversary, it is much more likely to develop as a defensive weapon than to attack the sources of injustice. Most of our respondents feel that collective action is useful and that labor unions are necessary. But many of them also suggest that there is a disconnect between perceived injustices and collective action because the latter appeals more to common interests than to feelings of justice, and, above all, because it necessitates a reduction of feelings of injustice to a sort of lowest common denominator, which will automatically pale beside the moral outrage of the individual victims. Ultimately, there's nothing new about any of these obstacles, and now as in the past, those who take action are generally those who can, rather than those who have good moral grounds for doing so.

From Causes to Responsibilities

There can be no collective action against an injustice unless the group concerned can pinpoint the cause thereof. Furthermore, this cause must lie in the social realm and it must be ascribed to a person or persons responsible, who, in turn, must be deemed to have intentionally wronged and/or harmed others. To paraphrase Dodier's punning formula (1994), for a feeling of injustice to be turned into collective action, workers must make common cause against a cause of injustice that is neither strictly technical nor wholly random, but the effect of personal whims or personalities. They must also juggle with positions and persons, which is tricky when the boss is likable and the victim is not (Lerner 1980).

Resistance, Virtue, and Generosity

Resistance. Individuals can shield themselves from injustice by keeping themselves "out of the fray." Without being taken in or indifferent, they can get out of harm's way by "tending their own garden." Refusing to be ground down by injustice or to live in a permanent state of indignation, they divorce themselves from the world in order to preserve their individuality. This attitude engenders a sense of continuity and assurance. It is easier to bear the injustices of the workplace if one has a life on the side, if one refuses to be defined exclusively by one's work, if one seeks first to create a personal life that will be proof against the turmoil of the outside world.

Damien, a bartender of African origin, holds that *"inequalities aren't that big a deal as long as you don't get completely immersed in them. The more dangerous inequality gets for us, the more you got to defend yourself against it. Otherwise, you'll take a beating."* For him, it is not a matter of knowing where he is now, but where he is heading. He feels privileged to be around people who are *"on the move,"* people who motivate him and spur him on to think ahead and get ahead. His friends open up other perspectives to him, enabling him to "hold on," to bear up under a grueling job. *"As for inequalities, I make sure that, for me, there aren't any."*

The experience of being wronged impels individuals to question their priorities, their personal values, and their best interests. It puts things in perspective. Losing a job is nothing against losing a loved one. It is always comforting to reflect that one's family and friends, pastimes and passions, are far more important than one's work. Injustices experienced at work can then draw a smile, even a laugh. The irony proceeds from dissociating one's personality from one's professional role, and it is a means of keeping injustice at bay. It allays the shame, the guilt, the anger, and serves to discount everything that might cause pain and humiliation. The workaday world comes to resemble a comedy or farce that invites laughter from the spectators, while those "strutting and fretting their hour upon the stage" are required to take it all seriously. So people make fun of their coworkers and superiors. "I'm there without being there," and it's all about finding a way to be there without really being there. Keeping one's distance allows one to feel happy and free, not to be too upset by the goings-on. Work is a daily ordeal to be weathered as painlessly as possible. By seeking a good life outside their work, some attain wisdom and happiness.

Past representations of injustice at work were long dominated by the categories of a labor movement and, above all, of a critical social theory equating withdrawal into private life with forsaking "the struggle." The predilection for private life and leisure-time pursuits was viewed ambivalently, as a hard-earned right and, at the same time, as a "petit bourgeois" free-market desertion of "the cause" that would shore up the partition between the public and private spheres. Workers had to choose between two alternatives: revolt or escape. And at all events it seemed to be an established fact that work reigned supreme over the whole of social experience. Without contesting the continued ascendancy of work over people's lives, it may be observed that a society that has broadened the base and scope of consumption, in spite of all the abiding inequalities, and that has shortened working hours even while stepping up the work pace, is according its workforce more and more scope for action and initiative outside the workplace: in family life, love, hobbies, music and the arts, sports, and a thousand other private pursuits. The fact that some such activities are often denigrated as culturally objectionable or even anathema to revolutionary aspirations and cultivated tastes does not alter the fact that they allow individuals to see themselves as subjects disposing of a modicum of control over their own lives.

Virtue and generosity. Many people do not appear deeply affected by injustices, albeit without seeming indifferent, cynical, or fatalistic. Nor do they simply adapt to adverse circumstances. Rather, they endeavor to construct a positive, controlled experience in the face of injustices and to transform problems of justice into problems of virtue, not by leaving the world behind, but by seeking to act within the world in a just manner.

Insofar as the cause of injustice is not invariably viewed as a target at which to take aim and fire, insofar as some believe the cause lies in the maliciousness of mankind, one must mistrust one's own indignation and dissociate one's assessments of justice from oneself. The problem of justice then becomes a problem of virtue as a normative mode of the formation of the self. In firsthand experiences of injustice at work, human decency is a form of compromise in which, given that the radical denunciation of injustices is suspect in itself, one avoids "joining the fray," seeking instead to be more sensitive to situations and persons than to more-or-less abstract principles. In order to establish their identity, individuals need to orient themselves toward "goodness" through their actions and "ways of being," through virtues that define what is really the good life for them (MacIntyre 1997). Since perfect justice cannot be established, we need to give value to our own lives. Whether that is ultimately a matter of compassion, work ethic, or respect is up to each individual to weigh up and decide.

The figure of "the just" involves differing constructs of the self. Michèle Lamont (2002) identifies two different definitions of morality among American workers: the work ethic among whites and compassion among blacks. These moral priorities constitute alternative standards of valorization that enable workers to maintain their dignity. The "be disciplined" espoused by the former and "be generous" by the latter find an echo in our interviews. But although a distinction can be drawn between these two orientations, they seem to be intermingled in most individuals. A champion of self-discipline considers himself tough, hard-working, upright. He stresses dignity, a pervasive theme in the accounts of those who seem fairly unaffected and unscathed by injustices. This dignity finds expression in a pride in one's work that often eclipses all the wrongs the worker in question has suffered. The value he accords to his work transcends the injustice of working conditions because every job is, in his eyes, a creative endeavor. *"Work is a treasure.... I'm not against resting, I'm all for it, but I'm also for working,"* says a skilled housepainter. That is why he regrets that people do not take enough pride in their work. In fact, workers manage to distinguish between working for themselves, which imparts dignity, and working for the company, which leads to exploitation. These two attitudes coexist harmoniously: One can suffer from the contempt of coworkers and employers while at the same time feeling an almost visceral need to devote oneself to one's work. *"When you do your job, you've got to do it well, and if you don't do it well it's normal for the boss not to be happy,"* says Justine, a cashier in a supermarket.

The wounds life inflicts on us do not always exacerbate our shame, humiliation, rage, and resentment: They can, on the contrary, forge the will to be just. If we wish to rid the world of injustice, we have to be better and more just than others. Gerard, a winery manager who has been laid off, draws strength from the wrongs he has suffered, and believes that decency, dignity, and caring about others are a way of overcoming and defying adversity and constructing one's identity on that basis: *"I believe there will always be some injustice, c'est la vie. So then, it's be as fair as possible yourself."* On the job he eschews the brutality of the new forms of management. *"I hope to have a good rapport with my staff, to be evenhanded. Nowadays it's a system of management I don't accept and will never subscribe to. It's moral harassment of the employees, and that I can't accept. This management system is instilled into them. I just don't get it. That wouldn't spur me on, it puts me off, makes me back off. It scares me to see those youngsters react that way. They'd kill their own mother and father and that's really dangerous; we're not dogs. Everyone has the right to live, the right to screw up."*

The other side of virtue is generosity, the ability to open up to others. "Be generous" involves more collective aspects than "be disciplined," for it privileges altruism, sharing, and the warmth of personal relations.

Etienne, a poorly paid 53-year-old sports instructor, launched into a whole-sale denunciation of the loss of values, the widening rift between the "big shots" and the "small fry," the recent abolition of a national holiday, excessive social security taxes, the incompetence of a government that encourages people "to stay home—it's on the house!" But for him, *"things aren't all that bad."* He has set up his own fitness center to *"pep people up, get them back in shape."* He likes human contact and the friendly, informal atmosphere, and makes an effort to adjust his rates to his cus-tomers' financial situations, even if it means "being had." *"At a big gym, you accept the rates and you don't haggle. They don't give a shit, you don't get your money back. And me, well, they know I'm a good guy, too good, and I play the game just right and they really go for it."*

What counts for Nicole now is to live her life and be decent *"towards the people you serve and who serve you; when you respect people, when you respect their value, their work, and then you pay them accordingly, there's really no trouble."* She gives the impression of going through life and its attendant injustices unscathed. Though she does not believe in anything, she thinks an immanent justice exists, that the righteous and virtuous are rewarded, for what they give to others will always be given back to them in one form or another.

Injustices are sometimes considered trials from which one emerges stronger and more autonomous. Those who have struggled against the tide feel a sense of victory. So it is with Senam, a young saleswoman from Togo, who says she has built an identity for herself by defying injustice: *"I figure it could always be worse, when I take stock of my life. I turned 28 not too long ago. Considering where I started out and the shaky situation I was in, and the young woman I am today, I feel like saying: 'I'm not unhappy with the results.'"* How many "human interest" stories reveal the positive side of the experience of injustice! The world of sports, for instance, abounds with heroic tales of champions who overcame terrible afflictions before "making it big." The business community never tires of applauding the exploits of those who went "from rags to riches." And the art world incessantly associates genius with trials and tribulations and life's injustices. But in these grand legends and archetypal myths, everyone can find "little" stories as well, which, as they are not extraordinary, might not be mere fairy tales.

Though destructive, the shame of having suffered injustices also im-pels the victims to exist as subjects. Sartre (1964) described how it sparked in him the need to "awaken to himself." Injustice has a socializing effect when it compels the victim to adopt the position of one subject among others, to assert her uniqueness while becoming more modest. Through injustice we discover that we are neither better nor worse than others, that we are like others and, at the same time, unique. Just as anger and rage can always be suspected of being nothing but the ruses of resentment, the vaunting of virtue might merely be a ruse of narcissism and a means of consoling oneself. How can we know? Claims of virtuousness simply expose us to the same suspicions we level at others. Therefore, rather than dreaming of plumbing the secrets of the soul, let us accept things as they appear to be without being overly credulous or skeptical. Suffice it to observe that subjects are obliged to create their identity, with some measure of good faith, that this autogenesis involves them with others, and that sociologists are not all that different from those they observe.

*   *   *

Like activists, sociologists are overly inclined to expect subjective injustice to translate automatically into collective action. But a whole "moral economy" always obtains between perceived injustices and action. Since feelings of injustice are moral sentiments, they demand both moral and social causes and interpretations. In the first place, definitions of justice seem to be based on hypotheses about the immanent justice of the order of things and about human nature. These hypotheses may inhibit individuals from taking action, if they believe social positions are determined by a sort of lottery beyond their control; or, apparently more commonly, if they assume that the fundamental depravity of human nature precludes any hope of a better world. What appears even more astonishing is the fact that individuals denounce injustices without believing that the victims are entirely innocent. Assuming we are free and responsible beings, must we pity those who seem to bear the brunt of the world's injustice? Likewise, while the province of tolerable inequalities seems to be bounded by the outcasts of society and the utterly destitute, they are often perceived as dangerous and violent wards of the state instead of innocent victims of injustice.

Not all individuals subscribe to the "pharisaic" view that evil exists outside the self. Many, moreover, have a sense of contributing more or less actively to the injustices they denounce, either by causing them or by passively riding the tides of day-to-day life in society. What is more, after protracted accounts of grievances past and present and long litanies of denunciations, it is not unusual for agents to wonder whether they really have a right to complain and whether organized collective action is truly righteous. Thus, the problem of virtue supersedes the problem of justice, and individuals are tempted to act at a limited, proximate level rather than turning to collective action, which always seems by nature more or less remote from their sense of justice.

This somewhat pessimistic assessment does not deny any nexus between a sense of justice, collective action, and social movements; collective action is indeed grounded in injustice and is usually called upon to justify itself in terms of justice. It can easily be shown that a host of social movements directly co-opt feelings of injustice, triggering surges of solidarity and emotion that go far beyond the particularist interests of the group directly concerned. But it seems entirely as though the sphere of subjective justice and the sphere of representations of the social domain were relatively autonomous and independent of each other. We should, therefore, stop construing collective action as the direct expression of the individual experience of injustice.

Notes

1. The "injustice scores" are as follows: unionized labor 5.48, nonunionized 5.29, average 5.23; those who take part in collective action 5.58, those who do not 5.10. In any case, the disparity is not statistically significant.

2. *Baccalauréat*: French national standardized school-leaving exams to obtain the rough equivalent of a high school diploma—Translator's note.

3. This is one of Bourdieu's themes (1997): What he likes about being a sociologist is that it allows him to be indignant.

4. A charity organization that distributes free meals to the indigent, akin to Meals on Wheels.

Conclusion

An Unjust World

THE PRINCIPLE OF EQUALITY gives rise to two main types of criticism. The first denounces inequalities of position and, in this domain, the French have retained their revolutionary aversion to castes and aristocracies—along with a paradoxically aristocratic obsession with "rank" and "honor." The existing rifts between the social strata are felt to be hurtful and degrading: Those "at the bottom" feel those "at the top" treat them as an inferior race of abject, invisible, and interchangeable drones with neither the same needs nor the same aspirations as their "superiors." But, to varying degrees, this feeling of injustice permeates the entire social fabric: Everyone feels to some extent devalued, disdained, disregarded. It is entirely as though the French revolution had never been completed, and the classification struggle remains a touchier issue than the class struggle.

The second type of criticism is markedly different. It looks beyond the issue of unequal social positions to focus on inequalities of opportunity to compete on a fair and equal footing for those unequal positions. It is the *challengers,* the women, immigrants, and young people, who champion this more liberal conception of equality. Thus, the working world appears doubly unjust. For one thing, inequalities of caste are superimposed on inequalities that are deemed normal and functional; for another, there are no guarantees of initial equality at the level of entry into the labor market. In the former case, positional inequalities need to be reduced. In the latter, the obstacles to equal opportunity need to be removed, including various forms of discrimination and, specifically, the perpetuation of educational inequalities, contend those with the highest academic qualifications. Workers are all for equality, but clearly not for the same brand of equality.

Similarly, the principle of merit yields a set of mutually distinct critiques. The most vehement remains the critique of exploitation born of a sense of a profound imbalance between contributions and compensations, a sense of spoliation. This feeling is particularly widespread among laborers whose working conditions are the most grueling and whose earnings are directly tied to day-to-day performance. Further, as merit is measured by comparisons within one's immediate circle, the principle of merit generates a continuous chain of frustrations, a concatenation of envy and petty jealousies. Finally, everyone suspects "objective" merit assessments of being skewed by favoritism and privilege on the one hand, and hounding and harassment on the other. But the vigor of these criticisms does not diminish the sway of the merit principle, and disregard for merit in the work organization is invariably condemned. Thus, despite its apparent clarity and ascendancy, the merit principle is one of the least stable principles of justice. Should merit be assessed on the basis of effort or results? How should professional and scholastic merit be linked, if at all? We all believe in merit without quite knowing how to handle it. No doubt it would be wrong to say the French put no faith in merit, but it is a faith tempered by suspicion and skepticism. And yet this very leap of faith is a prerequisite for the construction of just inequalities.

Most workers find an interest in their work—or, more precisely, something that interests them: the responsibility, the vocation, the interaction, etc. Autonomy hinges on a valorization of work for its own sake and breeds a critique whose yardstick is the subject's sense of self-fulfillment. This strictly subjective standard involves yet another twofold critique. On the one hand, workers revile inane, alienating, exhausting, destructive work, and in so doing, perpetuate a long-established tradition of vilifying mechanical and fatiguing labor. Work ought to provide an autonomous subject with a rewarding activity, but in many cases it breaks him down instead. On the other hand, workers denounce excessive autonomy as a corporate ruse aimed at appropriating their liberty. Hence the ongoing entanglement between the "age-old" critique of alienation and the condemnation of the "new" capitalist spirit.

The various families of criticism intrinsic to each principle of justice breed even more intense and unstable denunciations of combinations of those principles.

Injustice is often perceived in terms of violations of labor regulations and collective agreements. And yet procedural justice cannot be considered a real principle in itself: for labor-code enforcement is elastic, sometimes erratic, and in general the letter of the law is only applied as a last resort in situations of crisis and conflict. The most vulnerable workers believe the rules are simply a codified expression of the existing power imbalance, yet another tool to stultify them and keep them down. Sometimes the very excess of rules seems unfair. In the final analysis, everyone finds virtues in the labor code and fears any attempt to undermine it, yet everyone makes strategic use of its unstable combination of the principles of equality and merit.

The critique of power is likewise enmired in inexhaustible contradictions. Power may be regarded as the mediator between rational work organization and individual autonomy, but there always seems to be too much or too little of it. The most helpless workers feel subjected to the tyranny and whims of slave drivers, and their descriptions of shop-floor relations evoke a strikingly brutal world in which threats, contempt, and insults are the order of the day. Then again, those at the mercy of the whims of their superiors and coworkers do not know who wields the real authority to decide and protect, so authority seems to them by and large something weak, chaotic, uncertain. The actual owner or employer seems to be dissolved in the anonymous operation of the system.

Finally, the demand for recognition is endemic because it is at once an appeal for respect based on individual equality and a claim for the recognition of each person's uniqueness and autonomy. Contempt, dirty work, the decline of professional honor attaching to certain institutions, sexism, racism, denigration of the working class—everything concurs to engender a sense of nonrecognition. But the subjective importance of the craving for recognition should not mislead us into believing that this is the very core of injustice in the workplace. Rather, the need for recognition has grown as we become more and more individualistic and, concomitantly, more and more equal, and this profound evolution of democratic societies is reproduced in the workplace itself. The old ideologies of the dignity of suffering at work are on the wane, making way for an ever-increasing desire for recognition.

Classes Without Society

Social reformers of the past envisioned a classless society. Today we are confronted with societyless classes. To be sure, the assessments of justice by company heads and the most mistreated blue-collar workers are pretty much diametrically opposed, which is by no means inconsequential. For the rest, however, it is hardly possible to correlate beliefs about justice with social class. Once again, what we are witnessing is not the end of class domination, but the breakdown of class-based society—or, more precisely, of our long-cherished model of modern industrial society. In essence, this was a society identified with a nation-state and made up of social classes that were, concomitantly, communities and ways of life, particularly for the working class. Within this framework, it seemed easy to establish solid correlations between social positions and whole matrices of attitudes and dispositions. But the disparate elements that the very idea of society was able to assimilate and integrate are now breaking up and drawing apart. Workers perceive the economy as an objective force, alien and remote, over which they have no control—over which perhaps no one has any control. In our interviews we heard intermittent echoes of nineteenth-century social theorists describing capitalism as a blind force, a torrent bearing everything before it in its onward rush. The nation, so self-assured for so long, now seems enfeebled by cultural globalization and by all the immigrants and foreigners closing in on every side. Society and the economy are diverging, and though work remains as central as ever to the lives and subjectivity of individuals, it is no longer at the heart of our institutions or the welfare state. We have seen that employees at institutions identified with the public interest and the Republic are now seized with a profound sense of crisis. Hospitals and schools, for example, fear they will become mere service providers, no longer revered as pillars of society. We all expect the state to protect us, but we can't help thinking that politicians have lost the ability to steer the course of change. As a result, criticisms of inequalities and injustices are constantly interwoven with condemnations of selfishness and anomie, with a fear of the future and an idealization of the past. Though people admit that the times were even more unjust in their youth than they are today, the denunciation of injustices is still bound up with a nostalgia for a world that is "gone for good." And precisely because that age is no longer with us, it has acquired the enduring charm of a landscape painting.

The decline of the class-based image of society does not necessarily give rise to radically new schisms, but it heightens workers' awareness of them. In addition to sizable income disparities within each socioprofessional group, there is considerable variation in working conditions, which largely determine whether workers feel ill treated. Working hours; stress and fatigue; respect for collective agreements; and relations with superiors, peers, and customers have a far more decisive influence on perceptions of exploitation and ill treatment than social stratification. Naturally, the further down we look in the social hierarchy, the greater the odds that unfavorable working conditions will overlap, but it turns out that is not true of all blue-collar and unskilled white-collar workers, while it is true of more and more mid-level personnel. Ultimately, feelings of injustice are chiefly engendered by one's immediate working conditions and on-the-job social relations. As a result, a great many injustices are ascribed to persons rather than to the system. Each realm of work possesses its own grammar of subjective injustice, which, however, cannot be readily correlated with positions in the social structure. Moreover, criticisms arising out of the local context are also influenced by the spectacle of the world served up in the media, which considerably enlarges the field of comparison and confronts unhappy workers with the suffering of their counterparts in the farthest corners of the earth. The daily display of "remote suffering" and the horror of the human condition put the adversities of French workers in perspective, and impact their perceptions of injustice as forcefully as their own experiences in the workplace.

Various mixed-class groups in society contribute to the dispersal of perceived injustices. Most women feel subjected to sexism, either in the form of discrimination and inequalities or in the form of condescending or denigrating attitudes. Although men and women apply the same principles of justice, they do not necessarily combine them in the same way according to the occupations that are reserved for them, particularly inasmuch as the relationship between professional and family life remains profoundly different for men and women. Racial segregation and outright racism create a similar mixed-class group of victims. But racism is experienced as being more vicious and unjust than sexism because it imposes identities and stereotypes on individuals, in society and at work, which they do not necessarily accept, or which they sometimes affirm only in order to resist the destructive effects of stigmatization.

Different degrees of job security attaching to differences in employment status cause profound rifts within each socioprofessional group. Those with the most precarious status are wont to begrudge the privileges of tenured staff, who in turn justify their privileges as established entitlements or even as the normal advantages of professions identified with public service, the general weal, or national interests. Our study points up the intensity of a critique that is clearly not reducible to the vestiges of a *"poujadist"* (from Poujadism, a lower-middle-class authoritarian populist movement in the 1950s, now meaning narrow-minded shopkeeper mentality) vilification of the civil service. Even if they do equivalent jobs for equivalent pay, the situations of permanent and casual staff are poles apart. The former can make plans for the future and envisage a career; the latter simply cannot. In the face of this perceived injustice, those without job security and those who have known unemployment are more favorably disposed to criteria of merit than protected employees, who cleave to qualifications and competitive examinations and insist on the fairness of the resultant hierarchies.

The conception of injustice and inequalities at work takes shape within a representation of a society bounded by those *above* and those *below* the society of equals. Above the employers, bosses, coworkers, customers, and users who either cause or trigger the injustices to which workers react, there is an élite class of decision makers that seems increasingly abstract and remote. It is regarded as being outside of society, an aristocracy of sorts, but this is a virtual aristocracy, with which there is no contact, at least not any more. Corporate managers no longer organize the social realm the way industrialists once could, for they represent the stockholders more than the interests of their companies. The media offer glimpses of these "masters of the universe," these select few set apart from humanity by their income, their lifestyle, and their cosmopolitan-ism. Workers cannot be quite sure any more that the manager standing in front of them is the *real* boss. She is not the one who decides economic policy; she has no leverage in an economy ruled by the abstract forces of finance, by the global market that holds the fate of the workforce in its hands. Ultimately, the target of criticism is not capitalist society, but capitalism itself, which is accused of breaking away from society.

Beneath society are all those who are not really part of it: the indigent, the outcasts, the long-term unemployed, the welfare dependent, the home-less, the disenfranchised. However disputable at the level of sociological theory, the notion of an *underclass* really means something to workers. It signifies that beneath the acceptable stratifications and inequalities are all those inhabitants who are no longer part of society, those who are no longer exploited or exploitable. All the injustices converge here: the segregation of immigrants and French nationals of "ethnic" origin, slums, crime, poverty, broken homes, etc. This ghettoized underclass forms the *lower boundary* of the social realm, an abyss into which gainful em-ployment keeps us from falling. Urban riots serve to give this frontier an ambiguous visibility, a blend of outrage at such appalling injustices and the widespread dread of the dangerous classes.

These upper and lower internal boundaries are external boundaries as well. The economic élite are global players, while the excluded inhabit enclaves of the underdeveloped South that happen to be situated in the North. This sociogeographical configuration inside the country poses a threat to the very idea of a national society. The state of being sandwiched between the more or less abstract and invisible "masters of the universe," on one side, and the immigrants and outcasts who are often close at hand, on the other, heavily impacts our perceptions of injustice. Inequalities seem fairly acceptable as long as they lie *this side* of the two extremes. Our study, among others, shows that there is a broad consensus on what constitute tolerable inequalities: those that do not shatter the impression of belonging to the same world. After an extended diatribe against any number of social wrongs, many an interviewee would conclude with a disclaimer to the effect that "As for me, I'm OK." Though working condi-tions may spark outrage at perceived injustices, the structure of a society bounded above and below by groups that no longer seem to form part of that society significantly attenuates the reach of those injustices and contextually displaces them from the workplace to the nation.

For the most vulnerable segments of the working class, the threat of exclusion is not abstract: Their neighbors are pariahs, they have social outcasts in the family, they have known unemployment and job insecurity themselves. This proximity and this enduring threat give rise to both an egalitarian aspiration and a vigorous moral condemnation of the "danger-ous classes." The image of the waiting line at the welfare office where immigrant families are said to have cornered the benefits market came up in many of our interviews, and many workers see the near-equivalence of welfare benefits and the statutory minimum wage as a gross injustice and a threat to the dignity of French workers and citizens. A desire for equality and a moral condemnation of victims, especially those regarded as "outsiders," are frequently mixed, as Tocqueville observed in the attitudes of white Americans toward freed slaves migrating to the Northern states.

The highest-paid employees with the steadiest jobs generally advocate a policy of redistribution and the implementation of minimum safeguards, even while pointing out the ineffectiveness and pernicious effects thereof. And yet they are also in favor of the perpetuation of vast inequalities arising out of the free play of merit, whether in the professional or scholastic realm. In practice, however, they keep their distance, socially and geographically, from the fringes of society. They agree to pay taxes, but they shun the locations where they might run into the "underclass"— slum neighborhoods, schools, recreational facilities, and so on. They can be said to have both a social conscience and a liberal mindset.

Injustice and Action

A sense of injustice arises out of three relatively distinct social contexts: that of working conditions, that of disparities in hiring conditions, and that of a society bounded on one side by a quasi-invisible and all-powerful ultra-élite and, on the other, by the excluded elements, who are viewed as being both victims and a menace. These three different arenas of subjective injustice make it extremely difficult to transform feelings of injustice into action, for neither the same representations nor the same contexts of action obtain at each level. Collective movements pass through a multitude of different channels, which the same individuals may take one after another.

One such channel is an altruistic disposition, the indignation that philanthropic organizations and NGOs draw on to collect ad hoc donations and commitments to the causes that are the most sensational, the most heartrending, the most exposed to public compassion. If in a position to do so, we give a little or a lot of our time and money to organizations that are out combating the most shocking injustices. "Humanitarian aid" is an apt appellation, for it is a matter of saving certain groups from being excluded from humanity, though the humanity in question may well be far, far away from us.

The second vector of action is that of advocacy groups that combine a cultural critique with a commitment to democratic values in their struggle against any of various forms of discrimination. On behalf of women, immigrants, the handicapped, the disenfranchised, etc., they adopt a stance of liberal egalitarianism, opposing the initial inequalities that bar equitable access to unequal positions in the division of labor. Even if these groups may seem to have limited leverage, they are fairly effective at rousing public opinion and putting pressure on policymakers, who respond by reaffirming their commitment and reinforcing measures to fight discrimination. Interest groups have ultimately succeeded in imposing the prevailing conception of equality in our day: namely, equal opportunity.

Finally, labor unions draw attention to many perceived injustices, especially in decrying mass layoffs and closures of companies that seem to be viable and competitive. As they also oppose unfair dismissals, infringements of collective agreements, and inadequate wages, there is no denying the prominent role of organized struggle in the fight against injustice. At the same time, however, they remain preoccupied with the defense of social benefits, the public sector, and the most powerful trades and organizations. As a result, they tend to overlook other injustices, and many of the workers we interviewed think the unions reinforce deep-seated social inequalities by defending only those who are capable of defending themselves, thereby staking out a social turf for powerful and widespread corporatism.

The focus of mass movements seems to be shifting from strictly social struggles to issues of national concern. The 1995 strikes in France, the extreme right-wing's impressive election results, the rejection of the proposed European Constitution, the authoritarian and nationalistic public reaction to the youth riots in the slums—all of these highlight the extent to which, in diverse and often mutually opposed ideological registers, the defense of a republican national model overlaps with the struggle for social justice. Faced with economic globalization, the remoteness of the managerial élite, the dwindling capacity of national governments to control their own economies, the people clamor for a state capable of re-establishing social relations, which are currently dissolving in a morass over which no one seems to have any control anymore. In a restored nation, in a restored republic, they would reconstruct the nexus between capitalism and society that once held industrial society together for so long.[1]

In this respect, the sense of justice is becoming detached from the workplace and subsumed in an overall view of the nation and of global social change. These judgments stabilize on an essentially political plane, though without directly affecting individual judgments formed in firsthand experience of work.

In the "nationalistic/republican" camp of those who hold that change and globalization constitute a menace to the French nation and society, two configurations emerge:

- The right side of the political spectrum sees equality as a legitimate hierarchy, merit as objective performance rather than as a virtue, and autonomy as the individual's ability to resist the centrifugal forces of anomie and moral decadence. The resultant paradigm fuses several themes of the conservative revolution: A society bolstered by the legitimacy of its hierarchies, by its morally assured members, and by its economic performance is the only one capable of standing its ground and asserting itself in the global arena. A powerful central authority and an assertive national consciousness will enable us to rebuild a dynamic economy, so the argument goes, once we are rid of onerous regulations and the prodigal welfare state. Essentially, this view calls for the re-creation of a national entrepreneurial class.

- On the left, equality is also a legitimate hierarchical order, the individual is also defined by his moral self-control, but "true" (i.e., primarily academic) merit cannot be reduced to economic performance. A strong society will resist the threats of globalization by regrouping around the state and its civil service in order to withstand the corrosive forces of rampant individualism. We are also witnessing the return of a left-wing extremist sensibility that is actually more nationalistic than social, since it sees the state as the sole means of opposing injustices whose root causes lie outside society and the nation.

These two major ideological families disagree on merit and the economy, but they share the same conceptions of autonomy and equality. Proceeding from an essentially defensive view of national society, they appeal chiefly to the socioprofessional groups that feel threatened by change: small-scale entrepreneurs on one side of the spectrum, state-protected sectors on the other.

In the other camp are two "liberal" stances with similar conceptions of equality and autonomy, but different views on merit and, consequently, on the economy.

- On the right, equality is identified with equal opportunity and the struggle against discrimination, while merit is equated with economic performance, and individual autonomy with a right to difference and identity. It should be noted that this liberal configuration has never really found widespread political expression in France.
- On the left, one observes the same liberal schema with regard to equal opportunity and moral individualism, but the feeling is that merit should be heavily counterbalanced by social safeguards in order not to exclude the most vulnerable elements of society, including large-scale redistribution to protect against social fragmentation.[2] This is the aspiration of the "new left," or of an "American left," as it was called in the 1970s; of a left wing whose vague politics and

unionism remain dispersed among certain currents of the socialists, Greens, reformist unions, and the like. While the other left-wing contingent rejects social democracy, this one espouses it.

These two ideological sensibilities concern groups that do not feel threatened by change, but are ready to take it on, armed with their qualifications, mobility, skills, activity, and cosmopolitan culture.

This double divide is the manifestation of a profound social transformation. On the one hand, there are the problems of work itself; on the other, those of a society dominated by change and at the mercy of economic mechanisms it no longer controls. The upshot is a "social dislocation" in which the problems of order and those of change seem to be drifting apart. It probably wouldn't be hard to trace the twists and turns of this double divide running through French political life. Nonetheless, it seems to be part of a "superstructure" holding the moral representations of society in place rather than a direct consequence of workers' subjective notions of justice. It is, in all likelihood, because they are remote from workplace experiences that these configurations are so resistant to being shaped into assertive political forces. Ultimately, feelings of injustice at work find a relatively stable form of political expression only in a series of transformations of collective representations or institutional mechanisms at some remove from individual experience. So it is that agents feel entitled to censure political parties, unions, and governments without ever really having supported them; they tend to be censors rather than politically committed citizens.

Connected and Conflicting Principles

In the firmament of ideas, equality, merit, and autonomy form a set of principles that are highly integrated and connected by necessary links. But, as we have reiterated—doubtless ad nauseam—in the foregoing chapters, judgments of justice are formed somewhere between autonomous and antinomic principles. Agents adopt them by turns, never remaining faithful to any one principle. No single principle stands out as being central, and any appeal to one of them immediately entails a twofold critical activity: an internal critique carried out in the name of the chosen principle, and an external critique of the other two principles. The whole complexity of the system of judgments arises from the fact that individuals engage in this exercise for each of the three principles. Thus, there is always too much or too little equality, too much or too little merit, too much or too little autonomy. The nonhierarchic polyarchy of the principles of justice engenders an ongoing critical process in which no judgment is every truly stabilized. We want to engrave *Liberté, Egalité, Fraternité* on the pediment of every town hall in France, even though we know this motto is inherently contradictory; what was long considered the answer is now becoming the question.

A society that chose to promote any one principle at the expense of the others would doubtless prove utterly unjust. Pure equality would eradicate autonomy and merit, since they pose a threat to equality, and the history of the twentieth century teaches us that those who chose this course annihilated freedom and, above all, that this equality was, in some cases, merely a modern way of defining the nation and the people as a pure community. Choosing performance-based merit would mechanically generate a "Darwinian" world in which the just triumph of the fittest would entail the equally just defeat of the less fit. Finally, the hegemony of pure autonomy would be a blueprint for a sort of "nonsocial" libertarian society in which individuals—and one wonders where such individuals would be found—or communities with nothing in common but shared roots would live and work side by side rather than living and working together in any meaningful sense.

To all appearances, individuals have a sort of tacit awareness of these dead ends, at least for the injustices that concern them. The workers we interviewed opt for the full set of justice principles because, taken together, they balance one another out. Even if agents are not fully clear on the implications of their judgments, they do have a confused sense that one has to mix perspectives to live in a world that is less unjust, since an absolutely just world would doubtless prove a living hell. In essence, from the viewpoint of justice, individuals cherish several principles in order to ward off the tragedy of an inexhaustible war. They are, in this sense, wiser than critics who play at taking a single principle of justice to its logical conclusion. From the start, they embrace a plurality of principles in which they will never fully believe.

Indeed, these principles are probably best conceived of as necessary fictions we adopt for practical purposes, enabling us to steer action, arbitrate conflicts, and resolve tensions. It matters little whether these fictions are "true" or their foundations "solid." We can act only by availing ourselves thereof and reflecting that they are far more reasonable and plausible than purely rational. The principles are, in a word, both "pure" and pragmatic.

Yearning by turns for more equality, merit, and autonomy, we become disillusioned, less susceptible to believing in what Weber called the "metaphysical pathos," the assumption that someday, on some distant horizon, the principles of justice and moral values will ultimately be reconciled once and for all. So we are left with the prospect of a just society fundamentally destabilized by the inalterable antinomies between the principles of justice. Though a great deal of anger was expressed in our interviews, none of it was leveled at the image of a society reconciled with itself. We are, it would seem, more capable of saying what we don't want than what we do. For the people we interviewed, neither reason, nor science, nor the nation seems to bring us any closer to the utopia of a just world. Indeed, ordinary social criticism is of a nonutopian cast, and today's political leaders and intellectuals are not much further along in mapping out a just future for our society. French politicians who speak of "*rupture*" know what they want to break away *from,* but hardly ever intimate where they're heading *to.* Though we sometimes hear rumblings of yearnings for revolution, we never hear plans for the postrevolutionary society. Some would break with capitalism, but no one wants a totally planned economy. Others would strengthen the bonds that hold the nation together, but no one wants autarchy. Many want more freedom, but everyone fears the consequences thereof.

Many people ponder on the true causes of injustice. But when the causes are not found within the social realm, they are deemed unactionable. That there will always be injustice seems undeniable. Even though we are all equal under the law, it seems clear, in fact, that we are not; and there will always be winners and losers in the great lottery that awards strength, beauty, intelligence, talent, courage, virtue, in unequal measure. And the more we equate equality with equal opportunity, the ruder the awakening to the apparently inalterable results of the lottery. Worse still, our spontaneous moral anthropology is not entirely optimistic. In more or less secularized form, rationalized by a latent suspicion of the pernicious effects of change, a belief in man's inherent evil endures, a vestige of the doctrine of original sin. If men are not good, if the victims can be just as wicked as the oppressors, "protesting too much" becomes suspect.

In fact, we may not even have any right to protest. Now that the media have brought the world into our living rooms, its myriad egregious injustices are eclipsing ours, for many of us realize we live in a rich and fairly cosseted world. So we may have no right to complain, and many workers curb their invective when they compare their lot in life to that of the planet's many true have-nots. In fact, those who complain too loud and too long are sometimes suspected of solipsism.

The autonomy principle undermines the legitimacy of many complaints even more effectively. If we want to be free agents, responsible for our own lives, we cannot bear to see ourselves as mere victims. As a result, the principles of autonomy and, to a lesser degree, merit markedly dilute our compassion for victims and our indignation at their plight. There is no denying that the victims are put in an unfair position: Unemployment is unjust, as are the social inequalities at the root of educational inequality; the treatment of women is unfair, as is that of minorities. Still, it is not a foregone conclusion that that particular fellow on the unemployment line deserves a job, that that underprivileged child over there is not himself to blame for failing out of school, that that particular woman is not actively sabotaging herself, that that immigrant is really making an effort to assimilate.

In fact, the norms of justice are not necessarily conducive to indulgence, and it might even be that the more seriously we take them, the harsher we will be toward those found wanting. Whereas old-fashioned Christian compassion turned a blind eye to social injustice while showing charity to its victims, modern critics inveigh against social injustice, but without always showing quite as much charity toward the victims.

In denouncing injustice, agents are obliged to distinguish between persons and positions, between intentional harm and the objective mechanisms of the working world. And these two conceptions of the causes of affliction may lie far apart. When injustice is wholly attributed to persons, the workplace becomes a private world in which everything is a function of personality and human relations, and injustice remains within the confines of this microcosm. When injustice is blamed on the system alone, it becomes without cause, at any rate without actionable cause. This cognitive problem is also a social one: Beyond indiscriminately raging against the system, it may be hard to identify the right targets on which to vent our righteous ire. When society is considered evil through and through, a factory for the production of injustices, as it were, the outrage is liable to be free-floating and only satisfying to those who vent it.

The Limits of Justice

The more the war of the gods rages on, the less we believe in the possibility of a perfectly just world. We are trapped, forced to make do with "living arrangements" and crazy-quilt combinations of the principles of justice. This conclusion is a bit sad, but not hopeless: After all, one can find reasons to take action without necessarily believing it will make a heaven of this worldly hell.

We should condemn the existence of a border inside our own society, for it is a moral outrage and a social danger that we exacerbate by blaming the victims for their own exclusion and fearing them as dangerous outcasts. In other words, the fight against joblessness must be upheld as the paramount issue of social justice, for it is anterior to work itself, along with the fight against the privileges of an ultra-élite ensconced in a world of its own. This assertion is so obvious, so incantatory, that it would sound ridiculous if it were limited to "rooting out the evil," the designated culprits being "fat cats," immigrants, the market, globalization, and all the rest. Instead, the fight against these inequalities will require a paradigm shift. It will involve shifting the social divides and overhauling the guiding lines of social policy, educational policy, tax policy, and city planning, which are clearly less and less equal to the task of keeping our tattered social fabric together.

In this regard, the people we encountered in the course of our research sometimes seemed more lucid and courageous than those who represent them, who all too often claim that since we can't change the whole system, we must simply keep defending traditional political stances and slogans devoid of substance. Though they are as hollow and artificial as Potemkin villages, we cling to them on the pretext that things could only get worse if we abandoned the delusions we take for the core of our national identity. To state the case more plainly: We must become "social democrats" who refuse to believe that all the inequalities that have emerged over the past 50 years are just and that the fight against outrageous injustice will not involve certain sacrifices and realignments of the social divides.

For example, the muted struggle between liberal equality and hierarchical equalities probably concerns each and every one of us, and promoting the former will take its toll on the latter. Fewer restrictions on hiring and firing, albeit with stronger safeguards for temporary employment, would improve the prospects for some at the expense of the job security of others. In this sense, the independence of the spheres of justice must remain a core objective in the face of overlapping, mutually reinforcing inequalities in the workplace, as in the domains of education and housing.

The only way to conceive of a just world in the workplace itself is in terms of local adjustments between conflicting principles. The evil arises from monomaniacal management methods, and every work organization needs to be reconceived along more political, democratic lines. The sentiment may seem hackneyed, even "old hat," but it seems as though democracy stops at the factory gates, as though it were banned from the company premises, where threats vie with consent for supremacy. Wherever work relations supplant human relations, wherever the bosses' tyranny supplants good governance, employees may be reduced to adjustable variables. But in the workplace, where we combine antinomic principles of justice, our combinations must be ruled by some central principle, which, as it cannot be any of the principles of justice, must be a conception of the good, an idea of the good life.

As a perfectly just world lies beyond the horizons of criticism and action, as we are doomed to combining conflicting principles, the object of justice shifts to the individual. The paramount injustice is then whatever undermines the individual, whatever prevents her from being the subject of her life, from attaining self-realization in opposition to, or in spite of, injustice. A just society is neither perfect nor virtuous: It is a society that enables individuals to be fully fledged subjects combining the principles of justice themselves, so as to live their idea of the good life.

As justice cannot be ordained from the top down, it must be grounded in the individual, enabling each to assert what is good for him and for his working community.

The individual is regarded here as a subject capable of producing meaning, of structuring his world at a distance from, and in a state of constant tension with, society. The individual is a subject not because she has already attained to that state, but because she is not completely socialized, because she is still determined to wring a moral conception of the good life from the lives imposed on her by the constraints of work, exploitation, and consumerism, and from the identities foisted on her by her society. From this angle, the individual appears a sort of "micro labor movement," a movement mustering his body, emotions, individuality, dignity, and his inner circle of family and friends to defy those representations of himself and the various social controls that would reduce him either to his functional roles or his socioeconomic interests. In this perspective, the individual is both a social agent and the issue at stake, for she appears as a subject only in her determination or desire to construct herself as such. This is how our study saw those who are striving to forge their identity against the forces of injustice by asserting their own ethical value and forging what to them seems to be the good.

From this viewpoint, the problem of the individual exactly corresponds to that of the sociologist attempting to recompose the unit of social life. And just as society is an ongoing production, the individual is his own production. His "essence" is his ongoing work on himself, so injustice is any impediment to that work: contempt, exhaustion, mindless toil, the inflexibility of rules to special cases and life's agenda, the fixation on or uselessness of continued education, etc. Ultimately, if being an individual involves no end of tribulation, the tribulations lie in the social realm. Yet they are not the sole injustice, for it is unjust that agents are not equipped to face them, for want of both subjective recognition and social resources. Because the individual is at once the fulfillment of a socialization agenda, a cognitive machine, and a desire for autonomy, she has to learn to see how to go about being a subject. Like a good society, a good organization is one that supports her in this endeavor. So we should probably individualize social policies, equip workers with skills and a trade they can call their own, strengthen their education, give them mobility without disorientation—in short, we should probably face the fact that we live in a society of individuals.

One can always strike a pose and declare what a just society is—and how far ours falls short of it. On the latter head, the workers who have spoken out in this book did a better job than we could ever do. But if we have devoted some discussion to the individual's part in these matters, it is to stress that he is both the measure and the end of injustice. Each of the principles of justice is cruel and unjust in the end, and a just society is one that enables workers to forge an identity as subjects capable of saying where their dignity lies and what constitutes a good and acceptable life: subjects capable of resisting the chain of injustices. Thus, a good society is not a just one. It is, rather, the least unjust society possible, for it allows individuals to combine conflicting principles in the subjectivity of their own minds. Though unlikely ever to succeed, it should enable them to resist the destructive effects of injustice. A good society should prevent the formation of overlapping social divides and ghettoized injustices. No one sector of activity should be allowed sway over all the others at the expense of part of the population. Basically, the "miracle" is that individuals strive to be just in a society that is not, and perhaps can never be. Without ever giving up the anger and the struggle, each of us also resists the tyranny and impossibilities of the just by seeking the good.

Notes

1. This trend is not exclusively French. Witness the shift in a large part of the U.S. Democratic working-class electorate toward a Republican conservatism espousing economic policies that are ruinous for that very segment of the population (Frank 2004).

2. This is the model generally attributed to Denmark: a deregulated job market, moral liberalism, and strong social safeguards. This is also the model Giddens explores in his study of the "new egalitarianism" (Diamond/Giddens 2005).

Reference List

Allardt, E. 1971. "Emile Durkheim et la sociologie politique," in *Sociologie politique*, edited by P. Birnbaum and F. Chazel. Paris: Armand Colin.

Arendt, H. 1983. *Condition de l'homme moderne*. Paris: Calmann-Lévy.

Askenazy, P. 2004. *Les désordres du travail: Enquête sur le nouveau productivisme*. Paris: Seuil.

Aubert, N., and M. Pagès. 1998. *Le stress professionnel*. Paris: Klincksieck.

Aubert, N., and V. de Gauléjac. 1991. *Le coût de l'excellence*. Paris: Seuil.

Bataille, P. 1998. *Le racisme au travail*. Paris: La Découverte.

Baudelot, C., M. Gollac, et al. 2003. *Travailler pour être heureux?* Paris: Fayard.

Baudelot, C., and F. Leclerc, eds. 2005. *Les effets de l'éducation*. Paris: La Documentation française.

Bauman, Z. 1988. *Freedom*. Minneapolis: University of Minnesota Press.

———. 1991. *Modernity and Ambivalence*. Cambridge, UK: Polity Press.

Beck, U. 2001. *La société du risque*. Paris: Flammarion.

Bègue, L. 1998. "De la 'cognition morale' à l'étude des stratégies de positionnement moral: Aperçu théorique et controverses culturelles en psychologie morale," in *L'Année psychologique*. Paris: Armand Colin.

Birnbaum, P. 1979. *Le peuple et les gros: Histoire d'un mythe*. Paris: Grasset.

Blöss, T., ed. 2001. *La dialectique des rapports hommes-femmes*. Paris: PUF.

Boltanski, L., and L. Thévenot. 1991. *De la justification. Les économies de la grandeur*. Paris: Gallimard.

Boltanski, L. 1993. *La souffrance à distance*. Paris: Métailié.

Boltanski, L., and E. Chiapello. 1999. *Le nouvel esprit du capitalisme*. Paris: Gallimard.

Boudon, R. 1973. *L'inégalité des chances: La mobilité sociale dans les sociétés industrielles*. Paris: A. Colin.

———. 1996. *Le juste et le vrai*. Paris: Fayard.

———. 2004. *Raison, bonnes raisons*. Paris: PUF.

Bourdieu, P. 1989. *La noblesse d'Etat*. Paris: Editions de Minuit.

———. 1997. *Méditations pascaliennes*. Paris: Seuil.

Bowles, S., and H. Gintis. 1976. *Schooling in Capitalist America: Educational Reform and the Contradictions of Economic Life.* New York: Basic Books.

Bréchon, P. 2000. "Qu'est-ce qu'une société juste?" in *Les valeurs des Français (1980–2000).* Edited by P. Bréchon. Paris: Armand Colin.

Browning, C. 1994. *Des hommes ordinaires.* Paris: Les Belles lettres.

Caillet, V. 2001. *Le sentiment d'injustice à l'école.* Thesis, Université de Bordeaux 2.

Cam, P. 1981. *Les prud'hommes, juges ou arbitres? Les fonctions sociales de la justice du travail.* Paris: PFNSP.

Castel, R. 1995. *Les métamorphoses de la question sociale.* Paris: Fayard.

Castells, M. 1996. *The Rise of the Network Society,* London: Blackwell.

de Certeau, M. 1980. *L'invention du quotidien: Arts de faire.* Paris: UGE.

Chateauraynaud, F. 1991. *La faute professionnelle: Une sociologie des conflits de responsabilité.* Paris: Métailié.

Chauvel, L. 1998. *Le destin des générations.* Paris: PUF.

Chevalier, L. 1978. *Classes laborieuses et classes dangereuses* (1958). Paris: UGE.

Clair, D. 2001. Le travail vu de gauche, vu de droite, *Travailler est-il (bien) naturel? Recherches,* 18.

Cohn, N. 1983. *Les fanatiques de l'apocalypse.* Paris: Payot.

Costéséro, R. 2004. *De la norme à la responsabilité: L'expérience morale des bénévoles d'associations caritatives,* Thesis, Université de Bordeaux 2.

Courpasson, D. 2000. *L'action contrainte.* Paris: PUF.

Cousin, O. 2004. *Les cadres: Grandeur et incertitude.* Paris: L'Harmattan.

Crozier, M., and E. Friedberg. 1977. *L'acteur et le système.* Paris: Seuil.

Davies, J. C. 1962. "Toward a Theory of Revolution." *American Sociological Review* XXVII.

Dejours, C. 1998. *Souffrance en France.* Paris: Seuil.

Delamotte, Y. 1983. *Le droit du travail en pratique.* Paris: Editions de l'organisation.

Della Fave, L. R. 1974. "On the Structure of Egalitarianism." *Social Problems,* 22.

Desrosières, A. 1997. *Eléments pour une histoire des nomenclatures professionnelles.* Paris. INSEE.

Deutsch, M. 1985. *Distributive Justice.* New Haven, CT: Yale University Press.

Diamond, P., and A. Giddens. 2005. *Social Justice: Building a Fairer Britain.* London: Polity.

Dodier, N. 1994. "Causes et mise en cause: Innovations socio techniques et jugement moral face aux jugements du travail." *Revue française de sociologie* 35.

———. 1995. *Les Hommes et les Machines.* Paris: Metailié.

Donzelot, J. 2003. *Faire société.* Paris: Seuil.

Douglas, M. 2000. *Comment pensent les institutions.* Paris: La Découverte.

Dubet, F. 1987. *La galère.* Paris: Fayard.

———. 1994. *Sociologie de l'expérience.* Paris: Seuil.

———. 2000. *Les inégalités multipliées.* La Tour d'Aigues: Ed. de l'Aube.

———. 2000. "L'égalité et le mérite dans l'école démocratique de masse." *L'Année sociologique* 2.

———. 2002 *Le déclin de l'institution.* Paris: Le Seuil.

———. 2004. *L'école des chances*. Paris: Le Seuil.

Dubet, F., and A. Vérétout. 2001. "Pourquoi sortir du RMI?" *Revue Française de Sociologie* 3.

Dubet, F., and D. Martuccelli. 1996. *A l'école*. Paris: Seuil.

Dubet, F., and D. Martuccelli. 1998. *Dans quelle société vivons-nous?* Paris: Seuil.

Dumont, L. 1985. *Homo Equalis I*. Paris: Gallimard.

Dupuy, J.-P. 2004. "Les affaires sont les affaires," in *La justice: L'obligation impossible*. Paris: Autrement.

Durand, J.-P. 2004. *La chaîne invisible. Travailler aujourd'hui: Flux tendus et servitude volontaire*. Paris: Seuil.

Duret, P. 2004. *Les larmes de Marianne*. Paris: A. Colin.

Durkheim, E. 1967. *De la division du travail social* (1893). Paris: PUF.

———. 1967. *Le suicide* (1897). Paris: PUF.

Duru-Bellat, M. 2002. *Les inégalités sociales à l'école*. Paris: PUF.

———. 2006. *L'inflation scolaire: Les désillusions de la méritocratie*. Paris: Seuil.

Dworkin, R. 1986. *The Theory and Practice of Autonomy*. Cambridge: Cambridge University Press.

Ehrenberg, A. 1991. *Le culte de la performance*. Paris: Calmann-Lévy.

———. 1998. *La Fatigue d'être soi*. Paris: Odile Jacob.

Élias, N. 1997. *Logiques de l'exclusion*. Paris: Fayard.

Fitoussi, J.-P., and P. Rosanvallon. 1996. *Le nouvel âge des inégalités*. Paris: Seuil.

Forsé, M. 2005. *La priorité du juste: Application à des données européennes*. Paris and Caen: LASMAS.

Forsé, M., and M. Parodi. 2004. *La priorité du juste: Eléments pour une théorie des choix moraux*. Paris: PUF.

Forsyth, R. 1980. "A taxonomy of ethical ideology." *Journal of Personality and Social Psychology*, 39.

Fortino, S. 2002. *La mixité au travail*. Paris: La Dispute.

Frank, T. 2004. *What's the Matter with Kansas? How Conservatives Won the Heart of America*. New York: Metropolitan Books.

Fraser, N. 2005. *Qu'est-ce que la justice sociale? Reconnaissance et distribution*. Paris: La Découverte.

Freud, S. 1981. "Psychologie des foules et analyse du moi," in *Essais de psychanalyse*. Paris: Payot.

Friedberg, E. 1993. *Le pouvoir et la règle*. Paris: Le Seuil.

Frohlich, N., and J. A. Oppenheimer. 1992. *Choosing Justice: An Experimental Approach to Ethical Theory*. Berkeley and Oxford: University of California Press.

Galland, O. 2004. "Les jeunes Français forment-ils une génération?" *Comprendre* 5.

de Gauléjac, V. 1996. *Les sources de la honte*. Paris: Desclée de Brouwer.

Genet, J. 1949. *Journal du voleur*. Paris: Gallimard.

Gilligan, C. 1986. *Une si grande différence*. Paris: Flammarion.

Goblot, E. 1967. *La barrière et le niveau: Etude sociologique de la bourgeoisie française moderne*. Paris: PUF.

Godechot, O., and M. Gurgand. 2000. "Quand les salariés jugent leur salaire." *Economie et statistique* 3331, 1.

Goldthorpe, J. H., and C. W. Mills. 2004. "Trends in Intergenerational Class Mobility in Britain in the Late Twentieth Century" in *National Patterns of Social Mobility: Convergence or Divergence?* Edited by R. Breen. Oxford: Oxford University Press.

Goux, D., and E. Maurin. 1998. *La nouvelle condition ouvrière.* Paris: Fondation Saint Simon.

Gurr, T. R. 1970. *Why Men Rebel.* Princeton, NJ: Princeton University Press.

Gutman, A. 1988. *Democracy and the Welfare State.* Princeton, NJ: Princeton University Press.

Halbwachs, M. 1970. *La classe ouvrière et les niveaux de vie* (1912). Paris: Gordon & Breach.

Hamilton, V., and L. S. Rytina, 1980. "Social Consensus on Norms of Justice: Should the Punishment Fit the Crime?" *American Journal of Sociology* 85.

Hayek, F. 1976. *Law, Legislative and Liberty, t. II: The Mirage of Social Justice.* London. Routlege and Kegan Paul.

Hayek, F. 1985. *La route de la servitude.* Paris: PUF.

Hegel, F. 1969. *La première philosophie de l'esprit.* Paris: PUF.

Hervieu-Léger, D. 1999. *Le pèlerin et le converti.* Paris: Flammarion.

Herzberg, F. 1966. *Work and the Nature of Man.* New York: World Publishing Company.

Hirschman, A. O. 1980. *Les passions et les intérêts: Justifications politiques du capitalisme avant son apogée.* Paris: PUF.

———. 1991. *Deux siècles de rhétorique réactionnaire.* Paris: Fayard.

Hobsbawm, E. 1989. "Farewell to the Labour Movement," in *Politics for a Rational Left.* London: Verso.

Hochschild, J. 1981. *What's Fair? American Beliefs About Distributive Justice.* Cambridge, MA: Harvard University Press.

Homans, G. 1974. *Social Behavior: Its Elementary Forms.* New York: Harcourt Brace Jovanovich.

Honneth, A. 2000. *La lutte pour la reconnaissance.* Paris: Cerf.

———. 2004. "Recognition and Justice." *Acta Sociologica* 47.

Hugues, E. C. 1996. *Le regard sociologique: Essais choisis.* Paris: Editions de l'EHESS.

Hunout, P. 1987. "Conseil de prud'hommes: un exemple de décision dans un cadre institutionnel." *Revue française de sociologie* 28.

INSEE. 2005. *Tableaux de l'économie française.* Paris: INSEE

d'Iribarne, P. 1989. *La logique de l'honneur.* Paris: Seuil.

———. 1996. *Vous serez tous des maîtres.* Paris: Seuil.

Israël, J. 1972. *L'aliénation de Marx à la sociologie contemporaine.* Paris: Anthropos.

Joas, H. 1999. *La créativité de l'agir.* Paris: Cerf.

Kant, E. 1984. *Fondements de la métaphysique des mœurs,* in *Œuvres philosophiques.* Paris. Gallimard, coll. Bibliothèque de la Pléiade, t.II

Kaufmann, J.-C. 1992. *La trame conjugale.* Paris: Nathan.

Kellerhals, J., J. Coenen-Huther, and M. Modak. 1988. *Figures de l'équité: La construction des normes de justice dans les groupes.* Paris: PUF.

Kellerhals, J., M. Modak, and D. Perrenoud. 1997. *Le sentiment de justice dans les relations sociales.* Paris: PUF-Que sais-je?.

Kelley, J., and M. D. R. Evans. 1993. "The Legitimation of Inequality: Occupational Earnings in Nine Nations." *The American Journal of Sociology* 1.

Kokoreff, M. 2003. *La force des quartiers.* Paris: Payot.

Kruegel, J. S., and E. R. Smith. 1986. *Beliefs About Inequality: American Views of What Is and What Ought to Be.* New York: Aldine de Gruyter.

Kymlicka, W. 1999. *Les théories de la justice: Une introduction.* Paris: La Découverte.

de La Boëtie, E. 1976. *Discours sur la servitude volontaire.* Paris: Payot.

Lagrange, H. 2003. *Demandes de sécurité.* Paris: Seuil.

Lallement, M. 1997. *Sociologie des relations professionnelles.* Paris: La Découverte.

———. 2001. "Daedalus laborans," in *Travailler est-il (bien) naturel? Recherches* 18.

Lamont, M. 1995. *La morale et l'argent.* Paris: Métailié.

———. 2002. *La dignité des travailleurs.* Paris: FNSP.

Lanternari, V. 1979. *Les mouvements religieux des peuples opprimés.* Paris: Maspero.

Laufer, J., C. Marry, and M. Maruani, eds. 2003. *Le travail du genre: Les sciences sociales du travail à l'épreuve des différences de sexe.* Paris: La Découverte, MAUSS.

Legendre, P. 1999. *Sur la question dogmatique en Occident.* Paris: Fayard.

Le Goff, J. 1977. *Pour un autre Moyen Age: Temps, travail et culture en Occident: 18 essais.* Paris: Gallimard.

Lerner, J. M. 1980. *The Belief in a Just World: A Fundamental Delusion.* New York: Plenum Press.

Lerner, J. M. 1986. Le thème de la justice ou le besoin de justifier. *Bulletin de psychologie,* 374.

Lévi-Strauss, C. 1955. *Tristes tropiques.* Paris: Plon.

Leiris, M. 1939. *L'âge d'homme.* Paris: Gallimard.

Linhart, V. 2000. *Enquête aux prud'hommes.* Paris: Stock.

Locke, J. 1984. *Second traité du gouvernement civil* (1690). Paris: Flammarion.

Loriol, M. 2003. "Donner un sens à la plainte de fatigue au travail." *Année sociologique* 52, 2.

Loriol, M., ed. 2004. *Construction du stress, psychologisation du social et rapport au public,* Laboratoire Georges Friedmann.

Lucchesi, M. 1996. *A chacun selon son mérite?* Paris. Ellipses.

MacIntyre, A. 1994. *Quelle justice? Quelle rationalité?* Paris: PUF.

———. 1997. *Après la vertu.* Paris: PUF.

Marchand, O., and C. Thélot. 1998. *Le travail en France, 1800–2000.* Paris: Nathan.

Manent, P. 1987. *Histoire intellectuelle du libéralisme.* Paris: Calmann Lévy.

Martuccelli, D. 2005. *La consistance du social.* Rennes: PUR.

Maruani, M. 2000. *Travail et emploi des femmes.* Paris: La Découverte.

Maruani, M., ed. 2005. *Femmes, genre et société: L'état des savoirs.* Paris: La Découverte.

Marx, K. 1963. *Critique du programme du parti ouvrier allemand*, in *Œuvres complètes*, I. Paris: La Pléiade, Gallimard.

Maurin, L. 2004. "Portrait d'une France inégalitaire," *Comprendre*, 4

Mauss, M. 1950. "Essai sur le don," in *Sociologie et anthropologie*. Paris: PUF.

Mead, G. H. 1963. *L'Esprit, le Soi et la Société*. Paris: PUF.

Méda, D. 1995. *Le travail: Une valeur en voie de disparition*. Paris: Aubier.

———. 2002. *Le temps des femmes: Pour un nouveau partage des rôles*. Paris: Flammarion.

Méda, D., and F. Vernant, eds. 2004. *Le travail non qualifié: Recherches*. Paris: La Découverte.

Merle, P. 1996. *L'évaluation des élèves*. Paris: PUF.

Miller, D. 1999. *Principles of Social Justice*. Cambridge, MA: Harvard University Press.

Moore, B. 1978. *Injustice: Social Bases of Obedience and Revolt*. London: MacMillan Press.

Nagel, E. 1994. *Egalité et partialité*. Paris: PUF.

Nietzsche, F. 1985. *Ainsi parlait Zarathoustra*. Paris: Gallimard.

Nozick, R. 1988. *Anarchie, Etat et Utopie*. Paris: PUF.

Parsons, T. 1955. "Nouvelle ébauche d'une théorie de la stratification," in *Eléments pour une sociologie de l'action*. Paris: Plon.

Pascal, B. 2000. *Pensées* (1670). Paris: Librairie Générale Française.

Passeron, J.-C. 1982. "L'inflation des diplômes: Remarques sur l'usage de quelques concepts analogiques en sociologie." *Revue Française de Sociologie* 4.

Paugam, S. 2000. *Le salarié de la précarité*. Paris: PUF.

Perrineau, P. 1998. *Le symptôme Le Pen, radiographie des électeurs du Front national*. Paris: Fayard.

Pharo, P. 2004. *Morale et sociologie*. Paris: Gallimard.

Piaget, J. 1969. *L'évolution du jugement moral chez les enfants*. Paris: PUF.

Piketty, T. 2003. "Attitudes vis-à-vis des inégalités de revenus en France: Existerait-il un consensus?" *Comprendre* 4.

Polanyi, K. 1983. *La Grande Transformation: Aux origines économiques et politiques de notre temps*. Paris: Gallimard.

Rainwater, L. 1974. *What Money Buys: Inequality and the Social Meaning of Income*. New York, Basic Books.

Rawls, J. 1987. *Théorie de la justice*. Paris: Seuil.

Renaut, A. 1989. *L'ère de l'individu: Contribution à une histoire de la subjectivité*. Paris: Gallimard.

Reynaud, J.-D. 1989. *Les Règles du jeu: L'action collective et la régulation sociale*. Paris: A. Colin.

Riffault, H. 1994. "Travail et représentation sociale de l'économie," in *Les valeurs des Français*. Edited by H. Riffault. Paris: PUF.

Riffault, H., and J.-F. Tchernia. 2000. "Sens du travail et valeur économique," in *Les valeurs des Français: Evolutions de 1989 à 2000*. Edited by P. Bréchon. Paris: Armand Colin.

Robert, P. 1999. *Le citoyen, le crime et l'Etat*. Geneva: Droz.

Rotenberg, E. 2005. *Les prud'hommes, de la décision de justice au sentiment d'injustice*. Université de Bordeaux 2.

Saglio, J. 2001. "Les relations professionnelles entre négociation et consultation," in *Sociologie du travail: Quarante ans après.* Edited by A. Pouchet. Paris: Elsevier.

Sartre, J.-P. 1964. *Les mots.* Paris: Gallimard.

Schelling, T. 1960. *The Strategy of Conflict.* Cambridge, MA: Harvard University Press.

Schnapper, D. 1994. *La communauté des citoyens.* Paris: Gallimard.

———. 1997. *Contre la fin du travail.* Paris: Textuel.

Seeman, M. 1967. "Les composants de l'aliénation dans le travail." *Sociologie du travail 2.*

Selznick, P. 1969. *Law, Society and Industrial Justice.* New York: Russell Sage Foundation.

Sen, A. 2000. *Repenser l'inégalité.* Paris: Seuil.

Sennett, R. 1982. *Autorité.* Paris: Fayard.

———. 2002. *Le travail sans qualité: Les conséquences humaines de la flexibilité.* Paris: Albin Michel.

———. 2003. *Respect: De la dignité de l'homme dans un monde d'inégalité.* Paris: Albin Michel.

Shepalak, N. J., and D. F. Alwin. 1986. "Beliefs about Inequality and Perception of Distributive Justice." *American Sociological Review 51.*

Simmel, G. 1987. *La philosophie de l'argent.* (1900). Paris: PUF.

———. 1988. *La tragédie de la culture et autres essais.* Marseille: Rivages.

———. 1998. *Les pauvres.* Paris: PUF.

Supiot, A. 1994. *Critique du droit du travail.* Paris: PUF.

———. 2005. *Homo juridicus: Essai sur la fonction anthropologique du droit.* Paris: Seuil.

Taylor, C. 1997. *Multiculturalisme: différence et démocratie.* Paris: Flammarion.

———. 1998. *Les sources du moi.* Paris: Seuil.

Toernblom, K. Y., and U. G. Foa. 1983. "Choice of distribution principle: Cross-cultural evidence on the effects of resources." *Acta Sociologica 26.*

Touraine, A. 1964. *La conscience ouvrière.* Paris: Le Seuil.

———. 1973. *Production de la société.* Paris: Le Seuil.

———. 1988. *La parole et le sang.* Paris: Odile Jacob.

———. 1992. *Critique de la modernité.* Paris: Fayard.

Touraine, A., F. Dubet, and M. Wieviorka. 1982. *Solidarité.* Paris: Fayard.

Touraine, A., M. Wieviorka, and F. Dubet. 1984. *Le mouvement ouvrier.* Paris: Fayard. English translation: 1987. *The Workers' Movement.* Cambridge University Press

Van Parijs, P. 1991. *Qu'est-ce qu'une société juste? Introduction à la pratique d'une philosophie politique de la justice.* Paris: Seuil.

Véga, A. 2000. *Une ethnologue à l'hôpital: L'ambiguïté du quotidien infirmier.* Paris: Editions des Archives contemporaines.

Walzer, M. 1990. *Essais sur la critique sociale et son interprétation.* Paris: La Découverte.

———. 1997. *Sphères de justice.* Paris: Seuil.

Wieviorka, M. 1995. *La France raciste.* Paris: Seuil.

About the Author

François Dubet is a well-known French sociologist. After writing several books on social movements in France, Poland, and Chile, he published a landmark book on marginal suburban youth in 1986. He then turned to education, institutions, and finally to workers' experience of justice, all cast in the frame of his theories of the sociology of experience.